New German Critique

Number 132 · November 2017

Transatlantic Theory Transfer: Missed Encounters?

Special Issue Editors: Andreas Huyssen and Anson Rabinbach

Koselleck in America

Niklas Luhmann

The Kittler Effect

"Half a Heart and Double Zeal":
Critical Theory's Afterlife in the United States

Contributors

YAACOB DWECK teaches history at Princeton University.

PHILIPP FELSCH teaches the history of the human sciences at Humboldt University, Berlin.

PAUL FLEMING teaches in the Departments of German Studies and Comparative Literature at Cornell University.

DAGMAR HERZOG is Distinguished Professor of History at the Graduate Center, City University of New York.

STEFAN-LUDWIG HOFFMANN teaches late modern European history at the University of California, Berkeley.

MARTIN JAY is Sidney Hellman Ehrman Professor Emeritus of History at the University of California, Berkeley.

ANNA KINDER is research assistant at the German Literature Archive Marbach and lecturer at Stuttgart University.

JOE PAUL KROLL is an editor at the Leibniz Institute of European History in Mainz, Germany.

JOHANNES VON MOLTKE teaches in the Departments of Germanic Languages and Literatures and of Screen Arts and Cultures at the University of Michigan.

WILLIAM RASCH teaches in the Department of Germanic Studies at Indiana University.

GEOFFREY WINTHROP-YOUNG teaches in the German and Scandinavian programs within the Department of Central, Eastern and Northern European Studies at the University of British Columbia–Vancouver.

ROBERT ZWARG is a research assistant at the German Literature Archive Marbach.

DOI 10.1215/0094033X-4162949

TRANSATLANTIC THEORY TRANSFER
MISSED ENCOUNTERS ?

A conference organized by
Deutsches Literaturarchiv Marbach
and New German Critique

Co-presented with the Goethe-Institut New York

Co-sponsored by the
Department of Germanic Languages and the
Institute for Comparative Literature and Society

Deutsches Haus
Columbia University
March 27-28, 2015

To RSVP: please email pq2@columbia.edu

SPEAKERS

Anna Kinder
Philipp Felsch
Joe Paul Kroll
Yaacob Dweck
Johannes von Moltke
Robert Zwarg
Paul Fleming
Stefan-Ludwig Hoffmann
William Rasch
Dagmar Herzog
Geoffrey Winthrop-Young
Devin Fore

Kittler   Scholem   Kluge   Mitscherlich

Blumenberg   Kracauer   Luhmann   Koselleck

deutsches literatur archiv marbach   GOETHE INSTITUT   NGC NEW GERMAN CRITIQUE   ICLS The Institute for Comparative Literature and Society

Introduction: Transatlantic Theory Transfer: Missed Encounters?

Andreas Huyssen and Anson Rabinbach

In one of the miniatures of *Minima Moralia*, "To Them Shall No Thoughts Be Turned," Theodor W. Adorno reflected on the fate of émigrés in the United States, lamenting that their past life and their intellectual experiences are "declared non-transferable and un-naturalizable."[1] Whether true or not in the 1930s and 1940s, he raised the issue of transferability and naturalization of intellectual work and experience that confronts not just émigrés and exiles but transnational exchanges of ideas and transfers of theory in general. But he underestimated the multiple ways that intellectual ideas and experiences migrate and can be appropriated or truncated, transformed or projected, into a new context.

Several decades later, in the 1970s and 1980s, the United States experienced a boom in theory from Europe that was often accompanied by hostility between what was problematically called French versus German theory, a rather debilitating by-product of the postmodernism debates. All the more so as figures like Karl Marx, Friedrich Nietzsche, and Sigmund Freud were central to both traditions. If this special issue focuses on theory transfer from Germany alone, the last thing we have in mind is a revival of that old trope and its national resonances, which had more to do with the political legacies of Enlightenment thought and the academic institutionalization of theory in this country than with hard-and-fast national borders. As many contributions to this issue show,

1. Adorno, *Minima Moralia*, 47.

New German Critique 132, Vol. 44, No. 3, November 2017
DOI 10.1215/0094033X-4162190   © 2017 by New German Critique, Inc.

the transnational dynamics in the theory world are very much part of our retrospective taking stock of neglected aspects of those earlier years.

So how did we arrive at the choice of figures discussed in this issue? We did not want to focus on the big success stories, mainly associated with the Frankfurt School, whose work has been so central to *New German Critique* and other theory journals. Nor did we want to focus on those authors whose work was translated to an extent but failed to leave traces in the intellectual life of this country. Instead, we wanted to focus on the more complicated cases where there was reception, but perhaps not as intense as one might have imagined or hoped for—thus the question mark after the issue's title. What is it that may have been missed in these encounters?

We wanted to investigate different modes of transfer between intellectual and political environments. Our project raised broader questions about theory transfer, whether from Germany or elsewhere to the United States and vice versa. What makes one theory coming from abroad *anschlussfähig* and prevents another from having impact? What is the role of academic disciplines, of publishers' initiatives, of translation projects, of journals in this process of transfer and reception? Translation is a major and often problematic factor in reception. Especially in the German case, it is easy to point to bad translations that have impeded and distorted reception. In some cases, whole books had to be retranslated to begin to make sense in English. Residues of untranslatability will haunt even the best translations. But translation is never the only transformation a text undergoes when transplanted. Apart from cases of outright misconception and misrecognition, we need to ask more broadly: What transformations does theoretical work developed in one intellectual context undergo when it travels into other constellations? What role does (un)timeliness play in nurturing or blocking the transfer of theoretical work into another space/time? Why do some theories have an effect in a specific disciplinary context only, and not beyond, even when the times have increasingly privileged interdisciplinary theorizing in the humanities and social sciences? In what circumstances does theory transfer cause ruptures and paradigm changes in the receiving context rather than smoothly merging with it? What are the conditions of acceptance or resistance as theories begin to travel into other geographic and intellectual zones?

Finally, what exactly motivated the obsessions with "theory" as a mode of intellectual life in those last Cold War decades, and how do we gauge the relationship of theory to the humanities and social sciences today? Clearly, the heyday of theory as a dominant mode of intellectual and political thought has come and gone. But the "end of theory" thesis is simply nonsense when it comes with the demand to forget it all and to return to time-honored academic practices. Too much of theory has filtered into all our intellectual disciplines and critical endeavors. Theory's effects on the culture of reading and thinking about the world are still very much alive in the present.

Movement from one environment to another, however, is never unimpeded, as Edward W. Said pointed out in his influential essay "Traveling Theory" years ago. It always involves processes of mediation and institutionalization different from those at the point of origin. All of these questions, and others, are at the center of this special issue. Even if we have not been exhaustive in offering specific cases of theory transfer, we hope to stimulate further research on the very different kinds of transfer, translation, and reception. Such work seems all the more important at a time when intellectual openness and exchange are increasingly under attack from a nationalist turning inward and exclusionary politics worldwide.

This special issue contains the reworked and expanded papers first offered at a conference at Columbia University's Deutsches Haus, March 27–28, 2015. We wish to thank our generous sponsors who, together with *NGC*, funded the conference: the German Literature Archive in Marbach and the Goethe-Institut New York. For cosponsorship, we thank the Institute for Comparative Literature and Society at Columbia and, of course, the Department of Germanic Languages. Special thanks to Kelly Lemons, who designed the poster and program, and to departmental staff Peggy Quisenberry and William Dellinger, whose care of logistical detail has made all of this smoother sailing than the image of the sinking *Titanic* on the poster might suggest.

References

Adorno, Theodor W. 2005. *Minima Moralia: Reflections on a Damaged Life*, translated by E. F. N. Jephcott. London: Verso.

Said, Edward W. 1983. "Traveling Theory." In *The World, the Text, and the Critic*, 226–47. Cambridge, MA: Harvard University Press.

What Was Theory? Toward a Generic History

Philipp Felsch

In 1968 Siegfried Unseld, the publisher of the West German Suhrkamp Verlag, found himself confronted with a demand that he revoke his entrepreneurial arbitrament and grant his staff of editors an equal say. For the editors who were responsible for the proposition, these measures were but the first step on the way to "disappropriate the literary means of production"—in the parlance of the day. Not only personally offended but worried about his company's future, Unseld sought support from his authors, whom he could consider his natural allies if only because the new "constitution" did not allude to them in any significant way. Martin Walser, the novelist, considered the editors' challenge simply ridiculous. The Polish poet Zbigniew Herbert, who had been Unseld's guest during the Frankfurt Book Fair, pitied the editors as frustrated intellectuals who envied their boss for his young girlfriend and the fast car he used to take her out for joyrides in the nearby Taunus mountains. In need of harder arguments, Unseld also called Theodor W. Adorno. The editors' demands had to be considered a relapse into the most primitive form of syndicalism that would eventually lead to anarchy, Adorno replied, and he referred explicitly to Karl Marx's *Capital* to corroborate this claim. According to Marx, the authors, who wrote the books, as well as the publisher, who gave the money, had to be regarded as "productive resources," whereas the editors were only "third persons" in the economic sense. "When I asked Adorno what he meant," Unseld continues, "he told me that 'third persons,' for Marx, were parasites not unlike prostitutes and procurers." Four days later, when he convened with the insurgents to discuss

New German Critique 132, Vol. 44, No. 3, November 2017
DOI 10.1215/0094033X-4162202   © 2017 by New German Critique, Inc.

the matter, Unseld used Adorno's line of argument to reject their claims. With little further resistance they gave in. Several of them resigned. The rest agreed to continue to work for the capitalist Suhrkamp Verlag.[1]

The episode, which Unseld relates in his *Chronicles*, seems to belong to a distant past. It is just as unthinkable today that a bunch of employees would turn their company into a socialist enterprise as that their CEO would turn to theory to fight their claims. "Theory is something that no one sees," Hans Blumenberg writes at the beginning of *The Laughter of the Thracian Woman*, which bears the subtitle *A Protohistory of Theory*. What follows, though, is the attempt to write the history of its visible side. Sifting through centuries of European intellectual history, Blumenberg highlights the "exotic behaviour" of theorists and thinkers and how it has been amusing their beholders ever since the Greek philosopher Thales, while gazing at the stars, fell into a well.[2] Blumenberg's study reaches far into the postwar period. The transformation that lay behind the above-mentioned anecdote, however, is absent from his account. Yet his behavioral history of theory could have proved especially fruitful with respect to the 1960s and 1970s. Resuming older developments from the prewar period and even the intellectual history of the nineteenth century, the meaning and status of "theory" underwent significant changes during this time.

Abolishing disciplinary boundaries through claims of "totality," theory lost its status as expert knowledge and turned into a collective singular denominating a wide range of paradigms and schools. Just as high modernism began to dispute the virtues of commonsensical thinking, the generation of the New Left gained momentum against political pragmatism as a movement of abstract-minded theory devotees. From the West German *edition suhrkamp* to Louis Althusser's *Théorie* series, from *Tel Quel* to the Marxist literary journal *Alternative*, from the *New Left Review* to the poststructuralist periodical *Semiotext(e)*, "theory" (*Theorie*, *théorie*) began to circulate within a rapidly emerging field of publishing. Texts spread widely between France, West Germany, the United States, Italy, and England and were adapted to local circumstances. A new intellectual culture based on reading and discussing appealed to growing cohorts of student generations, as the "paperback revolution" produced a hitherto unknown quantity of difficult texts.[3] From the rhetoric of the student leader to the jargon of poststructuralism and the utterly sober scientism of Niklas Luhmann's systems theory, the heyday of theory unfolded through the emergence of new language

1. Unseld, *Chronik*, 25.
2. Blumenberg, *Laughter of the Thracian Woman*, 1.
3. See Mercer, "Paperback Revolution."

games inside and outside academe. Becoming an intellectual habitus, theory gradually lost its limitation to leftist thought, incorporating conservative and even reactionary thinkers.[4] The plethora of theory debates attests to the widespread urge to theorize that had taken hold of the humanities, from philology to · history. In the long run these tensions had a polarizing effect that made many academic departments break up into theory-friendly and theory-hostile camps.[5] But the realm of theory was not limited to academe. On the contrary, ever since its neo-Marxist self-fashioning as "theoretical practice," theory defined itself as a genre opposed to academic philosophy and became the indispensable legitimation for all sorts of political activity—at least in the eyes of those who believed in it.[6] Even the West German Red Army Faction (RAF) took pains to devise a "revolutionary theory" to put its assaults into a wider reference frame. When Andreas Baader, the charismatic patriarch of the RAF, killed himself in 1977, he left a library of more than four hundred volumes in his cell.[7]

The intellectual content of paradigms such as Critical Theory, neo-Marxism, and poststructuralism has been abundantly traced. What remains to be studied, however, is the tremendous impact these schools of thought had on both academe and Western countercultures during the Cold War. For this purpose, it is necessary to adopt a different approach. In this article I propose to conceive of theory as a genre. To prevent false expectations, especially from literary scholars, I hasten to say that I am talking of "genre" in a rather wide and explorative—albeit thoroughly deliberate—sense. The concept of genre and the scholarship it has inspired since the 1970s can provide a heuristic framework to address questions such as the following:[8] How did the transformation of the book market since the 1950s affect the production of theory? How was the emergence of theory connected to the crisis and subsequent growth of many humanities since the 1960s that led to an ongoing interrogation of Western epistemology? Which new language games emerged inside and outside academe, as being difficult became the hallmark of intellectual ambition? How can we explain the peculiar fascination for difficult texts so typical for Western countercultures between the 1960s and the 1980s?[9]

---

4. In West Germany this is exemplified by the case of the widely rediscovered Carl Schmitt.
5. See Wegmann, "'Wer von der Sache nichts versteht, macht Theorie.'"
6. See Judt, "Elucubrations."
7. See Stern and Herrmann, *Andreas Baader*, 110–16, 177.
8. For a recent overview, see Frow, *Genre*. Apart from literary studies, the concept of genre has recently been picked up by historians of science and knowledge. See Pomata, "Medical Case Narrative."
9. For a related programmatic approach, see Lepper, "Ce qui restera [. . .], c'est un style."

In terms of genre, theory turns out to be more than a succession of mere ideas. It has to be considered an "institution" comprising such mundane entities as authors and readers and publishers and media, that is, a material culture and intellectual practices that went along with it.[10] What is more, relevant scholarship has taught us to trace the emergence of genres by paying particular attention to the dissemination and reception—as opposed to the production—of texts. In Wilhelm Voßkamp's terms, genres require readers' "expectations" (*Erwartungen*), which in turn stimulate the anticipation of such expectations (*Erwartungserwartung*) by authors and publishers. It is only through this dialectics that genres originate and acquire stability.[11] To move away from the sphere of production to the sphere of circulation and use seems especially promising for theory, since the question whether and how a certain author or a certain text found its way into the canon of counterphilosophy was mostly decided by publishers such as Unseld and by readers for whom the exposure to the new theory paperbacks sometimes amounted to a way of life.

In recent years Franco Moretti has revolutionized the study of genre and of generic conventions by devising a method he calls "distant reading."[12] I find the term utterly inspiring for the study of theory. Undoubtedly, Moretti's idea of detecting regularities that become apparent in large numbers of texts could yield fascinating insights into the different theory cultures that have evolved since the 1960s. In this article, however, I am aiming at a much more modest goal. The distance I seek is not the distance of quantification. Instead, I have an ethnographical defamiliarization in mind that intends to suspend our customary preconception of theory by considering the curious behavior of its readers, publishers, and partisans. In this sense I intend to take a position not completely unlike Blumenberg's Thracian maid, who burst into laughter when she witnessed the stumbling philosopher with his eyes fixed on the sky. My case study, however, is situated not in Greece but in West Germany.

In 1973 George Steiner coined the famous phrase *Suhrkamp culture*, implying that the policy of a single publishing house shaped the reading habits of educated West Germans.[13] As a matter of fact, publishers like Suhrkamp and the West Berlin Merve Verlag have exerted a tremendous influence on the emergence of theory. Without their respective policies, the genre would have

10. See Voßkamp, "Gattungen als literarisch-soziale Institutionen."
11. See ibid. The role of reciprocal expectations for the stabilization of communication has been a key topic for systems theory as well. See Luhmann, *Love as Passion*.
12. See Moretti, *Distant Reading*.
13. Steiner, "Adorno," 253.

never flourished and influenced the West German student movement as it did. Consequently—and as a first attempt to test the feasibility of the new approach—I turn my attention to publishing. To understand the impact of theory on academe as well as on counterculture, it seems a particularly rewarding field. Moreover, to write the history of publishing is a timely endeavor. In recent years, both Suhrkamp and Merve have invited historians to engage with their past by handing over their papers to public archives.[14]

The Paperback Revolution

Tracing the use of the word *theory* as a collective singular in postwar Germany, one has to consider various mutually intertwined contexts: the so-called *Theoriearbeit* (theory work) of the New Left; the Frankfurt School, of course, which elevated Critical Theory to a trademark in the mid-1960s;[15] and—last but not least—the expanding paperback market, since theory has to be viewed as a paperback phenomenon. The first German paperbacks came out in the late 1940s. Heinrich Maria Ledig-Rowohlt, the publisher of Rowohlt Verlag, had become acquainted with paperbacks in the United States. At first Rowohlt confined its new format to fiction. However, with the *Deutsche Enzyklopädie*, which started in 1955, titles in philosophy, art history, and popular science were added to the pocket book program.[16]

Since the new series proved unexpectedly successful, Unseld tried something similar with Suhrkamp Verlag. In 1963 he launched the rainbow-colored *edition suhrkamp*, which turned into the hallmark of the Suhrkamp culture during the next decade. In the new series, "philosophical" titles (as they were still called) and works of fiction appeared in turn. To Unseld's surprise, difficult authors such as Ernst Bloch, Adorno, and Ludwig Wittgenstein led the sales figures—even in nonacademic bookstores such as West Germany's infamous Bahnhofsbuchhandlungen, which Hans Magnus Enzensberger had denounced as agencies of unculture around this time. While Martin Heidegger's *Sein und Zeit*, the long seller of twentieth-century German philosophy, had barely sold forty thousand copies by 1966, *Kultur und Gesellschaft I*, a collection of essays by Heidegger's disciple Herbert Marcuse that came out in the same year in the *edition suhrkamp*, reached eighty thousand copies in two years.[17] Such figures

14. The Suhrkamp papers are in the German Literature Archive, Marbach (under the name of Siegfried Unseld Archiv); the Merve papers can be found in the Center for Art and Media, Karlsruhe.

15. For the canonization of Critical Theory, see Behrmann, "Die Theorie, das Institut, die Zeitschrift und das Buch."

16. See Raddatz, *Jahre mit Ledig*; and Klimmt and Rössler, *Reihenweise*.

17. See N.N., "Wißbar wohin."

convey a sense that readers' habits in postwar Germany and other Western countries were changing dramatically. The heyday of theory, I argue, was part of a silent reading revolution.

Drawing the conclusions from his previous endeavor, Unseld set out in 1965 to launch a second paperback series dedicated to theoretical texts. For the *edition* he had secured the advice of such young, thriving authors as Enzensberger, Walser, and Uwe Johnson. For the new project, he recruited a board of editors comprising the luminaries of West German humanities, namely, Blumenberg, Jürgen Habermas, Dieter Henrich, and Jacob Taubes. A few years later Luhmann joined the group. According to Karl Markus Michel, the responsible editor, the series in question should be "well made" but also "inexpensive." It should be distinguishable from the "ubiquitous paperbacks" but stand out from "traditional volumes."[18] At the end of a lengthy conception period, the new series was presented to the public at the 1966 Frankfurt Book Fair. After considering alternatives such as "konzept," "kritik," and "argument"—all of them set in fashionable minuscules—the board and the publisher agreed on the title *Theorie*. Because of its bland, white-grayish jacket, one is tempted to regard it as the *White Album* of Suhrkamp Verlag—and the dazzling *edition suhrkamp*, respectively, as *Sgt. Pepper.*[19]

The launch of the *Theorie* series came along with the sweeping ambition to create or at least implement a genre distinct from academic philosophy. For Taubes, who held a chair for Jewish studies (*Judaistik*) at the Free University of Berlin, the birth of "theory" was nothing but the logical consequence of the "end of philosophy" that he dated back to G. W. F. Hegel's work. In Hegel the philosophical endeavor to build a unified body of knowledge had succeeded for the last time. Ever since, Western thought was spread across various disciplines. "There is no doubt," Taubes wrote in one of his many communiqués to Michel, "that philosophy lags behind the state of the art today. Anthropology, linguistics, psychoanalysis, literature studies, film theory, and even archaeology and history are contemporary modes of thinking. What we don't need is the kind of philosophy fashioned by philosophy professors."[20]

The renunciation of academic philosophy that Taubes, himself a professor, uttered has to be considered a characteristic trait of theory. In this sense,

---

18. Karl Markus Michel to Hans Blumenberg, January 20, 1965, Siegfried Unseld Archiv.

19. For the relationship between minimalism and pop art, and for the Beatles albums mentioned above, see Diederichsen, "Psychedelische Begabungen."

20. Jacob Taubes to Karl Markus Michel, August 26, 1965, Siegfried Unseld Archiv. For Taubes's considerations about the "end of philosophy," see Rötzer, "Jacob Taubes."

the genre's birth can be traced back to the nineteenth century. In the 1830s the Young Hegelians had started out to reform German academic philosophy. In their eyes, the capacity to change the social order was the hallmark of truth of any given philosophy. After promising beginnings, however, they fell victim to state repression. Because of their political and religious agenda, thinkers such as Ludwig Feuerbach, Arnold Ruge, and Marx were banned from civil service and forced to earn their livings as independent authors and journalists. Ironically, they had pinned their hopes on the liberal spirit of academe. But after his dismissal Feuerbach declared the irreconcilability of philosophy and the university as an institution. "It is a fact," he wrote in the late 1830s, "that philosophy and a chair of philosophy must be considered a contradiction."[21]

Of course, the philosophy professors of the time had a different view. Feuerbach expressed his intellectual contempt at a time when philosophy was transforming into an academic discipline. The 1850s saw the first professional conventions and the first journals of philosophy. Apart from these networks of communication, the constitution of an academic discipline relies on boundary work.[22] Thus, after the failure of the revolution of 1848, academic philosophers explicitly renounced the kind of political thinking seen as the trademark of the Young Hegelian School. In their editorial of 1852 the editors of the newly founded *Zeitschrift für Philosophie und philosophische Kritik* declared that philosophy, as they understood it, "will no longer refer to the ecclesiastical, political, and social questions of the day."[23]

In this article the history of anti-academicism in philosophy cannot be further pursued. A century later, when Taubes expressed his scorn for philosophy professors, he bore witness to the persistence of the old dichotomy. "Theory," as it was by now generally labeled, defined itself in opposition to a disciplinary regime. It is also for this reason that the paperback must be regarded as the genre's congenial form. According to the standards of professional philosophers, it was not a legitimate medium. When invited to publish his *Legitimacy of the Modern Age* in the novel Suhrkamp series, even Blumenberg, like Taubes one of Unseld's consultants, expressed doubts about the publisher's reputation. He lamented Suhrkamp's "unspecific resonance" and worried that the publisher might tamper with his manuscript to increase its salability.[24]

---

21. Quoted in Essbach, *Junghegelianer*, 131.
22. See Stichweh, *Zur Entstehung des modernen Systems wissenschaftlicher Disziplinen*, chap. 1.
23. Quoted in Köhnke, *Entstehung und Aufstieg des Neukantianismus*, 122.
24. Hans Blumenberg to Karl Markus Michel, April 21, 1965, Siegfried Unseld Archiv.

In Blumenberg's reaction we can hear the echo of a platitude of contemporary critics who decried the paperback as a harbinger of "mass culture" and a nemesis of *Bildung*, so dear to members of the educated German middle class. At the Frankfurt Book Fair in 1959 it had dawned on Adorno that books "do not look like books anymore."[25] In the same year the Hessische Rundfunk broadcast a famous radio essay in which Enzensberger diagnosed the transformation of books into "commodities" and the degradation of reading into mere "consumption." His concern seemed all the more justified in the case of theory, since he doubted that the high circulation numbers of "difficult" authors indicated that these authors were actually studied or read. Even more striking than Enzensberger's assumption was the widespread apprehension that paperbacks were not collected but discarded after use. Only subsequent surveys among readers would reveal that private paperback libraries were a common phenomenon. The trope of the disposable soft cover therefore proves phantasmic in origin. It reveals that the paperback critics were driven by the deep anxieties of German *Bildungsbürgertum*.[26]

Neither Adorno nor Enzensberger foresaw that the success of their own oeuvres would be largely due to the paperback market. In 1974 Hans Schmoller, a German-Jewish émigré and a designer at Penguin in London, noted a paradox of what he originally labeled the "paperback revolution": "Though in the West paperbacks have become big business, this has not prevented their publishers from giving free rein to expressing ideas strongly exposed to established political and economic systems and indeed advocating their overthrow."[27] Moreover, the paperback itself conveyed a political message. As the critics had lamented, it stripped the book of its "aura" and made it accessible to an ever-growing readership. In the eyes of a younger generation familiar with Walter Benjamin's endorsement of "mechanical reproduction," this equaled a "cultural revolution" in publishing.

It is peculiar how progressive and conservative paperback critics sometimes closely resembled each other, as can be seen in a review of the *edition suhrkamp* by the leftist film student Harun Farocki in the *Spandauer Volksblatt* in 1964. For Farocki, the conspicuous branding of the series was tantamount to the defeat of content by design. Fortunately, he had a remedy. To resist the commodification of higher learning, his readers should, he advised, rip off the colored jacket before they even opened a book.[28] A spirit of irreverence toward the book as a token of highbrow culture can generally be regarded

25. Adorno, "Bibliographische Grillen."

26. Enzensberger, "Bildung als Konsumgut," 113, 120. See Mercer, "Paperback Revolution."

27. Schmoller, "Paperback Revolution," 314.

28. Quoted in Stanitzek, "Gebrauchswerte der Ideologiekritik," 243.

as the policy of the small leftist publishers who sprang up like mushrooms amid the student rebellion after 1968.[29]

Merve Verlag was one of them. It was founded in West Berlin in 1970. The publishers intended, they said, to defy the mechanisms of consumer culture by issuing their pamphlets in a simple gray cardboard jacket.[30] Fighting the "reification" of the book, the same minimalistic logic prevailed in the inner part. In the 1980s Merve composed a declaration for the trade magazine *Buchmarkt* in which the company proclaimed "badly made books" its official policy.[31]

Ultimately, the revolution of the book could lead to biblioclasm, as some of the notorious library sit-ins of the late 1960s show.[32] Guido Viale, a member of the Italian Operaist group Lotta Continua, has conveyed a telling episode. In *Contro l'università*, his 1968 account of the student rebellion in Turin, he described how he performed the "ultimately liberating act towards the god-book" with his reading group: "To dissect the books that we read and to distribute five pages, respectively, to each member of the group."[33]

The Birth of the Reader

Acting against the reification of the book must also entail exploring its manifold potential uses. The revolution of the book that publishers like Merve intended therefore extended to the practice of reading. Alongside the market for leftist books, new forums for literacy emerged in the 1960s: from the study groups of the socialist German Student Union to the *Capital* seminars of the early 1970s to the *Anti-Oedipus* reading groups of the late 1970s. In 1978 Helmut Lethen, an assistant professor of German studies at the Free University of Berlin who had spent the first half of the decade in a Maoist group, published a progress report on the collective reading of Bertolt Brecht's poetry. The text is a treasure trove for the reading atmosphere of the time. The participants in Lethen's seminar had read Althusser's ideology theory and knew—unlike the adherents to the Constance School—that the gaps in the text were filled not by the reader's spontaneous activity but by ideologically saturated "mechanisms of identification." To penetrate these mechanisms and avoid "unworldly immersion in the text," as Lethen writes, it was necessary that "the readers present their appropriations mutually in an audible production." Only then did "the real process of ideological criticism" get started.[34]

29. For the leftist book trade in West Germany, see Sonnenberg, *Von Marx zum Maulwurf.*
30. See Lowien, *Weibliche Produktivkraft*, 79.
31. Paris and Gente, "Für Buch-Markt."
32. See Lethen, *Suche nach dem Handorakel*, 92.
33. Quoted in Mercer, "Paperback Revolution," 631.
34. Lehmann and Lethen, "Das kollektive Lesen," 3–8.

The "death of the author" that Roland Barthes decreed in 1968 has long been a firmly established term. However, the conclusion of Barthes's famous declaration of death has largely been forgotten. The "death of the author," he writes, is the price for the "birth of the reader."[35] Yet beyond the much more suggestive image of a polyphonic écriture dissolving the author entity in the anonymity of a thousand codes, this reader figure has remained strangely pale. Various figures have emerged from the bankruptcy of the author's estate: writing and its "excessive theoratization," as Michel Foucault had already noted in 1977.[36] From "grammatology" to "writing systems," it still claims its uncontested place in the middle of our French theoretical apparatus. In its shadow, much more discreetly, the reader's career proceeds: from Althusser's *Reading "Capital,"* held to be the protocol of a collective reading of Marx, to Barthes's *Pleasure of the Text*; from Gilles Deleuze and Félix Guattari's school of reading *Rhizome* to Michel de Certeau's *Practice of Everyday Life*, which celebrates the reader as a joyful "poacher" in a thicket of texts; from Hans Robert Jauß and Wolfgang Iser's *Rezeptionsästhetik* to the East Berliner "Naumann Collective" around the Romance philologists Manfred Naumann and Karlheinz Barck, which puts forward a theory of reading for a socialist society. Even Foucault, for whom reading was barely interesting from a theoretical standpoint, is said to have answered a question on his own authorial identity when on a lecturing tour in Brazil with "Who am I? A reader."[37]

There is much to suggest linking this strong reader figure to the new book market of the 1970s and to the utopia of the book cultivated by the student movement. In many respects, this time recalls the period around 1800, when an expanding publishing landscape blew up the reading monopoly that the Bible once enjoyed and created a reading audience hungry for annual new releases. Just as in the 1970s, the *Goethezeit* also produced a theory of reading, Friedrich Schleiermacher's hermeneutics, to which readers of Barthes or Althusser, of course, tended to cultivate an intimate enmity because it sought to restore the author's intention, a term meanwhile considered ideological.[38]

The sympathies of the 1970s belonged to the reader. Epilogues, letters, and interviews of the time from Merve show how the lack of a talent for writing became a virtue over the years: "We're not professionals, we're bookworms." "We are enthusiastic readers and incompetent writers." "Why do we

35. Barthes, "Death of the Author," 55.
36. Foucault, *Dispositive der Macht*, 46.
37. Quoted in Certeau, "Foucaults Lachen," 45.
38. For the relationship between book market and hermeneutics, which is shown here very cursorily, see Kittler, "Vergessen."

publish this or that book? Because we can't write ourselves."[39] If there was a germ cell from where this new pleasure of the text originated, it must have been the reading group with which the publishers battled their way through *Anti-Oedipus* from 1975 to 1980, Deleuze and Guattari's cryptic introduction to the "Non-Fascist Life," as Foucault wrote in his preface to the American edition.[40] "We met once a week in the apartment of one of the members and read 'Anti-Oedipus' from beginning to end," recalled Merve founder Peter Gente. "We were not prepared, there was no protocol, but we read sentence by sentence in order in a book."[41] No preparation, no outside or self-imposed agitation: the notoriously serious Marxist student groups yielded to a programmatic lightness. But the reminiscence also has unmistakably premodern overtones. This reading aloud together, this deliberate stroll through the vineyard of text—that was a kind of reading known in the early modern era.[42] While historical reading research was beginning to reconstruct the transformation of reading habits in contrasting pairs, such as slow and loud (premodern) versus fast and quiet (modern), older reading practices were experiencing a boom in countercultural contexts.[43] Friedrich Nietzsche should be counted one of the godfathers of this new reading culture. His plea for reading slowly and aloud belongs to the context of his criticism of language.[44] Barthes, too, dreamed in *The Pleasure of the Text* of an "aristocratic reader" who rediscovered the "leisure of former reading habits": "not to devour, to gobble, but to graze, to browse scrupulously." Under the influence of Nietzsche, Barthes, and related authors, the Merve collective demonstrated its method of reading with one of the theoretical buzzwords of the 1970s: "intensity."[45]

"One never asks what a book intends to mean," wrote Deleuze and Guattari in 1976 in *Rhizome*, published by Merve in German the following year as *Rhizom*. "The question is how a book works, in which connections its intensities flow."[46] The desire to release themselves from the totalitarian ethics of understanding went so far that the authors retroactively declared their *Anti-Oedipus* a children's book. Despite its undeniable hermeticism, which cost their West Berlin readers five years of reading time, they insisted that *Anti-Oedipus* required no previous knowledge or hermeneutic horizon: "Félix says that our

39. Paris and Gente, "Editorial Note."
40. Foucault, preface, xii.
41. Paris and Gente, "Ping-Pong auf der Hochebene von Tibet," 130.
42. See Kopp and Wegmann, "'Wenige wissen noch, wie Leser lieset.'"
43. See ibid.; and Engelsing, *Der Bürger als Leser.*
44. See Bickenbach, *Von den Möglichkeiten einer "inneren" Geschichte des Lesens*, 40–54.
45. Barthes, *Pleasure of the Text*, 13.
46. Deleuze and Guattari, *Rhizom*, 7.

book is aimed at people who are now between seven and fifteen years of age."[47] With this statement, the authors combined the claim to dispossess the intellectual caste with the attempt to make "theory" a commonplace good for all. In the Nietzschean terminology of their peculiar brand of Freudo-Marxism, this meant the dissolution of the hierarchies of representation.[48]

Rhizom, the most successful Merve title of all time, reads over long stretches like a school of intensive reading: "Find the places in a book with which you can start something. We no longer read and write in the conventional way. There is no death of the book, only a new way of reading. A book contains nothing that must be understood, but a lot with which you can start something. Take what you want!"[49] When reading Nietzsche, the intellectuals of their generation realized that they could be subversive simply by reading. Deleuze and Guattari translated this idea into a set of instructions. For a habitual reader like Gente, the new Parisian thinking must have been full of happy surprises. During the student movement he could not live out his obsession with books without feelings of guilt. Now, in the 1970s, he suddenly came across emphatic theories of reading. The bard of this postheroic heroism was Barthes.[50] "Imagine someone who abolishes within himself all barriers, all classes, all exclusions," he wrote in *The Pleasure of the Text*, "a person who mixes every language; who remains passive in the face of Socratic irony and legal terrorism (how much penal evidence is based on a psychology of consistency!). Such a man would be the mockery of our society: court, school, asylum, polite conversation would cast him out: who endures contradiction without shame? Now this anti-hero exists: he is the reader of the text."[51]

When the Merve members stressed that they were "enthusiastic readers and incapable writers," when they declared that their reception constituted "another mode of production," they were working on a paradigm that had, for the New Left, been seen as almost unquestionable since the rediscovery of Marx: the paradigm of production. True to the Marxist doctrine that social change was possible only at the level of production, the neo-Marxists of the 1960s and 1970s tried at all costs to belong to the producers. Hence the typical vocabulary of the time, the "literary producers" (known commonly as "leftist publishers"), the "mode of production" of the left-wing counterpublic (Negt/Kluge), or the wild "desiring-production" of the schizophrenics in *Anti-Oedipus*.

---

47. Guattari, *Mikro-Politik des Wunsches*, 46.
48. See Descombes, *Modern French Philosophy*, 173–80.
49. Deleuze and Guattari, *Rhizom*, book jacket.
50. Ibid.
51. Barthes, *Pleasure of the Text*, 3.

In the contrast of productive versus unproductive, all these terms found their political guiding difference.

The apotheosis of the reader turned it upside down. Its most mature form can be grasped in Certeau's *Practice of Everyday Life*, another key Merve text, which stylized the reader as a postmodern antihero. The French original appeared in 1980. "The reader is a novelist," Certeau wrote.

> He deterritorializes himself, oscillating in a nowhere between what he invents and what changes him. Sometimes, in fact, like a hunter in the forest, he spots the written quarry, follows a trail, laughs, plays tricks, or else like a gambler, lets himself be taken in by it. Sometimes he loses the fictive securities of reality when he reads: his escapades exile him from the assurances that give the self its location on the social checkerboard.

As a "misunderstood activity," Certeau continued, reading always stood in the shadow of writing, and as a "passive" recipient, the reader was always in the author's shadow. No longer prepared to follow this myth of a system that "distinguishes and privileges authors, educators, revolutionaries, in a word, 'producers,' in contrast with those who do not produce," he reversed the conventional assignment of roles.[52]

For Certeau, who wrote his book on commission for the French Ministry of Culture, the reader was none other than the prototype of the sly consumer who encountered unexpected freedom in the niches of the world of goods. The paperback reader, who had disconcerted the cultural critics of the late 1950s, must therefore also be regarded as one of his ancestors. In 1959 Enzensberger had called paperback readers "consumers in the literary supermarket."[53] But even he came to see it differently. In 1976 he pounced on the reader's right to "flip backward and forward, to skip entire passages, to read sentences against the grain, to draw conclusions from the text of which the text knows nothing, and to throw the book in which it is written into the corner at any time."[54]

References
Adorno, Theodor W. 1959. "Bibliographische Grillen." *Frankfurter Allgemeine Zeitung*, October 16.

Barthes, Roland. 1975. *The Pleasure of the Text*, translated by Richard Miller. Toronto: HarperCollins Canada.

---

52. Certeau, *Practice of Everyday Life*, 168.
53. Enzensberger, "Bildung als Konsumgut," 111.
54. Enzensberger, *Mittelmaß und Wahn*, 33–34.

———. 1986. "The Death of the Author." In *The Rustle of Language*, translated by Richard Howard, 49–55. Oxford: Blackwell.

Behrmann, Günter C. 1999. "Die Theorie, das Institut, die Zeitschrift und das Buch: Zur Publikations- und Wirkungsgeschichte der Kritischen Theorie 1945 bis 1965." In *Die intellektuelle Gründung der Bundesrepublik: Eine Wirkungsgeschichte der Frankfurter Schule*, edited by Clemens Albrecht, Günter C. Behrmann, Michael Bock, Harald Homann, and Friedrich H. Tenbruck, 247–311. Frankfurt am Main: Campus.

Bickenbach, Matthias. 1999. *Von den Möglichkeiten einer "inneren" Geschichte des Lesens.* Tübingen: Niemeyer.

Blumenberg, Hans. 2015. *The Laughter of the Thracian Woman: A Protohistory of Theory*, translated by Spencer Hawkins. New York: Bloomsbury.

Certeau, Michel de. 1984. *The Practice of Everyday Life*, translated by Steven Rendall. Berkeley: University of California Press.

———. 1997. "Foucaults Lachen." In *Theoretische Fiktionen: Geschichte und Psychoanalyse*, 44–58. Vienna: Turia und Kant.

Deleuze, Gilles, and Félix Guattari. 1977. *Rhizom.* Berlin: Merve.

Descombes, Vincent. 1980. *Modern French Philosophy*, translated by L. Scott-Fox and J. M. Harding. Cambridge: Cambridge University Press.

Diederichsen, Diedrich. 2008. "Psychedelische Begabungen: Minimalismus und Pop." In *Kritik des Auges: Texte zur Kunst*, 75–105. Hamburg: Philo Fine Arts.

Engelsing, Rolf. 1974. *Der Bürger als Leser: Lesergeschichte in Deutschland, 1500–1800.* Stuttgart: Metzler.

Enzensberger, Hans Magnus. 1962. "Bildung als Konsumgut: Analyse der Taschenbuch-Produktion." In *Einzelheiten*, 110–36. Frankfurt am Main: Suhrkamp.

———. 1991. *Mittelmaß und Wahn: Gesammelte Zerstreuungen.* Frankfurt am Main: Suhrkamp.

Essbach, Wolfgang. 1988. *Junghegelianer: Soziologie einer Intellektuellengruppe.* Paderborn: Fink.

Foucault, Michel. 1978. *Dispositive der Macht.* Berlin: Merve.

———. 1983. Preface to *Anti-Oedipus: Capitalism and Schizophrenia*, by Gilles Deleuze and Félix Guattari, translated by Robert Hurley, Mark Seem, and Helen R. Lane, x–xiii. Minneapolis: University of Minnesota Press.

Frow, John. 2015. *Genre: The New Critical Idiom.* 2nd ed. London: Routledge.

Guattari, Félix. 1977. *Mikro-Politik des Wunsches.* Berlin: Merve.

Judt, Tony. 2008. "Elucubrations: The 'Marxism' of Louis Althusser." In *Reappraisals: Reflections on the Forgotten Twentieth Century*, 106–15. New York: Penguin.

Kittler, Friedrich A. 1979. "Vergessen." In *Texthermeneutik: Aktualität, Geschichte, Kritik*, edited by Ulrich Nassen, 195–221. Paderborn: Schöningh.

Klimmt, Reinhard, and Patrick Rössler. 2016. *Reihenweise: Die Taschenbücher der 1950er Jahre und ihre Gestalter.* Butjadingen: Achilla.

Köhnke, Klaus Christian. 1986. *Entstehung und Aufstieg des Neukantianismus: Die deutsche Universitätsphilosophie zwischen Idealismus und Positivismus.* Frankfurt am Main: Suhrkamp.

Kopp, Detlev, and Nikolaus Wegmann. 1988. "'Wenige wissen noch, wie Leser lieset': Anmerkungen zum Thema; Lesen und Geschwindigkeit." In vol. 1 of *Germanistik und Deutschunterricht im Zeitalter der Technologie: Selbstbestimmung und Anpassung; Vorträge des Germanistentages Berlin 1987*, edited by Norbert Oellers, 92–104. Tübingen: Niemeyer.

Lehmann, Hans-Thies, and Helmut Lethen. 1978. "Das kollektive Lesen." In *Berthold Brechts "Hauspostille": Text und kollektives Lesen*, edited by Hans-Thies Lehmann and Helmut Lethen, 3–8. Stuttgart: Metzler.

Lepper, Marcel. 2005. "'Ce qui restera [. . .], c'est un style': Eine institutionengeschichtliche Projektskizze (1960–1989)." In *Jenseits des Poststrukturalismus? Eine Sondierung*, edited by Marcel Lepper, Steffen Siegel, and Sophie Wennerscheid, 51–76. Frankfurt am Main: Lang.

Lethen, Helmut. 2012. *Suche nach dem Handorakel: Ein Bericht*. Göttingen: Wallstein.

Lowien, Merve. 1977. *Weibliche Produktivkraft—gibt es eine andere Ökonomie? Erfahrungen aus einem linken Projekt*. Berlin: Merve.

Luhmann, Niklas. 1998. *Love as Passion: The Codification of Intimacy*, translated by Jeremy Gaines and Doris L. Jones. Stanford, CA: Stanford University Press.

Mercer, Ben. 2011. "The Paperback Revolution: Mass-Circulation Books and the Cultural Origins of 1968 in Western Europe." *Journal of the History of Ideas* 72, no. 4: 613–36.

Moretti, Franco. 2013. *Distant Reading*. New York: Verso.

N.N. 1966. "Wißbar wohin: Philosophie." *Der Spiegel*, July 11, 76.

Paris, Heidi, and Peter Gente. 1981. "Editorial Note." In *Museum der Obsessionen*, by Harald Szeemann, 225. Berlin: Merve.

———. 1986. "Für Buch-Markt." Typescript, Berlin. www.heidi-paris.de/verlag/wider-das-kostbare (accessed November 16, 2016).

———. 1998. "Ping-Pong auf der Hochebene von Tibet: Gespräch mit den Betreibern des Merve Verlages." In *Dagegen–Dabei: Texte, Gespräche und Dokumente zu Strategien der Selbstorganisation seit 1969*, edited by Hans-Christian Dany et al., 127–36. Hamburg: Kellner.

Pomata, Gianna. 2014. "The Medical Case Narrative: Distant Reading of an Epistemic Genre." *Literature and Medicine* 32, no. 1: 1–23.

Raddatz, Fritz. 2015. *Jahre mit Ledig: Eine Erinnerung*. Reinbek bei Hamburg: Rowohlt.

Rötzer, Florian. 1987. "Jacob Taubes." In *Denken, das an der Zeit ist*, edited by Florian Rötzer, 305–19. Frankfurt am Main: Suhrkamp.

Schmoller, Hans. 1974. "The Paperback Revolution." In *Essays in the History of Publishing: In Celebration of the 250th Anniversary of the House of Longman, 1724–1974*, edited by Asa Briggs, 283–319. London: Longman.

Sonnenberg, Uwe. 2016. *Von Marx zum Maulwurf: Linker Buchhandel in Westdeutschland in den 1970er Jahren*. Göttingen: Wallstein.

Stanitzek, Georg. 2011. "Gebrauchswerte der Ideologiekritik." In *Theorietheorie: Wider die Theoriemüdigkeit in den Geisteswissenschaften*, edited by Mario Grizelj and Oliver Jahraus, 231–59. Paderborn: Fink.

Steiner, George. 1973. "Adorno: Love and Cognition." *Times Literary Supplement*, March 9, 253.

Stern, Klaus, and Jörg Herrmann. 2007. *Andreas Baader: Das Leben eines Staatsfeindes.* Munich: Deutscher Taschenbuch Verlag.

Stichweh, Rudolf. 1984. *Zur Entstehung des modernen Systems wissenschaftlicher Disziplinen: Physik in Deutschland, 1740–1890.* Frankfurt am Main: Suhrkamp.

Unseld, Siegfried. 2010. *Chronik 1970.* Frankfurt am Main: Suhrkamp.

Voßkamp, Wilhelm. 1977. "Gattungen als literarisch-soziale Institutionen." In *Textsortenlehre—Gattungsgeschichte,* edited by Walter Hinck, 27–44. Heidelberg: Quelle+Meyer.

Wegmann, Nikolaus. 2000. "'Wer von der Sache nichts versteht, macht Theorie': Ein Topos der philologischen 'Curiositas' der Literaturwissenschaft." In *Literaturwissenschaft und Wissenschaftsforschung: DFG Symposion 1998,* edited by Jörg Schönert, 509–28. Stuttgart: Germanistische Symposien Berichtsbände.

Narratives of Theory Transfer

Anna Kinder

In 1980 the German publishing house Suhrkamp tried to conquer the US market by establishing Suhrkamp/Insel Publishers Boston Inc.[1] However, creating a transatlantic basis for publishing literary fiction and academic nonfiction met with obstacles and difficulties. Titles successful in Europe did not necessarily meet with the same interest in the United States, as the following slogan for a newsletter demonstrates: "Suhrkamp's Bestsellers Sold Out in Europe—Still Available in the U.S.!"[2] Next to German literary writers, the newsletter listed best-selling theorists. This marginal note alludes not only to the challenges of selling "German Theory" in the United States but also to the more general question of the scope of German theoretical and philosophical traditions in a comprehensive context of reception. The international exchange of ideas, literature, and scholarship puts the question of German theory in the context of a narration of global intellectual exchange and reception.

Therefore, before focusing on case studies and individual thinkers and their respective stories of success or failure in the United States, it seems promising to sketch a baseline of the grand narrative of transatlantic theory transfer, to chart trends and traditions as well as developments. Which theories have been transferred from Germany to the United States, and which have

---

1. See Lützeler, "Suhrkamp Culture amerikanisch?," 166.
2. Draft of a newsletter, Suhrkamp Boston 1979–82, Siegfried Unseld Archives, Deutsches Literaturarchiv Marbach (call number: SUA:Suhrkamp/01 Verlagsleitung). All citations used by permission of Suhrkamp.

New German Critique 132, Vol. 44, No. 3, November 2017
DOI 10.1215/0094033X-4162214   © 2017 by New German Critique, Inc.

been accepted or adapted? To obtain an empirical overview of the main trends and traditions of German theory in the United States, this article provides some statistical data. Well aware of the methodological challenges and requirements of presenting a conclusive big picture, I use the quantitative approach as a heuristic way to establish an overview from which to pursue further inquiries.

But before looking at the main trends, I first discuss the terminological coordinates of what we call theory transfer and its implications, as there already are various narratives about and around the highly contested object that theory is. What do we mean when we talk about transfer and theory? In the following, the article therefore makes its argument on two levels and considers the methodological challenges as well as the empirical dimension of defining theory transfer.

What Transfer?

Transfer is a concept that has long been challenged in its "original" meaning by the social sciences and by the humanities. Transfer as a simple process of transmission or translation, of bringing something from one point to another, invokes the idea of a linear process with an identifiable point of origin and a clear destination. Of course, transfer never can be that simple, especially when one is dealing with theory, with concepts and ideas that are in themselves unstable and cannot be moved without changing. Instead of a linear path there is circulation; one encounters ambiguous directions, with sharp discursive turns as well as questions of transformation, appropriation, reimport, or renewal. Germany and the United States are not two separate, hermetically sealed systems; the modes of exchange are much more complex, complicated, and interconnected.[3]

For example, the case of Max Weber, a key figure of German sociology in the early 1920s, can be described in terms of a game of table tennis between Heidelberg and the United States.[4] Weber himself, holding a chair at Heidelberg University since 1896, traveled to the United States in 1904, where he not only attended the International Congress of Arts and Sciences in St. Louis but also visited the Chicago Stockyards and Protestant communities—visits that probably influenced his works on the sociology of religion. Interestingly enough, the reception and dissemination of Weber's work in the United States started only after his death in 1920. The deployment of his ideas was facili-

3. From an archival point of view, when looking at the archives of individuals as well as those of vital protagonists of theory transfer, such as editorial and publishing archives, theory, like all knowledge production in a more general sense, always seems to undermine and challenge the idea of a centralization inherent in archives.

4. See Scaff, *Max Weber in America*.

tated first by the Chicago School and by scholars such as Frank Knight, followed by Talcott Parsons and by German immigrants, mainly at the New School for Social Research, who functioned as multipliers—a fact that then affected the remigration of Weber's work back to Germany after World War II.

The case of Talcott Parsons well demonstrates the interconnectedness of transfer: Parsons himself first came into contact with Weber's ideas in Heidelberg after Weber's death, when he studied with Edgar Salin. Parsons translated Weber's *Die protestantische Ethik und der Geist des Kapitalismus* (*The Protestant Ethic and the Spirit of Capitalism*) in the late 1920s and later, with his chair at Harvard, played a vital role in disseminating Weber's work in the United States—where, on the other hand, he was visited by Niklas Luhmann in 1960–61.

Recently the need for conceptualizing phenomena that transgress national borders has gained much academic attention from various sides. Take the discussions on world literature or on the untranslatability of philosophical concepts. In the field of transnational history there have been conceptualizations of a *histoire croisée*—an approach that not only analyzes the interconnectedness in history but also seeks to understand how this interconnectedness itself generates meaning in different contexts.[5]

Processes of transfer are much more complicated than the term itself suggests, which becomes clear from the modes, metaphors, and images employed when we describe transfer and exchange. For instance, in the 2009 reprint of "The German Issue" of *Semiotext(e)*, first published in 1982, Sylvère Lotringer talks about a "Moebius Strip."[6] He invokes the idea of an indefinite loop between the United States and West Berlin, between Wall Street and the Berlin Wall, when describing the mission of the magazine and the exchange it should facilitate. Similar ideas come to mind in regard to "travelling concepts" or "traveling theory."[7] James Clifford points to the common roots of theory and traveling in the Greek term *theorein*, a "practice of travel and observation," and thus describes "Theory" as a "product of displacement, comparison, a certain distance."[8] Theory itself, then, can be perceived as a mobile entity, moving (or being moved) between languages, cultures, and contexts, historical as well as geographic. It becomes apparent that with theory we have to deal with unstable concepts and take their variability into account. A traveling theory can always get enriched, invalidated, or altered on its way.[9]

5. See Werner and Zimmermann, "Vergleich, Transfer, Verflechtung."
6. Lotringer, "German Issues," v.
7. Bal, *Travelling Concepts in the Humanities*; Said, "Traveling Theory."
8. Clifford, "Notes on Travel and Theory."
9. See Lloyd, "Travelling Theories."

The idea of stability of theory and its unchangeability has long been dismissed. On the one hand, the focus of attention has shifted to the processes of reception. In the field of history, in regard to the history of transfer, questions are asked about the modes of selection and appropriation that set the course of import. Attention is brought to the traditions, contexts, and intentions of the recipient, the new "user."[10] On the other hand, the process of translation, in the linguistic as well as in the cultural sense of the term, has gained much attention. Next to the insight that every translation has to consider cultural, contextual differences, which has led the humanities and social sciences to proclaim the so-called translational turn,[11] the discussion on untranslatables, on untranslatability, as Emily Apter put it, seems worth noting in reference to theory transfer. In her preface to the translation of *Vocabulaire européen des philosophies* (*Dictionary of Untranslatables*), edited by Barbara Cassin, Apter emphasizes the French editor's notion of the interminability of translating, "the idea that one can never be done with translation."[12] Translation, then, no longer is a mere act of cultural transfer but gains philosophical value in itself. The act of translating—and translating over and over again in an infinite regress—is philosophically relevant, is in itself a philosophical event ("ein genuin philosophisches Ereignis").[13] In this sense, theory gains value through transfer; it cannot be moved without being productive. To translate theory means, to lean on Apter's words, to theorize in translation.[14]

Which Theory?

The metaphor of traveling reveals how difficult it is to locate theory, to tie theory to a certain time and place. Nevertheless, there are a lot of geographic labels of origin—just think of French theory, the Constance or Frankfurt School. Those labels allow a certain operationalizability and show that a certain set of assumptions enable us to label theory—and thus to talk about it. Overall, there seems to be a consensus about what we talk about when we speak of "theory." As Valentine Cunningham asserts, "Notwithstanding the looseness of the term, vague, ultra-compendious, a huge flag of convenience, it has stuck, and in practice we know more or less what it covers. . . . We all know what it means."[15] There seems to be a certain agreement on what posi-

---

10. See Zwarg, "Frankfurt in Madison"; and Cusset, *French Theory*.
11. See Bachmann-Medick, "Translational Turn."
12. Apter, preface, vii.
13. Geulen, "Begriffsgeschichten Go Global," 39.
14. See Apter, preface, vii.
15. Cunningham, "Theory? What Theory?," 26.

tions, concerns, and ideas the term comprises; for Cunningham, that is "an awful lot of things. An awful lot; an aweful lot."[16] Indeed, the idea of defining theory by listing the "things" it contains, thinkers as well as positions, is quite popular. Cunningham himself resorts to such a listing to define what he recognizes as "Theory" as it is found in (canonized) students' handbooks: "The scope is, of course, Structuralism and Feminism and Marxism and Reader-Response and Psychoanalysis and Deconstruction and Poststructuralism and Postmodernism and New Historicism and Postcolonialism," and the "modern gurus of Theory on these lines are, of course, the likes of Mikhail Bakhtin, Walter Benjamin, Roland Barthes, Louis Althusser, Jacques Derrida, Paul de Man, Jacques Lacan, Julia Kristeva, Luce Irigaray, Michel Foucault."[17] A similar definition of the Anglo-American term *theory* can be found in Apter's preface: "Theory is an imprecise catchall for a welter of postwar movements in the human sciences—existentialism, structural anthropology, sociolinguistics, semiotics, history of mentalités, post-Freudian psychoanalysis, deconstruction, poststructuralism, critical theory, identity politics, postcolonialism, biopolitics, nonphilosophy, speculative materialism—that has no equivalent in European languages."[18]

These examples point to the vagueness of the term and the difficulties in defining it that seem inherent to theory. Indeed, theory "has always been a difficult, unstable, and undisciplined concept, and this history of unruliness reaches back 2,500 years."[19] In his study David Rodowick argues that theory "has no stable or invariable sense in the present, nor can its meanings for us now be anchored in a unique origin in the near or distant past."[20] Rather, theory is a highly unstable practice of discourse, and defining theory, in Rodowick's sense, is always contingent and historical: "Theory is a tangled skein

---

16. Ibid.

17. Ibid., 27.

18. Apter, preface, viii. A similar scope can be found in the introduction to *Theory's Empire*: "When we began graduate work in literature in the late 1960s and 1970s a Marxist or, more generally speaking, sociological approach to literature was a new and promising area of study, excitingly different from the linguistic models of structuralism and formalism. North American scholars were (belatedly) discovering Gramsci, Brecht, Lukács, Adorno, Benjamin, and similar theorists, who quickly became icons of a critical establishment that pervaded literature departments and, to a lesser extent, related fields. In the years that followed, figures such as Althusser, Foucault, Derrida, Lacan, and Jameson . . . became touchstones of the craft of literary analysis. . . . At the same time, a feminist perspective became indispensable. . . . In the 1970s and well into the 1980s, reception theory, aesthetics, narratology, critical theory (basically the Frankfurt School), postcolonialism, and an all-encompassing preference for political approaches . . . became the norm" (Patai and Corral, introduction, 7–8).

19. Rodowick, *Elegy for Theory*, xi.

20. Ibid., 6.

composed from many threads whose filaments must be followed both individually and in the weave of their shifting patterns."[21]

Therefore, on the topic of transatlantic theory transfer from Germany to the United States, one has not only to bear in mind the detours and dead ends but also to look at the object being transferred. What theory do we refer to, exactly? Does the label *theory* have the same scope in Germany as in the United States, and which differences are there between the context of production and that of reception? Is Apter's assertion that "what is often referred to as theory in the Anglophone context would simply be called 'philosophy' in Europe" correct?[22]

It therefore is necessary to define the theory—or the concepts of theory—we talk about. One has to distinguish between "'a theory' as one approach among many, 'theory' as a system of concepts employed in the humanities, and Theory as an overarching 'practice' of our time."[23] It seems that the last definition of theory with a capital *T* refers to a phenomenon that can be historically determined and classified, in Germany as well as in the United States, albeit with differences.

Theory in the United States made its way mainly in academe and can be described as an academic phenomenon with the human sciences as protagonist. Starting in the 1960s, theory entered the universities through the literature departments. For example, French theory, as François Cusset has shown, was first recognized in literary studies, and the reception of Critical Theory occurred mainly in German studies.[24] As a result, in terms of theory in the United States, one essentially does talk about literary and cultural theory.

Interestingly, the main focus was disciplinary, not political, as Geoffrey Galt Harpham points out: "In the English-speaking world . . . the first stirrings of theory were marked not by political turbulence but by an interest in generalizing the findings of literary criticism from individual texts to literature at large, from interpretations of works to interpretation itself."[25] The US focus on interpretation—and not on social transformation—is in stark contrast to the practice of theory in the 1960s Federal Republic of Germany and as it has become the center of interest in recent German studies:[26] "'Theorie'—das

21. Ibid., xv.

22. Apter, preface, viii.

23. Patai and Corral, introduction, 1.

24. See Cusset, *French Theory*, 76; and Zwarg, "Frankfurt in Madison," 92.

25. Harpham, "From Revolution to Canon," 170.

26. See Felsch, *Der lange Sommer der Theorie*; Raulff, *Wiedersehen mit den Siebzigern*; Paul, "Theorieproduktion als Vermittlungsproblem"; Raulff and Schlak, "Droge Theorie"; and Felsch, "Der Leser als Partisan."

bedeutete 1965 in erster Linie kritische Gesellschaftstheorie auf der Linie der Neuen Linken" ("Theory"—in 1965 that first of all meant critical social theory along the lines of the New Left), as Philipp Felsch put it.[27] Whereas the definitions mentioned above concentrated on the paradigms covered under the umbrella of theory, research on the history of "German" theory centers on the non-, or even anti-, academic practice that characterizes it. Theory as a "Lifestyle-Accessoire" (lifestyle accessory) can be described as a way of living, of discussing, and, most of all, of reading.[28] Whereas in the United States theory was disseminated through journals, in Germany it was the paperback that became a shibboleth of theory. For the protagonists of theory's paperback empire—at the publishing houses of Suhrkamp and Merve—the difference in what was labeled theory in the United States and Germany is not such a big one, and there seems to be quite an overlap. Just take French theory, poststructuralism, or Critical Theory as examples.

Apter's assertion that theory in the Anglophone context covers what in Europe is called philosophy has at least to be specified. As Eva Geulen indicates in her review of the *Dictionary of Untranslatables*, there is a German history of theorizing—from romanticism to Critical and System Theory by way of Georg Lukács's *Theory of the Novel* ("zumal es auch im Deutschen eine Geschichte der Theoriebildung gibt—von der Romantik über Lukács' *Theorie des Romans* bis zur Kritischen und zur Systemtheorie")[29]— that has to be taken into consideration. But instead of comparing lists of names and concepts of what may or may not be called theory, the main difference between the United States and Germany seems to be one of the scope or range of the term. In Germany theory as a collective singular (*Kollektivsingular*) can strictly be ascribed to the historical situation of West Germany between the late 1960s and the 1990s and its specific practice. With that in mind, figures like Friedrich Nietzsche or Goethe who are regularly featured in US American theory anthologies would not that easily be labeled theoreticians in Germany.

Consequently, in the case of transatlantic theory transfer between Germany and the United States, one has to differentiate which "theory" one is talking about: Which German thinkers (to avoid the difference between philosophers and theorists) have been canonized under the label of theory in the United States? Are they considered theorists in Germany as well?

27. Felsch, *Der lange Sommer der Theorie*, 59.
28. Ibid., 12.
29. Geulen, "Begriffsgeschichten Go Global," 44.

Success Stories

But before these questions stands another: When can we talk of a success story in the first place? What indicators tell us when a theory has been accepted, when it has been well received? I propose three fields of implementation as indicators for a successful dissemination of a theory or a theorist: (1) the communities, networks, and the alliances in which theories are discussed; (2) the number of translations available; and (3) the acceptance of a theory, or its "author," into the academic canon.

To operationalize these indicators, I provide some statistical data, well aware that to do justice to such a quantitative approach, the database would have to be much more solid. So in the following, selected empirical evidence is provided that in its agglomeration highlights some trends and tendencies. I provide and examine data from a US journal, dedicated to theory; the foreign rights department of the German publishing house Suhrkamp; and US theory anthologies. In these cases I determine how often German theorists were cited; which US rights were successfully sold and which of those titles actually have been translated and published in the United States; and which theorists received an entry in theory anthologies and can thus be considered canonized.

In "The Footnote, in Theory," published in *Critical Inquiry* in 2006, Anne H. Stevens and Jay Williams analyzed the footnotes of all editions of *Critical Inquiry* between 1974 and 2004. They set out to determine who and whose works were cited most often in order to track trends and sketch fashions as taken on by *Critical Inquiry*. Furthermore, they were interested in the status of footnotes in the journal. Stevens and Williams published a list of the top ninety-five most cited theorists, sorted by the number of total citations and of citations per five volumes.[30] From their table I extracted all German authors (fig. 1), providing their place on the top ninety-five list and their individual numbers of citation. From the German-only table, two things are striking. First, there is an increase of footnotes over the years, which Stevens and Williams discerned as a trend that "can be traced in part to the increasing professionalization of the humanities."[31] Second, there seem to be some trends, like Friedrich Kittler or Siegfried Kracauer, and exceptions like the number of Benjamin citations in volumes 21 to 25, which can be explained by a special issue on Benjamin in 1998. More generally, there is a predominance of the Frankfurt School and Critical Theory (with Benjamin and Max Horkheimer–Theodor W. Adorno ranking in the top ten, followed by Jürgen Habermas in

---

30. See Stevens and Williams, "Footnote, in Theory," 216–17.
31. Ibid., 220.

Critical Inquiry	1974–2004							
Top 95	Name	All Volumes 1974–2004	Vol. 1–5 1974–79	Vol. 6–10 1979–84	Vol. 11–15 1984–89	Vol. 16–20 1989–94	Vol. 21–25 1994–99	Vol. 26–30 1999–2004
2	Freud	174	4	15	30	38	44	43
4	Benjamin	147	3	7	3	8	91	35
9	Adorno/Horkheimer	65	7	4	4	5	17	28
10	Kant	59	3	8	11	8	10	19
11	Habermas	58	1	2	6	16	16	17
12	Nietzsche	57	6	10	6	11	8	16
14	Hegel	55	4	9	12	5	8	17
15	Marx/Engels	54	1	10	5	6	14	18
17	Heidegger	52	0	6	12	5	9	20
17	Wittgenstein	52	9	7	5	11	14	6
33	Arendt	35	2	3	1	5	7	17
46	Lukács	27	4	4	4	2	8	5
57	F. Kittler	24	0	0	0	0	5	19
59	Gadamer	23	2	4	7	5	1	4
72	Auerbach	19	4	1	3	1	6	4
76	Weber	18	0	3	2	5	1	7
86	Kracauer	15	0	1	0	2	6	6
90	H. Marcuse	14	3	0	1	3	4	3

Figure 1. The most frequently cited German theorists in *Critical Inquiry*, 1974–2004.

position eleven and Herbert Marcuse farther down) as well as of the big paradigms of Continental philosophy (Immanuel Kant, Friedrich Nietzsche, G. W. F. Hegel, Martin Heidegger, and Ludwig Wittgenstein) or what we might call big philosophical systems or German idiosyncrasies (like Karl Marx and Sigmund Freud). From a generational point of view (fig. 2), fifteen out of twenty of the cited theorists were born before 1900 and belong to schools that date back to before the 1960s.

We find a similar pattern in a study published in 1986 that lists the 250 most cited authors in the Arts and Humanities Citation Index between 1978 and 1983 (fig. 3).[32] Marx is by far the most cited overall, followed by Freud and Hegel in the top ten, the "citation *crème de la crème*,"[33] then Kant, Heidegger, Nietzsche, and Wittgenstein. Furthermore, there are again the Critical Theorists like Habermas, Adorno, Benjamin, and Marcuse. In addition, and probably because the analyzed data are much broader, we find some representatives of literary criticism, namely, Hans Robert Jauss and Wolfgang Iser as well as Erich Auerbach, Ernst Robert Curtius, and Leo Spitzer.

32. Garfield, "250 Most-Cited Authors."
33. Ibid., 382.

Critical Inquiry	1974–2004	
Name	**Year of Birth**
Kant	1724
Hegel	1770
Marx	1818
Engels	1820
Nietzsche	1844
Freud	1856
Weber	1864
Lukács	1885
Heidegger	1889
Wittgenstein	1889
Kracauer	1889
Benjamin	1892
Auerbach	1892
Horkheimer	1895
H. Marcuse	1898
Gadamer	1900
Adorno	1903
Arendt	1906
Habermas	1929
F. Kittler	1943

Figure 2. Year of birth of the most
frequently cited German theorists in
Critical Inquiry, 1974–2004.

To tackle the question of translations of German theory available in the United States, I looked at the Siegfried Unseld Archives, from Suhrkamp, kept at the German Literature Archive in Marbach.[34] I found a yearly report of the department of foreign rights in which the sales of the rights and the publications of all titles are listed by author and country. For the United States there were data from 1979–94 that provide a similar picture, with a clear peak of three authors whose rights were quite successfully sold to the United States, namely, Adorno, Benjamin, and, topping them all, Habermas. But there were also some rather surprising cases. First is the number of sold rights to the work of Niklas Luhmann and Gershom Scholem, which are both above the average with respect to the Suhrkamp data. Second, there is Ernst Bloch, in which the difference between sold options and published books is quite large.

34. For details on the Siegfried Unseld Archives (SUA), see www.dla-marbach.de/archiv/siegfried -unseld-archiv.

Arts & Humanities Citation Index I 1976–1983		
Name	Year of Birth	Total Citations
Marx	1818	10.788
Freud	1856	6.111
Hegel	1770	4.439
Kant	1724	4.216
Heidegger	1889	4.015
Nietzsche	1844	3.142
Wittgenstein	1889	2.611
Popper	1902	2.534
Engels	1820	2.312
Jung	1875	2.236
Lukács	1885	1.961
Habermas	1929	1.943
Adorno	1903	1.888
Weber	1864	1.878
Husserl	1859	1.864
Benjamin	1892	1.551
Gadamer	1900	1.114
Marcuse, H.	1898	1.085
Leibniz	1646	1.071
Arendt	1906	1.005
Curtius	1886	972
Jauss	1921	862
Auerbach	1892	846
Iser	1926	846
Feyerabend	1924	792
Spitzer	1887	691

Figure 3. The most frequently cited German theorists
in the Arts and Humanities Citation Index, 1976–83.

Before drawing conclusions, I would like to present one last data set that deals with the question of academic canonization of German-language theory. Given that theory in the United States is mainly an academic phenomenon, I turned to the materialization of academic canonization par excellence, the anthology, that is, as Harpham argues in his review of *The Norton Anthology of Theory and Criticism*, the "transformation of revolution into canon."[35] I put together a small sample of anthologies and handbooks dedicated to critical, literary, and cultural theory. For pragmatic reasons I narrowed the examples down to copies published after 2000, edited by US scholars and published on the US market. Furthermore, I limited the selection to editions with their

35. Harpham, "From Revolution to Canon," 170.

Anthologies I 2000–2014	
Name	**Entries**
Benjamin	10
Freud	10
Adorno	9
Lukács	9
Heidegger	8
Iser	8
Marx	8
Nietzsche	8
Habermas	5
Hegel	5
Kant	5
Auerbach	4
Horkheimer	4
Husserl	4
Engels	3
Jauss	3
Schiller	3

Figure 4. German theorists
in US-anthologies of
Theory after 2000.

tables of contents sorted by names.[36] Thirteen anthologies met these narrow
criteria. From these I extracted all German theorists and counted their appearances (fig. 4).[37] Again there is a familiar pattern congruent with the earlier data
presented above: Freud, Benjamin, and Adorno on top, followed by Lukács,
Heidegger, Iser, Marx, and Nietzsche. The same protagonists of Critical Theory and German philosophy are featured, as are prominent agents of German
literary theory (Lukács, Iser, Auerbach, and Jauss).

What conclusions can be drawn from these findings regarding the transfer
of German theory to the United States? Can we learn anything from these data?

36. The following anthologies were included: Castle, *Blackwell Guide to Literary Theory*; Castle,
Literary Theory Handbook; Groden, Kreiswirth, and Szeman, *Johns Hopkins Guide to Literary
Theory and Criticism*; Groden, Kreiswirth, and Szeman, *Contemporary Literary and Cultural The-
ory*; Habib, *History of Literary Criticism*; Habib, *Modern Literary Criticism and Theory*; John and
Lopes, *Philosophy of Literature*; Leitch, *Norton Anthology of Theory and Criticism*; Parker, *Critical
Theory*; Rivkin and Ryan, *Literary Theory*; Ryan et al., *Encyclopedia of Literary and Cultural The-
ory*; Richter, *Critical Tradition*.

37. Figure 4 features only those theorists mentioned in three or more anthologies.

First, we can establish that what has been successfully transferred to and labeled as theory in the United States is not necessarily classified as theory in Germany, understood as a practice as defined above. Scholars like Nietzsche, Hegel, and Heidegger are more likely to be classified as philosophers, although they may have been important references for the theoretical debates of the 1960s and after. Indeed, it is necessary to have a look at the overall picture and the alliances and connections that may become visible. For example, the predominance of Freud, Marx, and Heidegger may be juxtaposed to the emerging role of French theory. In the study on *Critical Inquiry*'s footnotes there is a clear "proliferation of poststructuralist theoretical approaches."[38] Next to Freud, Benjamin, Horkheimer-Adorno, and Kant, there are prominent figures of French theory among the top ten: Derrida at one, Foucault at three, Barthes at five, and Lacan at six.[39] Altogether, there are twenty-three French theorists listed, compared with eighteen German ones. A similar pattern is presented by Garfield's study of the Arts and Humanities Index: Barthes (4.146 citations), Derrida (2.891 citations), Foucault (2.673 citations), and Lacan (1.232 citations) rank between Hans-Georg Gadamer and Kant, though none of them in the top ten. In that light the success of some German philosophers, such as Heidegger and Nietzsche, and especially that of Freud, can be interpreted as a trickle-down effect from French theory. The same effect can be attributed to Critical Theory and the high ranking of Marx and Hegel.

The representatives of Critical Theory themselves suggest another correlation, namely, that of German intellectuals who went into exile in the United States and succeeded there. More generally, the presented data suggest a correlation between the internationalization of one's career and one's reception abroad. Furthermore, there is the question of the individual theories. Are the ones that offer a vision, some kind of political salvation, well received? Or are those that are relatively accessible? Is Adorno's pathos more digestible than Luhmann's administrative language? Or do theories become interesting if there is no corresponding counterpart, if they stand out by themselves?

One final point may play a crucial role in whether a theorist is successfully received: the political dimension and the geopolitical embeddedness of theory. Therefore I take a closer look at a rather unsuccessful transfer that may shed light on the issue: the case of the German philosopher Ernst Bloch.[40] At first, Bloch seems to fit rather nicely into the picture, being close to the ideas of

38. Stevens and Williams, "Footnote, in Theory," 220.

39. Ibid., 217.

40. More details can be found in Bloch's estate, held at the Ernst Bloch Center in Ludwigshafen, Germany. Thanks to Frank Dengler, head of the center, for his ideas on the subject.

the Frankfurt School, being exiled to the United States, and having quite a share of charismatic tendencies. He has the right generational peer group and is one of Suhrkamp's best-selling authors who, like Benjamin, Adorno, Kant, and Hegel, merited a *Werkausgabe* (edition of his complete works). Nevertheless, Bloch never established himself on the US market, as he himself admitted to Thomas Mann in 1940: "Es gelang mir bisher nicht, in Amerika ökonomisch zu landen. Weder gelang es, einen Aufsatz in einer Zeitschrift zu plazieren . . . , noch reüssierte irgendein Scholarship noch das Manuskript meines Buches über die Träume vom besseren Leben. Hier ist irgend eine, leider von mir noch nicht begriffene Sperre" (So far I have not managed to economically arrive in the United States. Neither did I succeed in placing an article in a journal, nor was any scholarship or the manuscript of my book on the dreams of a better life a success. There is some barrier that unfortunately I have not yet understood).[41]

When looking into the archive of his German publisher Siegfried Unseld, we can find two possible explanations. First, many difficulties attend the translations of Bloch's works. In 1975 Unseld writes, "Adorno, Benjamin, Bloch: sie sind weiter mehr und mehr gefragt, bei Bloch allerdings sind die Schwierigkeiten mit den Übersetzern groß. Merkwürdigerweise nicht in dem Maß bei Adorno und Benjamin" (Adorno, Benjamin, Bloch: they are still more and more in demand; with Bloch, however, the difficulties with the translators are huge. Strangely, not to the same degree with Adorno and Benjamin).[42] In 1977, the year of Bloch's death, Unseld noted: "Ernst Bloch: die Übersetzungen bleiben weiter ein Sorgenkind. In den USA konnte für 'Das Prinzip Hoffnung' noch nichts erreicht werden" (Ernst Bloch: the translations will stay a problem child. In the USA nothing could yet be achieved for "The Principle of Hope").[43] The difficulties with Bloch's texts partly seemed to lie in their inaccessibility, as the publisher Alfred O. Mendel pointed out to Bloch: "Es ist sehr schwer, sich einfach auszudrücken, besonders dann, wenn der Gegenstand kompliziert ist. Komplizierte, dunkle Ausdrucksweise geht oft auf Bequemlichkeit und auch Hochmut zurück" (It is difficult to express oneself simply, especially when the topic is complex. Complicated, dark diction often is based on idleness and arrogance).[44] Furthermore, and this may be the main reason for his failure in the United States, Bloch was seen as politically suspi-

41. Ernst Bloch to Thomas Mann, May 27, 1940, in Bloch et al., *Ernst Bloch*, 700.

42. Jahresbericht 1975, Siegfried Unseld Archives, Deutsches Literaturarchiv Marbach (call number: SUA:Suhrkamp/01 Verlagsleitung).

43. Jahresbericht 1977, Siegfried Unseld Archives, Deutsches Literaturarchiv Marbach (call number: SUA:Suhrkamp/01 Verlagsleitung).

44. Ernst-Bloch-Zentrum, *Bloch*, 141.

cious. His communist orientation—his proximity to the Communist Party and his statements on the Moscow Trials—had already estranged him from his fellow émigrés Horkheimer, Marcuse, and Adorno. Later on Unseld also was aware of the political implications and the difficulties they brought along, as the correspondence between him and Ernst and Karola Bloch reveals. In 1967 Karola Bloch wrote to Unseld that Bloch had never been an official member of the Sozialistische Einheitspartei Deutschlands (Socialist Unity Party; SED), or the Communist Party of Germany. Whereas Karola Bloch just seemed interested in rectifying this detail, Unseld was aware of the importance of this information and asked Ernst Bloch for confirmation, if it is true "daß Bloch der KPD [Kommunistische Partei Deutschlands] nahestand, ihr jedoch, wie auch der SED, nie beigetreten ist. Die Sache ist deshalb wichtig, weil derselbe Text noch einmal in der Messenummer des Börsenblatts gebracht wird und dort natürlich international sehr beachtet werden wird" (that Bloch was close to the KPD [Communist Party of Germany], but, like with the SED, never joined it. This matter is important, because the same text will again be published in [the Frankfurt Book] fair's edition of the "Börsenblatt" and there will naturally gain a lot of international attention).[45] In his answer Bloch confirms the information.

The impact of the political affiliation with communism and with the German Democratic Republic may also be the reason for the nonreception of Werner Krauss in the United States. Whereas Spitzer, Auerbach, and Curtius are well received and well known, Krauss, who is generally referred to along with the other three, does not appear. René Wellek, who recognizes the other three in his works, mentions Krauss only briefly in a piece on "comparative literature today" as "an East German professor . . . who severely criticized our journal *Comparative Literature* for willful and bad contributions."[46]

In recent years Stanford University Press has published a translation of Bloch's *Spuren* (*Traces*, 2006) as well as *Geist der Utopie* (*The Spirit of Utopia*, 2000), and there seems to have appeared something like a belated recognition of Bloch and his philosophy of the *Noch-Nicht* (not-yet).

To conclude, the case of Bloch brings us back to the methodological and terminological attempts to describe and define theory transfer as a concept whose attraction is its in-betweenness and its openness: the empirics of German theory transfer into the United States have to deal with the challenges of theoretical traveling.

45. Siegfried Unseld to Ernst Bloch, August 11, 1967, Siegfried Unseld Archives, Deutsches Literaturarchiv Marbach (call number: SUA:Suhrkamp /01 Verlagsleitung/Autorenkonvolute/Bloch, Ernst).
46. Wellek, "Comparative Literature Today," 331.

References

Apter, Emily. 2014. Preface to *Dictionary of Untranslatables: A Philosophical Lexicon*, edited by Barbara Cassin, translation edited by Emily Apter, Jacques Lezra, and Michael Wood, vii–xv. Princeton, NJ: Princeton University Press.

Bachmann-Medick, Doris. 2016. "Translational Turn." In *Cultural Turns: New Orientations in the Study of Culture*, edited by Doris Bachmann-Medick, translated by Adam Blauhut, 175–209. Berlin: de Gruyter.

Bal, Mieke. 2002. *Travelling Concepts in the Humanities: A Rough Guide.* Toronto: University of Toronto Press.

Bloch, Karola, et al., eds. 1985. *Ernst Bloch: Briefe, 1903–1975.* 2 vols. Frankfurt am Main: Suhrkamp.

Castle, Gregory. 2007. *The Blackwell Guide to Literary Theory.* Malden, MA: Blackwell.

———. 2013. *The Literary Theory Handbook.* Malden, MA: Wiley-Blackwell.

Clifford, James. 1989. "Notes on Travel and Theory." *Inscriptions* 5. www.complit.utoronto.ca/wp-content/uploads/COL1000-Week08_Nov4_JamesClifford.pdf.

Cunningham, Valentine. 2005. "Theory? What Theory?" In *Theory's Empire: An Anthology of Dissent*, edited by Daphne Patai and Will H. Corral, 24–41. New York: Columbia University Press.

Cusset, François. 2008. *French Theory: How Foucault, Derrida, Deleuze & Co. Transformed the Intellectual Life of the United States*, translated by Jeff Fort. Minneapolis: University of Minnesota Press.

Ernst-Bloch-Zentrum Ludwigshafen, eds. 2007. *Bloch: Eine Bildmonographie.* Frankfurt am Main: Suhrkamp.

Felsch, Philipp. 2012. "Der Leser als Partisan." *Zeitschrift für Ideengeschichte* 6, no. 4: 35–49.

———. 2015. *Der lange Sommer der Theorie: Geschichte einer Revolte, 1960–1990.* Munich: Beck.

Garfield, Eugene. 1986. "The 250 Most-Cited Authors in the Arts and Humanities Citation Index, 1976–1983." *Current Comments*, no. 48: 3–10.

Geulen, Eva. 2015. "Begriffsgeschichten Go Global (or Try To)." *Merkur*, no. 788: 38–48.

Groden, Michael, Martin Kreiswirth, and Imre Szeman, eds. 2005. *The Johns Hopkins Guide to Literary Theory and Criticism.* 2nd ed. Baltimore, MD: Johns Hopkins University Press.

———. 2012. *Contemporary Literary and Cultural Theory: The Johns Hopkins Guide.* Baltimore, MD: Johns Hopkins University Press.

Habib, Rafey. 2005. *A History of Literary Criticism: From Plato to the Present.* Malden, MA: Blackwell.

———. 2008. *Modern Literary Criticism and Theory: A History.* Malden, MA: Blackwell.

Hale, Dorothy J., ed. 2006. *The Novel: An Anthology of Criticism and Theory, 1900–2000.* Malden, MA: Blackwell.

Harpham, Geoffrey Galt. 2003. "From Revolution to Canon: On *The Norton Anthology of Theory and Criticism*." *Kenyon Review* 25, no. 2: 169–87.

John, Eileen, and Dominic Lopes, eds. 2004. *Philosophy of Literature: Contemporary and Classic Readings; An Anthology.* Malden, MA: Blackwell.

Leitch, Vincent B., ed. 2010. *The Norton Anthology of Theory and Criticism*. 2nd ed. New York: Norton.

Lloyd, Moya. 2015. "Travelling Theories." *Redescriptions* 18, no. 2: 121–25.

Lotringer, Sylvère. 2009. "German Issues." In *The German Issue*, edited by Sylvère Lotringer, v–viii. 2nd ed. Los Angeles: Semiotext(e).

Lützeler, Paul Michael. 2013. "Suhrkamp Culture amerikanisch? Siegfried Unseld in der neuen Welt (2011)." In *Transatlantische Germanistik: Kontakt, Transfer, Dialogik*, edited by Paul Michael Lützeler, 159–78. Berlin: de Gruyter.

Parker, Robert Dale. 2012. *Critical Theory: A Reader for Literary and Cultural Studies*. New York: Oxford University Press.

Patai, Daphne, and Will H. Corral. 2005. Introduction to *Theory's Empire: An Anthology of Dissent*, edited by Daphne Patai and Will H. Corral, 1–18. New York: Columbia University Press.

Paul, Morten. 2013. "Theorieproduktion als Vermittlungsproblem: Die Buchreihe 'Theorie' (1966–1986)." *Geschichte der Germanistik*, nos. 43–44: 143–45.

Raulff, Ulrich. 2014. *Wiedersehen mit den Siebzigern: Die wilden Jahre des Lesens*. Stuttgart: Klett-Cotta.

Raulff, Ulrich, and Stephan Schlak, eds. 2012. "Droge Theorie." Special issue. *Zeitschrift für Ideengeschichte* 6, no. 4.

Richter, David H. 2007. *The Critical Tradition: Classic Texts and Contemporary Trends*. 3rd ed. New York: Bedford / St. Martin's.

Rivkin, Julie, and Michael Ryan, eds. 2004. *Literary Theory: An Anthology*. 2nd ed. Malden, MA: Blackwell.

Rodowick, David Norman. 2014. *Elegy for Theory*. Cambridge, MA: Harvard University Press.

Ryan, Michael, Gregory Castle, Robert Eaglestone, and M. Keith Booker, eds. 2011. *The Encyclopedia of Literary and Cultural Theory*. Malden, MA: Wiley-Blackwell.

Said, Edward. 1983. "Traveling Theory." In *The World, the Text, and the Critic*, 226–46. Cambridge, MA: Harvard University Press.

Scaff, Lawrence A. 2011. *Max Weber in America*. Princeton, NJ: Princeton University Press.

Stevens, Anne H., and Jay Williams. 2006. "The Footnote, in Theory." *Critical Inquiry* 32, no. 2: 208–25.

Wellek, René. 1965. "Comparative Literature Today." *Comparative Literature* 17, no. 4: 325–37.

Werner, Michael, and Bénédicte Zimmermann. 2002. "Vergleich, Transfer, Verflechtung: Der Ansatz der Histoire croisée und die Herausforderungen des Transnationalen." *Geschichte und Gesellschaft* 28, no. 4: 607–36.

Zwarg, Robert. 2011. "Frankfurt in Madison—zur Rezeption der Kritischen Theorie in Amerika." *Simon Dubnow Institute Yearbook* 10: 89–111.

(Mis)reading the Market?
The Publishing Business and Theory Transfer

Joe Paul Kroll

At what point might theory transfer from a foreign language be said to begin? When a scholar or critic happens upon a writer and decides to promote that writer in the classroom or in his or her own work? When a theorist's reputation percolates through footnotes until enough readers decide to follow up the references? When a commissioning editor learns of an interesting new thinker at an international book fair? Or when a theorist becomes so celebrated in another country that an enterprising publisher decides to take a bet, hoping to bring home the next big thing?

All of these are plausible scenarios, though they are far from the only possibilities. As the case studies presented in this special issue show, there is also the factor of time to consider: how long before a thinker is translated, and then what interval between translation and reception—if reception takes place

For inspiration and information, I am grateful to Katharina Bensch (Börsenverein des Deutschen Buchhandels), Sebastian Budgen (Verso), Emily-Jane Cohen (Stanford University Press), Eva Gilmer (Suhrkamp), Petra Hardt (Suhrkamp), Christie Henry (University of Chicago Press), Philip Laughlin (MIT Press), Wendy Lochner (Columbia University Press), Ute Lütkenhaus (Börsenverein des Deutschen Buchhandels), Thomas McCarthy (Northwestern University), Timothy Nunan (Harvard University), Julia Schülli (Campus Verlag), Anke Simon (Börsenverein des Deutschen Buchhandels), William P. Sisler (Harvard University Press), Riky Stock (German Book Office, NYC), Judith Wilke-Primavesi (Campus Verlag, Geisteswissenschaften International). For the opportunity to research this topic and present my findings, I would like to thank the conference organizers, Anson Rabinbach and Andreas Huyssen, and, for the staff, William Dellinger.

New German Critique 132, Vol. 44, No. 3, November 2017
DOI 10.1215/0094033X-4162226   © 2017 by New German Critique, Inc.

at all, that is, beyond the circle of scholars dedicating themselves to a particular theorist's thought? The image used on flyers and posters for the conference that led to this issue, a sinking ship (most likely the *Titanic*), seems to have been chosen to evoke the notion of cargo and communications never reaching their destination (not to mention the shipwreck being one of Hans Blumenberg's favorite metaphors). But it might also put one in mind of another nautical metaphor, that of ships passing in the night, missed encounters in another sense: not so much the failure of communication as obliviousness to its very possibility.

Whether an encounter even takes place and whether it results in communication depends on many factors, of which translation is perhaps the most important—though it leaves open the intelligibility of "foreign" ideas, even when rendered into a familiar language. It is also worth bearing in mind questions of what perceived needs beyond "mere" curiosity translation may serve, what place new ideas may assume in the intellectual economy of the "buyer" country. The following study can, however, give at most indirect or partial answers to such questions, and it altogether excludes considerations of the theory of translation and cultural transfer, right up to the notion of "world literature."

Instead, this article attempts to contribute to an understanding of theory transfer by turning to a site beloved less of literary scholars than economists: the marketplace, where historians of intercultural communication and transfer have long begun their inquiries. My aim, in short, is to examine the market for translations from German into English of scholarly work in the humanities and,   . to the extent that it can be cleanly distinguished, "theory" in particular. The underlying assumption is that monetary transactions often accompany and indeed precede transfer of a more immaterial kind. In the case of the book, we are faced with a material commodity with an immaterial content, capable of being diffused independently, at least to some extent, of its material character. Trade in translation rights is the sale and purchase of the right to render ideas into another language and sell them in a material form, though it is neither a necessary nor a sufficient condition for theory transfer to take place: on the one hand, ideas may be diffused indirectly, secondhand, or by pirated translations; on the other hand, licensed translations may fail to find readers.

In any case, we would expect, at some point in *successful* theory transfer, official translations to appear on the market. Whether crowd-sourced translations will change this remains unknown. For the time being—and certainly for the time on which this issue looks back—licensed translations are the norm. In looking at the situation as it currently presents itself to individuals in or close to the publishing industry, I hope that this article provides some perspective to those working, knowingly or not, in cultural exchange:

publishers looking for new ideas, critics wondering why a favorite theorist has not yet become widely known or even been translated, and scholars hoping to broaden the exchange of ideas.

This issue is based on the assumption that there is a problem with translation, that is, with at least two distinct stages: getting books translated and getting people to read them. The problem extends across genres and categories. Apropos of the award of the Nobel Prize in Literature to the French novelist Patrick Modiano in 2014, the website *Daily Beast* noted that "about 3 percent of all the books published in the U.S. every year are translations. But the bulk of these are technical writings or reprints of literary classics; only 0.7 percent are first-time translations of fiction and poetry."[1] Assuming that this figure is correct, it would mean that 9,147 of 304,912 titles published in the United States in 2013 were translated from another language.[2] Compare the figure for Germany in the same year: 11.5 percent (10,731) of 93,600 titles published were translations, a larger number, in both absolute and relative terms, than in the United States.

Such figures may bear out anecdotal evidence and give some support to preconceived notions of American cultural insularity. But they tell us little about books sold, except by inference: American publishers seem less optimistic than their German counterparts about the market prospects for translated literature. Another question that simple statistics of this kind are unable to answer, and which it will be left to the case studies on individual thinkers to cast some light on, is the time lag between original publication and translation—and then again, perhaps, reception. A book that defines an era in its country of origin may arrive on foreign shores to find itself in the midst of another discourse entirely or, worse, none at all. Maybe the encounters we are considering here are not so much missed as delayed or ill-timed ones.

My aim here is to discuss the market situation of books published in the humanities in general and, wherever possible, "theory" in particular. I begin by giving some more detailed figures for recent translations from German into English and situating them in the context of the development of overall foreign rights sales by German publishers. After addressing these quantitative questions, I look at the institutional support the German book trade provides for translation in the humanities, especially the Geisteswissenschaften International program. Third, I bring together some voices from the publishing industry on both sides of the Atlantic in order to hear their views on the market and

1. Morris, "Why Americans Don't Read Foreign Fiction."
2. Ingenta, "IPA Report Says Global Publishing Productivity Is Up."

the institutional support available, as well as their ideas for improvement. This also includes a historical perspective, asking how the business has changed since the last great wave of exports to the United States began in the late 1960s, associated with the (re)discovery of the Frankfurt School.

The Foreign Rights Market in Numbers

The market for German foreign rights sales has remained stable over a decade (fig. 1). Yet a breakdown by languages (fig. 2) reveals the relative insignificance— in quantitative terms—of sales of translation rights to English-language countries by German publishers.[3] Indeed, neither the United States nor the United Kingdom has been among the top ten most important countries for foreign rights sales in recent years, though the sale of English-language rights to other countries gives English a greater role.[4] If German publishers nevertheless take particular satisfaction in making sales to English-language countries (though this statement is purely anecdotal), it surely has something to do with the prestige associated with cracking a market that, as was suggested above, is not without reason perceived as somewhat insular. Moreover, Germany's trade deficit in the foreign rights business (fig. 3) seems greater still when looking at publisher's catalogs and the best seller list, in which books translated from English figure prominently. Though there are signs that the German nonfiction market, in particular, is turning inward, to launch the next big thing from across the Atlantic remains a major ambition for German publishers. To reverse the flow must, under these circumstances, seem a little like breaking into Hollywood.

With regard to "theory," the statistics compiled by the Börsenverein, the powerful trade organization in Germany, put us at the mercy of fairly arbitrary classifications. "Theory" is most likely to be found in *Geisteswissenschaften* and *Philosophie* (in which not all works are necessarily "theory" for the purposes of this issue), but it may also include works from other categories, such as history. This uncertainty should not, however, trouble us unduly. Nor should we be too concerned that the translation of theory from German into English

---

3. In this context, it is worth remembering that the traditional distinction in the foreign rights market, between US rights, on the one hand, and UK and Commonwealth rights, on the other, still to some extent obtains, though multinational publishing corporations such as Holtzbrinck or Random House increasingly control the international translation and distribution of best-selling titles through their own subsidiaries. This barely applies, however, to the "theory" market under consideration here, in which independent publishers and university presses play a far more important role and in which English-language rights tend to be sold for distribution in all countries.

4. Börsenverein des Deutschen Buchhandels, *Buch und Buchhandel in Zahlen 2015*, tables 47–50. China and Chinese top the respective tables for countries and languages. While no English-speaking country has made the top ten in recent years, the English language was the second most important for foreign rights sales in 2014.

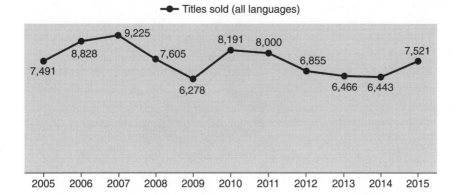

Figure 1. Foreign rights sales by German publishers, 2005–15

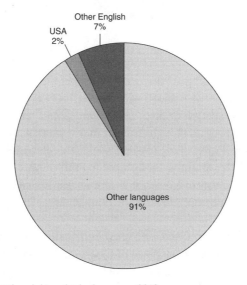

Figure 2. German foreign rights sales by language, 2012

represents a fraction of a fraction of the overall market, and from that perspective is commercially negligible, for it is precisely that small share that interests us. Placing it in a broader context can only help explain why market incentives alone are not enough to ensure that theory transfer by means of commercial translation takes place.

The latest figures released by the Börsenverein show that in 2015 German publishers sold ninety-eight licenses for English-language rights in the category *Geisteswissenschaften, Kunst, Musik*. In the subcategory *Philosophie*, English

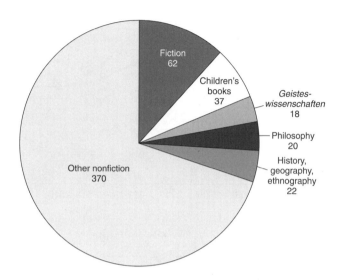

Figure 3. Foreign rights balance of trade for Germany, 2013

leads with thirty-two titles ahead of Chinese, Italian, and Spanish, tied for second place with twenty-four titles each.[5] *Geschichte*, perhaps surprisingly, is a weaker category overall, though stronger in general than in academic nonfiction, with combined sales of twenty-one titles. The categories used in the 2012 survey (fig. 4) differ slightly, though the overall picture is consistent. The catch-all category *Geisteswissenschaften* for unclassifiable work is diminished in 2015, at a mere five titles, down from 18 in 2012.

Supporting Translation: Geisteswissenschaften International
Unfortunately, establishing the place of theory in the translation market does not relate the number of relevant titles sold to the overall production of theory, nor can it explain what titles end up being translated in a commercial climate largely unfavorable to the undertaking. To help answer at least the second of these questions, this section considers some of the institutional support available to publishers on both sides of the deal.

5. *Lizenzumfrage 2016*, supplied to the author by e-mail from Katharina Bensch at the Börsenverein des Deutschen Buchhandels on July 5, 2016. *Geisteswissenschaften, Kunst, Musik* is product group 5 in this statistic; confusingly, however, many of its subcategories also turn up in product group 9, *Sachbuch*, or general as opposed to academic nonfiction. For philosophy (this time including religion), this puts English behind Chinese, adding another three and fifteen titles, respectively.

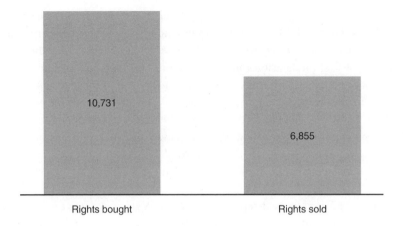

Figure 4. Distribution of English-language rights sales by subject, 2012

The single most important program dedicated to this end is Geisteswissenschaften International (GWI), which was founded in 2008 and is supported by the Fritz Thyssen Foundation, the VG Wort (the German copyright collecting agency), the Börsenverein, and the German Foreign Ministry—the inclusion of the latter suggesting that the promotion of German scholarship is not merely a matter of commercial or academic significance but one in which national prestige is at stake—and in which the country's representation abroad may be influenced, however gently. The stated aims of GWI are as follows:

> Geisteswissenschaften International's objective is to support wider international dissemination of the results of academic research carried out in Germany in the social sciences and the humanities and at the same time, to uphold and support the German language as an academic language and the language of first publication. The idea is to increase the number of licenses sold in the English-speaking world and to preserve the opportunity to continue publishing academic works in the German language.[6]

Since information on the technicalities of the application process is easily accessed online, it shall be noted here only that grants tend to cover the entire

6. The application process is described in some detail at www.boersenverein.de/de/portal/Terms_and_conditions_for_participation/255620; the German website www.boersenverein.de/de/portal/Uebersetzungsfoerderung/186810 also links directly to lists of awards for each session in the last seven years.

cost of translating a book, which may range, depending on length, from around three thousand to well over fifteen thousand dollars, as well as rendering practical assistance. GWI aims "to motivate active scholars to use German as the language of first publication for their academic findings in Germany." The principal beneficiaries are thus books "that have been published within the three years preceding the application year." GWI is not a means for introducing back catalogs of belatedly discovered theorists to Anglophone readers, though posthumously published works or newly prepared editions of extant titles may occasionally receive funding.[7] Applications are reviewed by a jury, currently eleven members, drawn from academe, the publishing industry, and the media (i.e., professional critics).

To get beyond the self-representation of GWI, I spoke to a recent member of the jury, Judith Wilke-Primavesi, editorial director at Campus Verlag in Frankfurt.[8] She explained that there are two awards sessions per year, with about fifty to eighty entries per semester. (A "letter of intent" from a potential licensee is not actually required, but is certainly helpful.) From this pool, between fifteen and thirty-five titles receive awards, depending on the strength of the field and the total cost. The beneficiaries of grants are ideally newcomers—that is, authors whose work has not yet been translated into English, though they may already have a reputation in Germany.

Of course, not all jurors can read all books: each book is assigned to two jurors. Agreement between the two tends to prefigure the final decision, positive or negative. Given the nature of this process, there is no single perspective from which the entire jury can decide, since only those jurors who have read the books can really discuss them. A further question concerns biases implicit in the process. Although GWI claims to make its selections purely on merit, and there is no official remit to shape Germany's image abroad, there does seem to be a sense among jurors that they are expected to choose "representative" works. Such books would be expected to convey not just a positive image of German scholarship but also one of a country addressing all aspects of its past, both Auschwitz and Goethe. There also appears to be a certain bias against essayistic works in favor of more rigorous *Wissenschaftlichkeit*.

If we expect "theory" as a genre to be replenished precisely by hard-to-classify work defying the academic mainstream, a program like GWI in its

7. E.g., Hans Blumenberg's *Paradigmen zu einer Metaphorologie* at the April 2010 session: www .boersenverein.de/de/portal/Ausgezeichnete_Werke_April_2010/381264.

8. The following two paragraphs are based on a telephone interview with Judith Wilke-Primavesi, June 17, 2014. The figures were checked with Anke Simon, Börsenverein des Deutschen Buchhandels, e-mail to author, September 14, 2016.

present form may not represent the best support for its translation, invaluable though its efforts may generally be. Both an appreciation and a critique comes from Sebastian Budgen, the commissioning editor at Verso, an independent publisher in both the United Kingdom and the United States.[9] Whereas the literary prizes and awards that influence sales in Germany are, as far as the Anglophone market is concerned, marginal incentives at most, he calls GWI "one of the most positive developments in German publishing," one without which it would be extremely hard to make translation from German viable at all. Yet its efforts tend to be hampered by remaining stuck in a somewhat inward-looking perspective. "I think we should be grateful to both the Goethe-Institut and GWI, but it seems to me that there's a lack of comprehension about cultural differences. Books that are big in Germany (or France or Italy or Spain, for that matter), may only sell 1,000 copies, and often may sell far less than that in the States." The problem here, in other words, is that critical attention and praise do not even reliably translate into sales in the domestic market, and still less so abroad, yet both publishers and organizations like GWI seem to accord disproportionate importance to a book's reception by the German literary critics.

Another problem with GWI, as this editor sees it, is that it tends to hide behind "a slippery concept of scientificity," which is defined as whatever the jury wants it to be at any given moment. He also sees a quest for "respectability," in which a six-hundred-page book on the Holocaust or Nazism is likely to beat out a slim volume of essays, however original the latter may be. Finally, he finds an unsubtle understanding of the Anglophone market reflected in the way German books are sold abroad. One problem is that market success and critical renown do not translate one to one. More frustrating still is the polarization he sees between the extremely populist and the highly academic, including the German practice of publishing dissertations without major revisions—books written with a committee rather than readers in mind. Independent publishers looking for support in translating less conventional work into English thus find their needs only partly met by GWI. This might be less problematic if publishers did not increasingly depend on GWI and organizations like the Goethe-Institut not just for financing but also for the selection of titles to be considered. That publishers should virtually outsource their acquisitions, however, points to another problem, which I address later on: a lack of knowledge of German and the German cultural scene in publishing houses.

9. Sebastian Budgen (commissioning editor, Verso Books), telephone conversation with author, June 12, 2014.

Less specific than GWI, but instead directed at promoting German literature in general, is the work of the German Book Office (GBO), which shares
its premises with the Goethe-Institut in New York City. The GBO was founded
in 1998 as a bureau of the Frankfurt Book Fair, and its mission is to connect
US publishers with German foreign rights managers, editors, translators, and
readers. Its projects include events in the United States as well as an annual
editors' trip to Germany, in which commissioning editors from US publishing
houses visit centers of the German publishing industry. The GBO also publishes a list of recent titles of interest as well as hosting the "New Books in
German" website,[10] which not only points out titles of interest (in what is obvi-
ously a curated selection) but also aims to connect translators and publishers.
Like GWI, the GBO is supported by the German foreign ministry. If the GBO
and the Goethe-Institut are given relatively short shrift in this article, it is because
only a small part of their activities have the promotion of scholarship in the
humanities, less still *theory*, as their specific aim. The work done by the
Goethe-Institut to create spaces for cultural exchange—not least by supporting
this conference that led to this issue—is invaluable, but its benefits reside less in
providing support to specific translation projects (as in the case of GWI) than in
promoting an awareness and understanding of the German cultural scene, which
many of the professionals consulted for this article see as a major desideratum.

Theory's Powerhouse: Suhrkamp Verlag

Although its hegemony has been challenged almost since it became established,
the most prestigious and important—not least in terms of volume—publisher
of theory in German remains Suhrkamp, founded in 1950 and now, after many
years down the road from the Institute for Social Research in Frankfurt, based
in Berlin. From the outset, Suhrkamp published both literature and theory,
notably the works of Theodor W. Adorno and Walter Benjamin. Its activities as
a publisher of scholarship in philosophy and the social sciences, however,
expanded greatly in the 1960s. Suhrkamp's paperback series in particular was
well adapted to the needs of a fast-growing market of politicized students. The
first installment of twenty paperbacks in the *edition suhrkamp* series, launched
in 1963 and still running, included *Eingriffe* by Adorno, *Waiting for Godot* by
Samuel Beckett, and *Tractatus Logico-Philosophicus* by Ludwig Wittgenstein.
This commingling of fiction and nonfiction in a single, affordable series was a
highly original concept in Germany at the time, and not uncontentious: Hans
Blumenberg, who was introduced to Suhrkamp's publisher, Siegfried Unseld,
by Jacob Taubes (Blumenberg and Taubes would go on to coedit the short-lived

---

10. New Books in German, www.new-books-in-german.com.

but influential *Theorie* series of paperbacks), was initially afraid that Suhrkamp lacked scholarly credibility, though he would ultimately remain with the house for the rest of his life.[11] As a case study, Suhrkamp is particularly relevant as the publisher of all the authors discussed in this special issue, at least for part of their work.

Today Suhrkamp publishes about 470 books per year across genres and under various imprints. Its catalog for spring 2015 contained about forty works by German authors classifiable as theory (some of them posthumous editions) and a further twenty translated from other languages. Suhrkamp's rights director, Petra Hardt,[12] told me that the firm sells about twenty English-language licenses a year, half of which are nonfiction. Whether the buyers are based in the United Kingdom, the United States, or elsewhere is of secondary concern, for Suhrkamp sells only global rights. The single largest buyer is Polity Press, based in Cambridge (UK). Against the idea of the 1960s as a golden age of theory, at least from a commercial perspective, Hardt notes that the global market gained its present momentum only after 1990. Between 1995 and 2014, Suhrkamp sold rights to about 160 *wissenschaftliche* titles to Anglophone publishers. Current major sellers in the international marketplace include Axel Honneth, Peter Sloterdijk, and a surprise best seller, *Gekaufte Zeit* by Wolfgang Streeck, an analysis of the global financial crisis and its repercussions within the Eurozone. Being the publisher of Jürgen Habermas, notes Hardt, still opens doors, and his works continue to sell very well.

In promoting new books, time is an important factor: licenses tend to sell within twelve months of first publication or not at all, though efforts are still being made for backlist authors such as Blumenberg and Niklas Luhmann. Problems that arise in promoting German authors abroad can have as much to do with business practices as with academic cultures. For instance, Suhrkamp's self-image is of an *Autorenverlag*, a publisher cultivating long-term relationships with authors and making a commitment to their work rather than marketing only individual books.[13] This practice is not reflected in the

11. Blumenberg to Taubes, March 22, 1965, in Blumenberg and Taubes, *Briefwechsel*, 49: "ob der äußere Habitus meiner Arbeiten, in denen ich auf den traditionellen 'gelehrten Apparat' nicht verzichten mag, in das Bild eines Verlages vorwiegend belletristischer Art und von Beweislasten unbeschwerter Philosophie passen würde" (whether the outward aspect of my works, in which I am loath to dispense with the traditional "scholarly apparatus," would sit comfortably with the image of a publishing house dealing mainly in literary fiction and the kind of philosophy that is unencumbered by burdens of evidence).

12. Petra Hardt (rights director, Suhrkamp Verlag), telephone conversation with author, May 22, 2014.

13. A British editor told me that this expectation on Suhrkamp's part made it harder to take a chance on a single book.

acquisitions by foreign publishers or their subsequent policies. Despite Suhrkamp's best efforts, in concert with Stanford University Press, it has so far been impossible to produce a uniform English-language edition of Adorno's works, because the rights are spread among too many publishers. On the other hand, Hardt is very pleased with the Harvard University Press edition of Benjamin's writings. As far as support by GWI is concerned, what she sees is not a political agenda but a good understanding of the target market.

From an editorial perspective, Hardt's colleague Eva Gilmer adds that while the editors naturally cannot directly influence rights sales, their potential does play some part in commissioning decisions.[14] Younger authors in particular are well connected abroad and make their contacts available for promoting their books. However, younger German authors are also increasingly likely to write in English, especially if they work abroad or in international research groups, evidence of the diminishing importance of German as a global academic language. Gilmer also points to different demarcations between and traditions within disciplines, which may mean that the marketing of an author, in particular a theorist, needs to be adapted to a different audience: for instance, in the United States, Blumenberg tends to be studied in literature rather than in philosophy departments. As for reception habits across the Atlantic, German editors can pick up hints from the footnotes to the American books they are sent for consideration, giving them at least an impression of how the traffic of ideas is flowing in each direction.

As the market leader and beneficiary of a long-established network, with the most impressive back catalog in the business, Suhrkamp may be a somewhat atypical example, but the conditions for its success convey a notion of the challenges smaller publishers face.

The 1970s: Theory's "Golden Age"?
The idea of a "golden age" not just of German theory but of its reception abroad has already been mentioned a few times in this study. Many scholars, journals, and publishers contributed to its success, from pirated editions and underground newsletters to university presses. Perhaps the single most important attempt by an American publisher to translate a canon of German theory into English is the series Studies in Contemporary German Social Thought, published by MIT Press. Its authors include Habermas, Blumenberg, Reinhart Koselleck, Carl Schmitt, Ernst Tugendhat, Karl-Otto Apel, Hans-Georg Gadamer, Ernst Bloch, and Adorno. The series comprises sixty-five transla-

---

14. Eva Gilmer (editor, Suhrkamp Verlag), telephone conversation with author, May 26, 2014.

tions as well as additional titles written in English. Although these translations appeared between 1981 and 2005 and thus somewhat later than the purported golden age, the project's roots lie in the late 1960s and early 1970s, as the series editor, Thomas McCarthy, explains.[15]

McCarthy became acquainted with the Critical Theory of the Frankfurt School while working as a research assistant at the University of Munich from 1968 to 1972. This was the time when Critical Theory was being "resurrected" in the form of new editions and commentaries, since much of it had never been published in Germany before or had been suppressed under the Nazi regime. McCarthy takes up the story:

> When I returned to the USA to take up a position at Boston University, I got in touch with Beacon Press, which was interested in the work of Jürgen Habermas, a contemporary, influential representative of the Frankfurt School, and agreed to do a translation of his *Legitimation Crisis* (1975) and a critical study of his work to date [*The Critical Theory of Jürgen Habermas*] (1978).
>
> At about that time, MIT Press met with great success in publishing a translation of Lukács's *History and Class Consciousness*, which had been urged upon them by one of my colleagues. In trying to understand (and perhaps duplicate) this unexpected success, they talked to a number of people who told them that there was publishing gold lying everywhere in Germany, as the process of reception had been seriously interrupted since the 1930s. They set about looking for an editor for some sort of translation project. They eventually came to me, and I proposed that there be a series of such translations dealing with important works and from before and after the War, which had not yet been translated. The result was a series of about one hundred works, at first mostly translations and later increasingly English language works that discussed or otherwise continued the reception of German traditions.[16]

McCarthy also stresses that, even in its supposed heyday, theory was unprofitable, and grants from German organizations were not yet available. A series like Studies in Contemporary German Social Thought could be published only because a university press decided that it could afford to subsidize such a project and would derive some prestige from it. This was not to be taken for granted but in turn depended on vigorous lobbying of the board by the acquisitions editor at the time, who was personally committed to the series. Personal commitment, McCarthy adds, also motivated many translators in the

---

15. Thomas McCarthy (former series editor, *Studies in Contemporary German Social Thought*), e-mail to author, May 28, 2014.

16. Ibid.

early 1970s, young Jewish scholars for whom the rediscovery of a German-Jewish tradition of thought in the form of the Frankfurt School "amounted
to a rescue of lost meaning."[17]

Asked why some theories seemed to travel better than others, and why
some of the authors discussed at the conference had failed to make much of an
impact despite the availability of their work in translation through Studies in
Contemporary German Social Thought, McCarthy replied:

> The differential reception you mention struck me as largely a reflection of
> already existing or clearly growing interests in the English-speaking world.
> Thus, initially the strongest reception was given to books that reflected inter-
> ests in critical social and political theory that had developed in the 1970s. In
> other cases (e.g. books on Hegel or Kant), the receptions reflected longer-
> standing interests. In cases of relatively unknown authors in relatively
> unknown traditions, like some of those you mention, the problem was that the
> German-proficient scholars who knew their work didn't need translations, and
> for the rest it was more a matter of scattered interests from different disciplin-
> ary angles.[18]

The "golden age," it emerges, came about through several factors, some of
which, like the conditions that made the student movement on both sides of the
Atlantic possible, belong in a broader consideration of social history. Others
are more specific: the conjunction of publishers' perception of an untapped
market and the initiative of a few people with experience in the field and access
to and familiarity with material that, in many cases, was not even officially in
print in German. The commitment of young Jewish scholars to reviving a tradition of thought that had almost been cut off by the Holocaust also played a
part. McCarthy's account also suggests, however, that the work of interest to a
sufficiently wide readership would always be limited, and its appeal depended
largely on external factors that were liable to change. But "disciplinary angles"
also play a part, suggesting that there are limits to the mobility not only of
ideas but of the work in which they are transported, their academic cultures.

How much communication between academic cultures and personal
contact in particular have mattered historically is confirmed by Sebastian
Budgen of Verso Books.[19] Verso emerged in the 1970s as the imprint of the

17. Thomas McCarthy, e-mail to author, August 10, 2016.
18. Thomas McCarthy, e-mail to author, May 28, 2014.
19. Sebastian Budgen (commissioning editor, Verso Books), telephone conversation with author,
June 12, 2014.

British *New Left Review*. At the time, the *NLR* circle was part of an international network of contacts, one that "withered on the vine" during the 1980s—except for the French contacts, who came to be more strongly represented in Verso's catalog. To rebuild such networks and to cultivate relations with small publishers in Germany, and to keep these relations mutual, has been a concern for Verso. The problems faced by German theory as a whole are not, however, unique: French theory, too, is perceived to be well past its own golden age, and the malaise is felt there, too, as another editor told me: "There are no real heirs to the big names of yore."[20]

An Eroding Market?

The previous case study, Studies in Contemporary German Social Thought, looked mostly at the past. This section gathers some arguments I heard from various professionals in the United Kingdom and United States, pointing to both structural and commercial difficulties in trying to find an audience for theory in German, though many apply to other and indeed all literary genres. Among the most frequently heard complaints is the lack of German-language skills in English-speaking countries, even in academe and the publishing business. Institutions like the German Book Office exist to counterbalance this problem by making crucial information and reviews available in English and by translating excerpts even before a contract has been signed, but it is necessarily a narrow conduit, unable to provide truly comprehensive coverage or reflect a wide diversity of taste and opinion, its best efforts notwithstanding. For their part, publishers tend to lack the time and resources to follow foreign book reviews, and foreign-language titles are seldom reviewed in English-language publications. The *Times Literary Supplement* is an exception, giving occasional space to books in German, French, and other languages, whereas the *London Review of Books* will every now and then review a book published only in French. Neither publication can offer a comprehensive idea of what is going on in other intellectual cultures, which would surely mean to ask too much of them, but the more difficult question to ask is whether a general awareness of what is happening elsewhere informs their outlook. Again, the importance of informal contacts across borders in generating such awareness should be emphasized.

Personal contacts are important for authors themselves, as are the presence and visibility of authors in foreign markets. "Visibility" in this context does not necessarily mean physical presence, though it may be an asset if an

---

20. Emily-Jane Cohen (editor, Stanford University Press), e-mail message to author, February 24, 2015.

author teaches and lectures away from home. It could also mean a strong online presence, writing for high-profile blogs and websites, and not all German academics, it seems, are comfortable with this. Physical or online presence also contributes to cultivating a network of contacts through which ideas and reputations can be diffused.

From an economic perspective, translation costs are a decisive factor, far more so than the actual licensing costs, and often exceed a book's physical production costs. This presents a particular problem for more specialized titles, where each copy printed has to recoup a larger proportion of the translation costs. Yet the more specialized a book is and the smaller the niche it is addressed to, the more likely the audience will consist of people able to read it in German. Meanwhile, scholars and students in search of a quick citation or looking just to get the gist of a book may make do with Google translate, further diminishing the market for professional translations. Moreover, sales to an academic audience are in any case unlikely to make translation commercially viable. But to reach an educated audience outside academe is, if anything, more difficult still. Surprise best sellers cannot be predicted, nor do they usually draw much else in their wake—Thomas Piketty's *Capital in the Twenty-First Century*, for instance, can barely be claimed to have inaugurated overwhelming public interest in the work of French economists.

Finally, a mismatch between what constitutes theory today and a broader educated audience may prove the most difficult obstacle: the best efforts of publishers and organizations such as the Goethe-Institut and the GBO are in vain if German theory is found to be unpalatable or irrelevant. While I shall reserve judgment on the state of theory per se, and indeed would warn against talk of its "death," it seems that the potential market is diminishing as the proportion of humanities degrees awarded in the United States declines, to 6.5 percent of all degrees in 2014.[21] Although it is as unclear what level of actual engagement with theory such a figure denotes as it is what it means for the market, it does suggest a diminution of the stature of an education in the humanities overall. That said, there is no necessary connection between such a quantitative indicator and the vitality of the discipline as perceived by its students and practitioners, and the much higher rate of humanities degrees awarded in Germany should, conversely, not be misunderstood as correlating with innovation in the field.[22]

21. Jaschik, "Shrinking Humanities Major."
22. Reliable statistics on actual degrees awarded are hard to come by, but about a quarter of all German students beginning a university education enroll in humanities programs. See Piatov, "Wer das Falsche studiert."

Conclusion: Beyond Provincialism

> Only by trying to use analytic means to unlock the strengths of our own tradition and by drawing on the sources from Immanuel Kant to G. W. F. Hegel and Karl Marx in addressing systematic problems was my generation able to gain the interest and respect of American and French, and sometimes also English, colleagues. I make so bold as to recommend this because I hope to be above suspicion of provincialism.[23]

Habermas is surely right to consider a widely understood philosophical tradition to be an important factor in enabling academic discourse across national and linguistic boundaries. What seems less obvious is that this should have been the decisive factor in enabling the international success of Critical Theory—though again, the arguments may differ depending on whether one considers student radicals or philosophy departments to be the principal vectors. One may also argue in detail how close the theorists of the Frankfurt School were to the philosophical "tradition" as Habermas defines it. In any case, closeness to tradition is not a sufficient condition: the work of Hans Heinz Holz, for instance, a Marxist steeped in the philosophical tradition from Leibniz to Hegel, has traveled even less well than that of Luhmann, whose intellectual formation took place largely outside it. What has distinguished the internationally most successful—that is to say, most widely received—theorists seems rather to be their heterodox adaptation of tradition and an ability to work in, indeed a preference for, an idiom quite unlike that of conventional academic philosophy. Again, though, this could also be said of many of the theories whose "missed encounters" with a transatlantic readership are under discussion here.

At this point, it becomes unavoidable to mention such a vague concept as "fashion," more specifically perhaps, the concurrence of a cultural need with the production or even belated discovery of a certain kind of theoretical work. This seems something of a truism when applied to the conditions subsumed, at least in Europe, under the cipher "1968." What this truism belies, of course, is that the relationship between the Frankfurt School and the student movement was never straightforward. Moreover, 1968 came at the end of the lives and careers of the first generation of the Frankfurt School, or indeed brought them posthumous recognition. Their intellectual formation and much of their most celebrated work took shape under conditions other than the Federal Republic

---

23. Habermas, "Die Lesarten von Demokratie." My translation.

nearly a quarter century after World War II and the Holocaust: persecution and exile, the experience of which is reflected in perhaps the most celebrated text of the Frankfurt School, *Dialectic of Enlightenment*. Its roots go back to the 1930s, its first version appeared in 1944, and it was circulated in various pirated versions before being officially republished in 1969. By this time, the student movement on both sides of the Atlantic had begun to fragment and, in some instances, degenerate into violence and paranoia. It was in and against this atmosphere, "the utter collapse of New Left or 'movement' politics," that *New German Critique* was founded: "This was perhaps our grande illusion—that what the American left needed most in 1970, was a strong dose of German theory."[24] "French Theory," on the other hand, seems to have flowered after the disappointed revolutionary hopes of 1968, and the 1970s and 1980s found its leading exponents at the height of their powers.[25] With regard to both France and Germany, it seems that the demise of these schools has left a sense of nostalgia for a golden age of theory, which somewhat improbably can embody a sense of national cultural influence and importance.[26]

Nostalgia can be a barrier to understanding, particularly if it elides historical circumstances that are impossible and undesirable to re-create. Intellectual history risks encouraging such nostalgia when it looks back at—and in the process creates—"golden ages" in which everything seemed possible and a little pamphlet set on an electric typewriter and mimeographed in a dingy loft could take the world by storm. Furthermore, the retrospective definition of a golden age of theory is in danger of giving implicit justification to the idea of theory's subsequent irrelevance or even "death." To proclaim the death of theory would not only give undeserved succor to those who never trusted it to begin with and would now gladly banish it from the classroom, but also stifle developments in the humanities and their transfer from Germany to the English-speaking world.[27] Of course, it remains to be seen if and how their work is "popularized" and if any "heirs to the big names of yore" emerge.

24. Huyssen and Rabinbach, "*New German Critique*," 9–10.

25. Concerning a broader shift in the humanities from German to French theory in the 1970s and 1980s, Atina Grossmann, speaking from the audience at the conference, suggested that a factor may have been the rather limited use of the German variety to feminist theory. Again, theory transfer depends not least on the needs of the recipients and developments in their academic cultures.

26. For the French case, see Anderson, *New Old World*, 142–44. Anderson outlines a comprehensive French renaissance in the early years of the Fifth Republic, in which the appearance on the scene of Jacques Derrida, Michel Foucault, Jacques Lacan, and others, the "vitality of France's culture under De Gaulle," are contrasted with the country's present sense of diminished stature.

27. To name but two centers of research whose work is beginning to be noticed internationally: Internationales Kolleg für Kulturtechnikforschung und Medienphilosophie, based in Weimar, and the Exzellenzcluster "Die Herausbildung normativer Ordnungen," in Frankfurt.

Far from being mere exercises in nostalgia, historical accounts and memoirs of supposed golden ages of theory may also be instructive for the present, not least when they reveal the importance of often informal international networks and the deeply committed individuals involved in them.[28] The importance of such informal links was emphasized by several industry figures consulted for this study. Yet it seems hard to credit the idea that, in an age of global communications and mobility such as ours, they should not exist or be impossible to maintain. One explanation might be that, as the overall market for books dwindles,[29] and any growth is achieved in such areas as cookery and children's books, publishers have become more risk averse, though this hypothesis is hard to test empirically. Moreover, even the best-connected commissioning editors are limited in their choices by the exigencies of satisfying the accounts department, in other words, turning a profit. This is increasingly true even for university presses. Though they are still less guided than commercial publishers by short-term sales targets, there is a limit to the number of loss-making books they can knowingly acquire.

What this entails for those committed to disseminating theory and other kinds of literature is taking on some of the work traditionally carried out or funded by publishing houses. This is true of translation, for instance: if publishers depend on grants to make translating books viable, academics may choose to translate them out of dedication to their authors rather than for financial gain. This means, of course, that they work either on the clock or in their free time, with the cost underwritten either by their primary employers (i.e., universities) or by themselves. In turn, this makes translating theory a risky business for professional translators, whose livelihood depends on paid work and who are already under pressure from stagnating fees. Yet it may be that initiatives by enthusiastic translators will be of increasing importance in bringing to the attention of publishers and ultimately the marketplace works that otherwise would not have been considered promising economic prospects.

The case of bloggers is more complicated. It would be tempting to say that the publishing industry had also outsourced the diffusion of new books and ideas to bloggers, but this is patently not the case, as the example of the German Book Office shows. Independent bloggers can, however, do much to augment such efforts. A good example would be Katy Derbyshire, a professional literary translator from German into English, whose blog gathers updates on works in

---

28. A case in point is Felsch, *Der lange Sommer der Theorie.*

29. Both in Germany and in the United States; on the website of the Börsenverein, figures for Germany may be found at www.boersenverein.de/de/182716, for the United States at www.buchmesse .de/images/fbm/dokumente-ua-pdfs/2014/us_book_market_2014_v29102014_48184.pdf.

progress and observations on the German literary scene.[30] Derbyshire's blogging is, of course, only a sideline to her work as a translator and makes no claims to comprehensiveness. It is also dependent on the continued economic viability of translation. This is not to say that any comparable project concentrating on theory would have to follow analogous lines, but merely to point out that any sustained engagement with literature of whatever kind, particularly if it involves writing on it, requires some kind of economic support, be it in simple cash, in the availability of free time, or in the form of institutional incentives: academics tend to be rewarded for scholarly articles rather than blog posts, even if the latter may end up reaching a far wider audience.

On the German side, the state of criticism has recently been the subject of some debate, amid claims that the daily and weekly newspapers, traditionally the main outlets for book reviews, have made less space available for the coverage of new releases and that the sheer diversity of the literary blogosphere is hard to navigate.[31] In the absence of a taste-defining print publication devoted to long-form book reviews and literary journalism, like the *New York Review of Books* and its London namesake, or one as far ranging as the *Times Literary Supplement*, this must also be of concern to anyone abroad hoping to keep abreast of debates and trends. Furthermore, any such publication would still come up against the language barrier. The idea of one editor interviewed for this article—a supplement dedicated to reviews of German books, in English, to be published (in print and, more important still, online) on the occasion of the Frankfurt Book Fair by a German newspaper, be it the *Frankfurter Allgemeine* or *die tageszeitung*—seems both charming and doomed to failure unless those already beleaguered institutions can find someone else to pay for it. The charm of such a project would lie in its representing the viewpoint of a particular paper with all its quirks and biases rather than a selection made by committee to please supposed international tastes.

Indeed, any initiative that raises international awareness of the literary and intellectual scene in Germany can only benefit theory. It is thus particularly sad that one of the boldest attempts at doing so, the website signandsight .com, was discontinued for lack of funding. The site offered translations into English of articles from newspapers and magazines, not only from Germany but from many other European languages and countries, in an attempt to create something like a European space for debate—based on the idea of English

---

30. Love German Books, lovegermanbooks.blogspot.de.

31. For an overview of this debate, see Perlentaucher.de, www.perlentaucher.de/essay/perlentaucher -debatte-literaturkritik-im-netz.html.

as a lingua franca.[32] An international project from a German perspective, the example of signandsight.com raises, though by no means answers, the question whether national initiatives are enough and whether to gain an international audience it might be necessary to dispense with so constitutive a factor of cultural identity as language.

As long as German remains a language of intellectual discourse and Germany retains a lively literary culture, some knowledge of German is undoubtedly the key to appreciating the diversity of what is thought, written, and said in that language. Yet to address the poor state of foreign-language instruction in English-speaking countries and elsewhere is more than German institutions, and certainly the German publishing industry, are able to do. What they can do is to address audiences abroad in their own language or in the de facto lingua franca, English, as the Goethe-Institut and the German Book Office already do. Yet is not enough merely to make information available. German organizations and publishers must cultivate an awareness of the specific needs and interests of their target markets. It is not only some German words that do not translate easily: this is also true of commercial success and academic cultures.

References

Anderson, Perry. 2013. *The New Old World*. London: Verso, 2009.

Blumenberg, Hans, and Jacob Taubes. 2013. *Briefwechsel, 1961–1981, und weitere Materialien*. Berlin: Suhrkamp.

Börsenverein des Deutschen Buchhandels, ed. 2015. *Buch und Buchhandel in Zahlen 2015*. Frankfurt am Main: Börsenverein des Deutschen Buchhandels.

Felsch, Philipp. 2015. *Der lange Sommer der Theorie: Geschichte einer Revolte, 1960–1990*. Munich: Beck.

Habermas, Jürgen. 2014. "Die Lesarten von Demokratie" (interview by Markus Schwering). *Berliner Zeitung*, June 16. www.berliner-zeitung.de/kultur/interview-mit-juergen-habermas-die-lesarten-von-demokratie-1159050-seite2.

Huyssen, Andreas, and Anson Rabinbach. 2005. "*New German Critique*: The First Decade." *New German Critique*, no. 95: 5–26.

32. Which, in turn, made it incompatible with official European Union policy. As the editors wrote in their farewell notice to readers: "Signandsight.com is not a business model. The editorial and translation costs are too high. Ideally signandsight.com would have become a project of an emerging European civil society, financed by European foundations and sponsors. But there proved to be hardly any foundations that operate on a truly European level. Many foundations wish to bring the voices of their own country into the European chorus, but are unable to support projects based in other countries. Approaching the EU was futile: it would never have funded a project dedicated to the pragmatic notion of English as a lingua franca. And a pared-down and efficient working structure was important." Seeliger and Chervel, "Signandsight.com Says Goodbye."

Ingenta. 2014. "IPA Report Says Global Publishing Productivity Is Up, but Growth Is Down." October 31. www.ingenta.com/blog-article/ipa-report-says-global-publishing-productivity-is-up-but-growth-is-down-2.

Jaschik, Scott. 2016. "The Shrinking Humanities Major: Number of Bachelor's Degrees Awarded Fell 8.7 Percent between 2012 and 2014, Study Finds." *Inside Higher Ed*, March 14. www.insidehighered.com/news/2016/03/14/study-shows-87-decline-humanities-bachelors-degrees-2-years.

Morris, Bill. 2015. "Why Americans Don't Read Foreign Fiction." *Daily Beast*, February 4. www.thedailybeast.com/articles/2015/02/04/why-americans-don-t-read-foreign-fiction.html.

Piatov, Filipp. 2015. "Wer das Falsche studiert, wird keinen Job finden." *Die Welt*, May 15. www.welt.de/debatte/kommentare/article140977655/Wer-das-Falsche-studiert-wird-keinen-Job-finden.html.

Seeliger, Anja, and Thierry Chervel. 2012. "Signandsight.com Says Goodbye." signandsight.com, March 28. www.signandsight.com/features/2234.html.

Gershom Scholem and America

Yaacob Dweck

"I rode with acquaintances in their car back here from Cincinnati across the Virginia mountains, a wonderful tour for the most part. Trying to see something of the country without a car is a project doomed to failure."[1] Thus Gershom Scholem wrote to Walter Benjamin from New York City in the spring of 1938. Scholem had come to the United States for the first time earlier that year to spend a semester in New York. He had made the trip to America from his adopted city of Jerusalem to deliver a series of lectures, the Stroock Lectures, on Jewish mysticism at the Jewish Institute of Religion. In New York and in Cincinnati Scholem visited libraries that contained Hebrew manuscripts and books essential to his work. In New York he met Theodor W. Adorno for the first time, a meeting that led to a long and productive friendship critical to the making of Benjamin's intellectual legacy.[2] Although Scholem encountered America as a fully formed scholar, the country would have a decisive impact on his later career and, to a lesser extent, on his scholarship.

Scholem and America thus seems a relatively straightforward subject. Dozens of correspondents, a number of distinguished speaking engagements, and a handful of visiting professorships all seem to make for a conventional story of a respected academic and intellectual for whom the United States was a source of patronage and validation over a long and celebrated career. There is a certain truth to this simple story. Yet, as with so much else relating to

---

1. Scholem to Benjamin, May 6, 1938, in *Complete Correspondence*, 219.
2. Adorno and Scholem, *Briefwechsel*.

New German Critique 132, Vol. 44, No. 3, November 2017
DOI 10.1215/0094033X-4162238   © 2017 by New German Critique, Inc.

Scholem, the harder one looks, the more opaque things appear. To recount the entirety of Scholem's reception in the United States would take far too long and would be far too tedious. Rather, I hope here to make a single point: Scholem's relationship with America is simultaneously a story of extraordinary success and one of abject failure. I insist on the coexistence of these two poles, but before doing so, I think it important to emphasize a sense of proportion. As the title of his memoir *From Berlin to Jerusalem* suggests, the two most significant places in Scholem's life were the Germany of his youth and the Palestine and later Israel of his adulthood.[3] America never competed for pride of place in Scholem's intellectual world.[4] Nonetheless, the country played an important role, particularly in the second half of his career. Scholem's reception in America turned a professor of mysticism in Jerusalem into an intellectual celebrity abroad. At the same time, in the 1960s and 1970s, Scholem increasingly defined himself against America.

Scholem's engagement with America begins in the late 1930s and continues until the years before his death in December 1982. By the time he died, Scholem was a household name among American intellectuals, particularly in and around New York City. This was no accident. Scholem was actively involved in curating his own reception in three distinct milieus: his adopted homeland, the country of his birth, and finally the United States. He interacted with two distinct intellectual circles in the United States. The first included close colleagues and friends, some of whom he knew from Germany or from Jerusalem, who had settled in the United States. These colleagues—Shalom Spiegel and Saul Lieberman, as well as Salo Baron and Harry Wolfson—were well-known scholars of Judaica and were roughly Scholem's contemporaries. Scholem corresponded with them, exchanged views in public and in private, dedicated articles in their honor, and contributed to their Festschriften for nearly half a century: in short, the stuff of academic life.

These colleagues were instrumental in arranging Scholem's initial visits to the United States and in overseeing the publication of some of his work in English. They were essential for the making of Scholem in America, but without a second and overlapping group Scholem probably would have remained simply another academic who had come to the United States, given a few talks, and published a few books in English. This second group can be catego-

---

3. Scholem, *From Berlin to Jerusalem*. On Scholem's memoirs, see Campanini, "Case for Sainte-Beuve."

4. Scholem himself emphasized the centrality of Palestine in his memoirs. For the centrality of Germany, see Mosse, "Gershom Scholem as a German Jew"; Zadoff, *From Berlin to Jerusalem and Back*; and Necker, Morlok, and Morgenstern, *Gershom Scholem in Deutschland*.

rized somewhat loosely as the New York Intellectuals: men such as Daniel Bell, Irving Howe, and Norman Podhoretz, and, significantly, women such as Hannah Arendt and Cynthia Ozick, all of whom played a vital role in turning Scholem into an intellectual icon.[5] Unlike the first group, many but not all the figures in the second group were younger than Scholem, and their encounter with him took place in the latter decades of Scholem's life. In this respect, as in so many others, Arendt was an exceptional figure. Within this group a certain paradox emerges, a critical point about Scholem and America: the very success of Scholem's reception in the United States was simultaneously its failure. This reception was a success in all the ways an academic could desire: Scholem was published, anthologized, translated, interviewed, and profiled. Yet his reception was also a missed encounter, less easy to define but no less important to articulate.

Scholem's meteoric rise in the literary world of America had the perverse effect that most of what he wrote was taken at face value. To make this point, I chart his engagement with the United States through a brief chronology and then turn to one example: a comparison between the reception of his monumental study of Sabbatai Sevi as a two-volume Hebrew work in Israel in the 1950s with the one-volume English translation in the United States in the 1970s. I conclude with a brief survey of remarks Scholem made in passing about American Jewish writers and scholars in the 1960s and 1970s. These comments offer another perspective about America's role in Scholem's life. Not only was America a source of patronage and prestige, but it also provided him with an alibi against which he defined himself.

Chronology
By the mid-1930s Scholem had lived in Jerusalem for well over a decade. Having first worked as a librarian at the Jewish and National University Library, he later taught courses on Jewish mysticism at the recently founded Hebrew University in Jerusalem.[6] In the late 1920s he published two substantial works of bibliography: a descriptive bibliographic guide to the literature of the Kabbalah, and descriptions of the kabbalistic manuscripts in the library where he worked.[7] First as a lecturer and then as a professor, Scholem assembled a glittering gallery of students. By the late 1930s this circle included Chaim Wirszubski,

---

5. On the term, see Howe, "New York Intellectuals." Howe's essay first appeared in *Commentary* in 1968. On Scholem as an icon, see Aschheim, *Beyond the Border*, chap. 3.

6. On Scholem's appointment, see Myers, *Re-inventing the Jewish Past*, 58n18, 159n40.

7. For the former, see Scholem, *Bibliographia Kabbalistica*; for the latter, see Scholem, *Hebrew Manuscripts in the National Library*.

Isaiah Tishby, and Moshe Perlmutter; later it included Joseph Weiss and Jacob Taubes. Between his immigration to Palestine in 1923 and his first visit to the United States in 1938, Scholem wrote a series of brilliant and highly technical articles in his native German and his adopted Hebrew. In the early 1930s Scholem was a regular contributor to *Kiryat Sefer*, the bibliographic journal of the Jewish and National University Library, and *Tarbiz*, the journal of Jewish studies founded by the great Talmudist J. N. Epstein and affiliated with the Institute of Jewish Studies at the Hebrew University.

In 1937 Scholem received an invitation from Shalom Spiegel to come to New York and lecture on Jewish mysticism. At the time Spiegel worked at the Jewish Institute of Religion, an educational institution loosely affiliated with Jewish Reform. A native of Habsburg Romania who had studied at the rabbinical seminary in Vienna, Spiegel had moved to Palestine before immigrating to New York. He was a scholar of medieval Hebrew literature whose writings on *piyyut* in Ashkenaz have the rare quality of being works of literature in and of themselves.[8] Spiegel and Scholem had known each other in Palestine, and the invitation marked the beginning of a long and fruitful correspondence.[9] Spiegel's invitation, first broached in a letter sent from New York in June 1937, had evidently been preceded by several discussions between the two when Spiegel was in Jerusalem.[10] Over two letters Spiegel made it clear that he and Stephen Wise, the head of the Jewish Institute of Religion who would serve as Scholem's official host, hoped that Scholem would deliver five or six lectures in English on Jewish mysticism. Spiegel specified that the lectures should be less technical than Scholem's earlier written work. As if to sweeten the deal, Spiegel emphasized that a visit to New York, with its vibrant intellectual life, would allow Scholem to consult the extraordinary collections of Hebrew manuscripts in the United States.

Spiegel's invitation was perfectly timed. Scholem was close to forty and at the height of his scholarly powers. He had recently discovered Sabbatianism and had just published one of his most important articles, "Mitzvah ha-ba-ah

---

8. For one instance that later appeared in English, see Spiegel, *Last Trial*; for an account of Spiegel, see Goldin, "About Shalom Spiegel."

9. A few samples of Scholem's letters to Spiegel were published posthumously. See Scholem, *Briefe*. For Spiegel's letters to Scholem, see below; Spiegel's papers, still unprocessed, are housed at the Jewish Theological Seminary Library in New York.

10. Shalom Spiegel to Gershom Scholem, June 18, 1937, in Gershom Scholem Papers, National Library of Israel, Jerusalem, Arc. 40 1599 01 2523.1. A second undated letter from Spiegel to Scholem appears in the same file. As it refers to the contents of the earlier letter from June 18, 1937, but discusses Scholem's upcoming lecture series in more specific terms, I assume that it dates to slightly later in 1937.

ba-averah: Le-havanat ha-shabtaut." One might render the full title in English as "Fulfillment by Transgression: Toward an Understanding of Sabbatianism." It eventually appeared in an English translation by Hillel Halkin as "Redemption through Sin."[11] Scholem had sent Spiegel a copy of the article, and in his response Spiegel had followed up on their earlier discussions about the possibility of Scholem's visit to New York. The pressure and challenge of delivering the public lectures that became "Major Trends in Jewish Mysticism" prompted Scholem to present a synthetic account of his field from rabbinic antiquity up to Hasidic modernity. Moreover, it forced him to improve his English. While Scholem drafted the lectures in German, he delivered six of them in English and one in Hebrew. For the English translations, Scholem had the help of George Lichtheim, a German intellectual who lived in Jerusalem, and Morton Smith, an American student at the Hebrew University who went on to a distinguished career as an ancient historian in the United States.[12] Over and above these substantial intellectual benefits, the invitation afforded Scholem the opportunity to leave Jerusalem at an opportune time. Mandate Palestine between 1936 and 1939 was punctuated by increasingly violent conflict, which Scholem referred to in letters to his mother, Betty Scholem, and to Benjamin. The extended stay in New York provided Scholem a respite from the violence and allowed him to travel through Europe on his return from Palestine.

Scholem delivered his lectures early in 1938. New York seems to have lived up to Spiegel's promise in his initial letters of invitation. In a March 1938 letter to Benjamin, Scholem referred to "the flood of New York life," mentioned the lectures that he had completed "with enormous success," and said that "I am now spending all my time studying the manuscripts."[13] Scholem spent much of the summer of 1938 traveling in Europe, where he attempted but failed to see Benjamin. He returned to Jerusalem in late September. In early November he wrote a long letter to Benjamin that picked up the thread of the latter's proposed book on Franz Kafka from earlier correspondence. The letter also included a short sketch of Scholem's stay in America, replete with gossip—he had gotten along with Adorno but could not stand Max Horkheimer—and general impressions of the United States. "It's a most attractive country," he declared, but added, "where life is easy only if you have sufficient means at your disposal." Scholem's impressions of life in New York

11. In Scholem, *Messianic Idea in Judaism*. On this article, see Alter, *Necessary Angels*, 37–38; Wasserstrom, *Religion after Religion*, chap. 14; and Lazier, *God Interrupted*, pt. 3. On Halkin's translation of the title, see Maciejko, *Mixed Multitude*, 21.

12. On Lichtheim, see Laqueur, "George Lichtheim." On Smith, see also Scholem and Smith, *Correspondence*.

13. Scholem to Benjamin, March 25, 1938, in *Complete Correspondence*, 214–15.

were written with sympathy, distance, and concern. He emphasized that "there is widespread openness to and interest in matters Americans aren't supposed to be interested in," and even conceded that "the intellectual atmosphere is better than we in Europe are accustomed to presume." Scholem's positioning of himself as a European would mark almost all his contact with America and his correspondence with Americans. He adopted the polite condescension of a European cosmopolitan rather than the cloying inferiority of a Jewish settler in the Orient. He also seems to have understood the parochialism that marked American life and even speculated on its causes: "The security they feel in their awareness that they are still essentially protected from airborne attack by the two oceans and the present state of technology influences their behavior in the extreme."[14] Scholem's letter to Benjamin, written over several days, was completed on November 8, 1938, the day before Kristallnacht.

For the next two and a half years, between his return to Jerusalem in September 1938 and May 1941, as the world descended into war, Scholem labored to revise the draft of the lectures into the text of a book. In 1941 the Schocken Publishing House in Palestine issued Scholem's *Major Trends in Jewish Mysticism*. Its dedication to Benjamin has been read as Scholem's epitaph for his recently deceased friend.[15] The book also contained a short preface that amounted to a declaration of war on any scholar who had written on the Kabbalah or any other aspect of Jewish mysticism prior to Scholem.[16] All the ambivalence and complexity that had characterized Scholem's discussion of America in his correspondence with Benjamin during and after his 1938 visit disappeared in the preface's final paragraph. Immediately before offering his thanks to Spiegel for serving as his host, Scholem referred to the scene of his lectures that made up the book as "the great desert of New York."[17]

It was over a decade before Scholem returned to the United States. In March 1946, as he prepared to return to Europe for the first time since the war, Scholem informed Morton Smith that he had been invited back by Stephen Wise to deliver another set of lectures at the Jewish Institute of Religion.[18]

---

14. Scholem to Benjamin, November 6–8, 1938, in *Complete Correspondence*, 234.

15. Anidjar, *"Our Place in al-Andalus,"* chap. 3.

16. On Scholem and his scholarly predecessors, see Schäfer, "Gershom Scholem und die 'Wissenschaft des Judentums'"; and Abrams, "Defining Modern Academic Scholarship."

17. Scholem, *Major Trends in Jewish Mysticism*, ix. For a recurrence of this phrase, see Scholem to Smith, July 3, 1961, in *Correspondence*, 128.

18. Scholem to Smith, March 24, 1946, in *Correspondence*, 14.

Scholem had originally planned to spend the late spring and early summer in Europe before continuing on to New York. This was not to be. As Scholem's many letters attest, the trip to Europe to assess the fate of Jewish books in the immediate wake of the war was a grueling experience. The Hebrew University had delegated Scholem, along with Abraham Yaari, to identify and, with luck, acquire Jewish books that the Nazis had stolen from Jews and their communities before and during the war and that were now in Allied hands. Scholem's trip, which was so difficult that he canceled his plans to continue on to the United States and returned to Jerusalem, has been vividly reconstructed by Noam Zadoff.[19] Scholem's change of plans meant that he did not travel to the United States until the spring of 1949, after most of the 1948 war had already occurred.

Scholem may not have traveled to America in the summer of 1946, but his journey to postwar Germany involved a prolonged and sustained contact with the US government and with American Jewry. The fate of Jewish property in Europe was of central concern to American Jews even before the war ended. In 1944 prominent American Jews led by Salo Baron established the Commission on European Jewish Cultural Reconstruction to coordinate the rescue and repatriation of Jewish property with other institutions worldwide, including the Hebrew University. In 1947 Baron's commission grew into Jewish Cultural Reconstruction Inc., which received authority from the US Office of Military Government to assume responsibility for the identification and dispersal of Jewish property in Allied zones.[20] Scholem's trip to the Allied depot in Offenbach occurred in the spring of 1946, as various Jewish institutions competed to assert their claims. During his time in Offenbach, Scholem examined and classified Hebrew manuscripts according to a system of roman numerals from I through V. With the help of the American military chaplain Herbert Friedman, who remained in Europe after Scholem had returned to Palestine, five boxes containing the most valuable manuscripts labeled I and II were transferred from Offenbach to the offices of the Jewish Agency in Paris. From Paris, Friedman drove the boxes to Antwerp, where they accompanied Chaim Weizman's personal library to Palestine.[21]

Scholem's involvement with the removal of Hebrew manuscripts from Allied-occupied Europe to Mandate Palestine points to a crucial aspect of his

19. Zadoff, *From Berlin to Jerusalem and Back*, chap. 5.
20. Herman, "*Hashavat Avedah*."
21. Ibid., 169–80.

encounter with America that an examination of his ideas and their circulation might otherwise leave unaccounted. In the immediate postwar period, Scholem fought for the priority of the Hebrew University and, by extension, for the Jewish settlement in Palestine to serve as the principal custodian of the Jewish cultural materials that remained in Europe. Yet the primary institution through which the examination and allocation of Jewish cultural possessions occurred was American and run by Americans. Between 1947 and 1950, when the Jewish Cultural Reconstruction carried out its most significant work, Scholem was often overwhelmed by his American colleagues. His correspondence with Hannah Arendt, who worked for long periods as the executive secretary of the Jewish Cultural Reconstruction, reflects his increasing frustration. In the spring of 1950 he wrote to Arendt about the fate of Jewish archival material from Germany that was designated for a memorial library to German Jewry at the Jewish Institute of Religion:

> I am sorry to say I have never been asked about this matter and I consider it of great importance that the position of the Hebrew University is made clear to everybody concerned. Archival material shipped to America is not a matter for the American institutions alone to be decided upon and we expect no decision to be taken without consultation with us. I fail to understand why the material has not in the first place been shipped to Israel, but, conceded the technical necessity for shipping it to the U.S.A., this does not change the claim in principle of the Hebrew University to have these materials assigned to it.[22]

Possession was nine-tenths of the law, both for the manuscripts that Scholem had identified in Offenbach and that ended up in Jerusalem and for the materials shipped to the United States. Scholem knew this all too well and repeatedly asserted the precedence of the Hebrew University of Jerusalem.

Scholem made two extended visits to the United States over the next decade. In the spring of 1949 he returned to New York to deliver a second set of Stroock lectures at the Jewish Institute of Religion. The final chapter of *Major Trends in Jewish Mysticism* had been titled "Hasidism: The Latest Phase," and Scholem devoted the entirety of these lectures to "major trends in Hasidism." Unlike the first series of lectures, which became Scholem's first English book and established his international reputation, "Major Trends in Hasidism" did not appear in print in his lifetime.[23] Although he repeatedly returned to the study of Hasidism in the ensuing decades, notably in a memo-

22. Scholem to Arendt, April, 6, 1950, in Arendt and Scholem, *Der Briefwechsel*, 255.
23. Meir, "From Scholem's Archive."

rial lecture for his student Joseph Weiss delivered in London, Scholem never wrote a synthetic account of the movement, as he did with Sabbatai Sevi and Sabbatianism and with the origins of the Kabbalah.[24]

Scholem next arrived in the United States in late 1956 to serve as a visiting professor in the spring of 1957 at Brown University, a position arranged for him by his longtime friend and former student Morton Smith. If Scholem's second set of lectures in America dealt with one of the most contemporary movements of Jewish mysticism, his third treated an ancient theme. Scholem gave the lectures, which treated gnosticism and the Hekhalot literature of late antiquity, in New York during the spring of 1957, and they subsequently appeared as an English book in 1960.[25] The book attempts to trace the relationship between gnosticism and early Jewish mysticism, a subject that Scholem had been interested in for many years. It remains one of his most speculative and challenging works. The level of difficulty may not have been accidental. Scholem was lecturing on this occasion at the Jewish Theological Seminary, at a time "when the faculty of the Jewish Theological Seminary was the most formidable array of Jewish scholars ever assembled in a single institution."[26] Spiegel, Lieberman, and H. L. Ginsberg were all on the faculty, and a few blocks south Baron taught at Columbia. Here again, one can see the intellectual relationships Scholem had formed in Jerusalem decades earlier on full display. Lieberman, who had been a student at the Institute for Jewish Studies at the Hebrew University in the 1930s, delivered perhaps the most celebrated introduction in Jewish studies for one of Scholem's lectures: "Nonsense is nonsense, but the history of nonsense is a very important science."[27] Allegedly as penance for his caustic remark, Lieberman furnished one of the appendixes to the published lectures that treated the Talmudic origins of an esoteric teaching discussed in Scholem's book.

The 1957 work on ancient Jewish mysticism marked the final time Scholem delivered a lecture series in the United States. Over the next twenty-five years Scholem returned on occasion to America, notably as a visiting professor at Boston University in 1975. If the period between 1938 and 1957 marked an intense exchange between Scholem and Jewish scholars in America, as well as considerable tension between Scholem and his American colleagues

24. On Scholem and Hasidism, see Scholem, *Final Phase.*
25. Scholem, *Jewish Gnosticism, Merkabah Mysticism, and Talmudic Tradition.*
26. Wieseltier, "Sidney," 34.
27. The phrase appears in Lieberman, "How Much Greek in Jewish Palestine?," 135, cited in Abrams, "Defining Modern Academic Scholarship," 267–68. Two lines later Lieberman cites Scholem's *Jewish Gnosticism, Merkabah Mysticism, and Talmudic Tradition* (135n4).

over the fate of Jewish books in postwar Europe, the succeeding two decades represented a different stage of Scholem's engagement with the United States.

Sabbatai Sevi *in America*

At almost the same time that Scholem was delivering his lectures in New York, his two-volume history of Sabbatai Sevi and the Sabbatian movement had appeared in Hebrew in Israel. The work built on Scholem's earlier studies of Sabbatianism, such as the chapter "Sabbatianism and Mystical Heresy" in *Major Trends in Jewish Mysticism* and his aforementioned article "Redemption through Sin." Scholem sought to recount the history of a movement that had formed around a Jewish messiah named Sabbatai Sevi and his prophet Nathan of Gaza in 1665–66. Drawing on a wealth of sources in print and in manuscript, but largely eschewing those that could have been found in state archives, Scholem demonstrated that the messianic enthusiasm had spread throughout the Jewish world from Yemen to England, Palestine to Poland. He reconstructed the frenzy in all its detail and sought to reconstruct the mind-set of the messiah and his prophet in the year and a half during which they spread their faith. Scholem focused on the spectacular suspension of norms within Jewish law that he identified as a defining feature of the Sabbatian movement. Equally, if not more important, he insisted on studying the development of Sabbatianism as a movement within Judaism even after Sabbatai Sevi's forced conversion to Islam at the behest of the Ottoman sultan in September 1666.

When *Sabbatai Sevi* appeared in Hebrew, Scholem was excoriated in the popular press and in scholarly journals. In the newspaper *Ha-aretz*, the literary critic Baruch Kurzweil attacked him on several fronts.[28] Kurzweil rejected Scholem's account of Sabbatianism as the point of origin for Jewish modernity, denied the political significance that Scholem had attributed to the movement, and dismissed Scholem's claims about the nature of Judaism, stating pointedly that "Judaism is whatever Gershom Scholem decides it is." In the academic journals, one of Scholem's colleagues, R. J. Zwi Werblowsky, and one of his former students, Isaiah Tishby, wrote extensive and disparaging reviews. In a wicked gesture, Werblowsky alluded to Scholem's attack on nineteenth-century German Jewish scholarship in the title of his review.[29] Tishby

---

28. Kurzweil, "Notes on 'Sabbatai Sevi' by Gershom Scholem." On Kurzweil and Scholem, see Myers, "Scholem-Kurzweil Debate and Modern Jewish Historiography"; and Zadoff, "Debate between Baruch Kurzweil and Gershom Scholem."

29. Werblowsky, "Reflections on 'Sabbatai Sevi' by G. Scholem." The title alludes to Scholem, "Reflections on Jewish Studies."

sought to chip away at Scholem's scholarly edifice and, in a way that neither Kurzweil nor Werblowsky had attempted, actually challenged Scholem's interpretation of specific sources and individuals.[30]

Shortly after Scholem published the Hebrew version of *Sabbatai Sevi*, he published in the *Eranos Jahrbuch* his celebrated essay "Towards an Understanding of the Messianic Idea in Judaism."[31] The essay expands on many of the ideas Scholem had developed about Jewish messianism in the opening chapter of *Sabbatai Sevi*. Yet its place of publication was hardly incidental. The *Eranos Jahrbuch* published papers from the annual conferences on the history of religions held in Ascona, Switzerland. From 1949 to 1979 Scholem addressed the Eranos Conferences, lecturing in his native German before a distinguished audience of scholars who did not hail from the narrow confines of Jewish studies.[32] Scholem's presence at Eranos echoed far beyond Switzerland. Many papers that first appeared in the *Eranos Jahrbuch* were later collected as volumes of essays published in German and in English.[33] Moreover, Scholem's presence at Eranos facilitated his contact with a new set of patrons that had a decisive impact on the making of *Sabbatai Sevi* as an English book.

The central figure at Eranos in its early years had been Carl Gustav Jung, about whose past Scholem had deep reservations.[34] Nevertheless, the Eranos Conferences and the Bollingen Foundation, a philanthropic organization founded by Mary Mellon and Paul Mellon that funded the Eranos Conferences for a time, proved decisive in the making of the English translation. The Bollingen Foundation had a publishing house devoted to issuing the works of Jung and other figures as diverse as Samuel Taylor Coleridge and Paul Valéry, as well as a fellowship program that supported scholarship such as Charles de Tolnay's work on Michelangelo and Alfred Kazin's study of American literature. At the 1952 Eranos Conference the publisher Kurt Wolff had urged Scholem to apply for a fellowship to complete the Hebrew edition of *Sabbatai Sevi*, a grant that he received and acknowledged in its preface. Yet after the book's appearance in Hebrew, it was hardly a matter of course that an English translation of *Sabbatai Sevi* would follow. An early adviser to the Bollingen Foundation who also had links to Jung, but who was not a Jungian, was the

30. Tishby, "On Gershom Scholem's Approach to the Study of Sabbatianism."
31. Scholem, "Towards an Understanding of the Messianic Idea in Judaism." The essay first appeared as "Zum Verständnis der messianischen Idee im Judentum."
32. On Scholem at Eranos, see Wasserstrom, *Religion after Religion*; Dan, "Gershom Scholem, *Eranos*, and *Religion after Religion*"; and Zadoff, *From Berlin to Jerusalem and Back*, 294–331.
33. Scholem, *Zur Kabbala und ihrer Symbolik*.
34. On Scholem and Jung, see Zadoff, *From Berlin to Jerusalem and Back*, 299–306.

Berkeley anthropologist Paul Radin. The son of a rabbi, Radin had been born in Poland in 1883 and raised in New York City. Radin understood the importance of *Sabbatai Sevi* and convinced the Bollingen Foundation and its president, John D. Barrett, to fund Werblowsky's translation into English.[35] In 1967 the Bollingen Foundation had signed an agreement to publish future works with Princeton University Press, and Werblowsky's translation duly appeared under their joint imprint in 1973.

It was thus due to a series of American patrons that *Sabbatai Sevi* appeared as a one-volume English book. The English publication of *Sabbatai Sevi* presents several contrasts to Scholem's earlier work in English and in Hebrew. His two previous book-length studies in English, *Major Trends in Jewish Mysticism* and *Jewish Gnosticism, Merkabah Mysticism, and Talmudic Tradition*, had both appeared under the imprint of Jewish publishing houses. While both books earned Scholem the respect and admiration of his colleagues, neither generated a sustained discussion in and of itself. The Hebrew edition of *Sabbatai Sevi*, by contrast, set off a storm of controversy about Scholem's ideological commitments to secular Zionism and anarchic nihilism in his scholarship. Between the Hebrew edition of *Sabbatai Sevi* in 1957 and its English translation in 1973, several events may have shaped the reception of the latter. The first was Scholem's participation in the controversy over Arendt's *Eichmann in Jerusalem*. This heated exchange placed Scholem at the center of a burning contemporary issue.[36] By virtue of her 1951 publication *The Origins of Totalitarianism* and the force of her presence in New York, Arendt was a well-known figure in American intellectual life.[37] This was hardly the case with Scholem, whose byline in *Encounter Magazine*, one of the many places where his exchange with Arendt was published, labeled him "a world-famous scholar who is Professor at the Hebrew University in Jerusalem."[38] The second was the publication in English of two volumes of Scholem's essays, *On the Kabbalah and Its Symbolism* in 1965 and *The Messianic Idea in Judaism and Other Essays on Jewish Spirituality* in 1971. These volumes, both of them paperbacks, presented a Scholem considerably more accessible than his previous book in English on Jewish gnosticism. They included some of his most celebrated pieces, some in German and others in English, in a sin-

---

35. McGuire, *Bollingen*, 152–54.

36. On Scholem and Arendt, see Raz-Krakotzkin, "Binationalism and Jewish Identity." On the reception of *Eichmann in Jerusalem*, see Rabinbach, "Eichmann in New York."

37. King, *Arendt and America*.

38. Arendt and Scholem, "*Eichmann in Jerusalem*," 51.

gle volume. Perhaps most important, many of them treated subjects in the modern period.

If the Hebrew edition of *Sabbatai Sevi* ignited controversy and sparked scholarly debate, the English edition brought Scholem fulsome praise.[39] In the *New York Review of Books*, D. P. Walker confessed: "Being unable to read Hebrew and Aramaic, I have no firsthand knowledge of the main sources of Professor Scholem's book; indeed what little acquaintance I have with Jewish religious thought comes almost entirely from his other works."[40] What Walker had the decency to acknowledge, other writers about Scholem covered over with bombastic rhetoric. In the *New Yorker* George Steiner compared Scholem to Joseph Needham and Frances Yates: "These scholar-artists are, consciously or not, the legatees of the classic novel, and in particular of Proust. Theirs also is a 'remembrance of things past' so vivid that we enter into their world of documents and analysis so confidently as into our native scene. Gershom Scholem is of this family."[41] In the *New York Times Book Review* Ozick declared:

> There are certain magisterial works of the human mind that alter ordinary comprehension so unpredictably and on so prodigious a scale that culture itself is set awry. . . . An accretion of fundamental insight takes on the power of a natural force. Gershom Scholem's oeuvre has such a force and its massive keystone, "Sabbatai Sevi," presses down on the gasping consciousness with the strength not simply of its invulnerable, almost tidal, scholarship, but of its singular instruction in the nature of man.[42]

Rather than write about Sabbatai Sevi and Sabbatianism using Scholem's work as a point of departure, as Kurzweil, Werblowsky, and Tishby had done, those writing about the English translation wrote about Scholem himself. The author had overwhelmed his subject.

Moreover, Scholem's scholarly project had begun to make its way into American culture. Harold Bloom used Scholem's work as the basis for his misguided attempt to trace a theory of literary influence with concepts from the Kabbalah.[43] Barnett Newman pointed to Scholem's writings on the Kabbalah as the source of inspiration for his paintings and sculpture. In *Gravity's*

---

39. The text of this paragraph appears in substantially the same form in Dweck, "Introduction to the Princeton Classics Edition," lix–lx.
40. Walker, "Mystery in History."
41. Steiner, "Inner Lights," 172–73.
42. Ozick, "Slouching toward Smyrna."
43. Bloom, *Kabbalah and Criticism*. On this work, see Wieseltier, "Summoning Up the Kabbalah."

Rainbow Thomas Pynchon invoked kabbalistic concepts so frequently that they constitute a leitmotif. Early on, Pynchon described Captain Geoffrey "Pirate" Prentice listening to a record on the gramophone: "There to stumble into an orgy held by a Messiah no one has quite recognized yet, and to know, as your eyes meet, that you are his John the Baptist, his Nathan of Gaza, that it is you who must convince him of his Godhead, proclaim him to others, love him both profanely and in the Name of what he is."[44] In *Sabbatai Sevi* Scholem had written: "Borrowing a metaphor from an earlier but in many ways analogous messianic movement, Nathan [of Gaza] was at once the John the Baptist and the Paul of the New Messiah."[45] Later on in the novel, in a description of Nora Dodson-Truck, the wife of Sir Stephen Dodson-Truck, who had tutored one of the central characters, Slothrop, in rocketry, Pynchon wrote: "She must prove herself now—find some deeper forms of renunciation, deeper than Sabbatai Zvi's apostasy before the sublime port."[46] I cannot point with certainty to Pynchon's reading of Scholem prior to the writing of *Gravity's Rainbow*. Yet Scholem's chapter on Sabbatai Sevi in *Major Trends in Jewish Mysticism*, the repeated references to him in the essays in *On the Kabbalah and Its Symbolism*, and the long discussion of him in "Redemption through Sin" would have made such a reading possible.[47] Leon Wieseltier's rebuke of Thomas B. Hess in the correspondence pages of the *New York Review of Books* should give one pause before pointing to sources about Sabbatai Sevi and the Kabbalah other than Scholem. Hess had written a monograph on Newman, which Wieseltier referred to in his discussion of Scholem's impact on Newman's art. When Hess wrote a fulminating letter to the *New York Review of Books* disavowing Scholem's influence but maintaining Newman's interest in the Kabbalah, Wieseltier responded: "He [Newman], like so many others, would certainly have known most of what he knew about Kabbalah from Scholem."[48] The same could easily be said of Pynchon.

In the years that followed, this trend only increased.[49] Scholem became a field of study unto himself.[50] In 1979 David Biale wrote a book about

44. Pynchon, *Gravity's Rainbow*, 14.

45. Scholem, *Sabbatai Sevi*, 207.

46. Pynchon, *Gravity's Rainbow*, 639.

47. Scholem, *On the Kabbalah and Its Symbolism*, 74, 83, 90, 135. For Scholem as a source for Pynchon, see Weisenburger, *"Gravity's Rainbow" Companion*, 144, 305, 377.

48. Wieseltier, "Response to Justus George Lawler."

49. The text of this paragraph appears in substantially the same form in Dweck, "Introduction to the Princeton Classics Edition," lx.

50. Weidener, *Gershom Scholem*; Aschheim, "Metaphysical Psychologist"; Kriegel, *Gershom Scholem*.

Scholem's thought that accepted his portrayal of Sabbatai Sevi and respect-
fully relegated the criticism the Hebrew edition had received to a brief summary.[51] Bloom's contribution to a volume of essays he edited on Scholem constitutes the apotheosis of this trend: "The negative moment opens up, and what
appears by the light of the sparks generated through that opening might be
called Scholem's final and unstated paradox. Sabbatai Zevi, Nathan of Gaza,
and Jacob Frank are no more and no less representative of Jewish spirituality
than are, say, Maimonides, Judah Halevi, and Franz Rosenzweig."[52] Bloom,
Ozick, and Steiner were tourists in the subject, and like tourists they saw what
they wanted to see. Scholem was taken at his word and had come to serve as a
stand-in for Judaism itself. Very few people who wrote about *Sabbatai Sevi* in
English had any firsthand knowledge of the material on which it was based.
Instead of a sustained engagement with the actual sources that Scholem had
used, his reviewers read Scholem and wrote about Scholem. He thus served as
an alibi for engaging with something that had the patina of authenticity, that
offered a touch of the real, an encounter with the Jewish tradition that enabled
his readers to avoid the rabbis. Scholem's work in English enabled its readers
to avoid the law.

Scholem on American Jewish Writers

Yet just as Scholem was becoming an icon in America, he had harsher and
harsher things to say about it. When Philip Roth's *Portnoy's Complaint* appeared
in 1969, Scholem wrote a scathing review of the book for *Ha-aretz*. He accused
Roth of Jewish self-hatred and claimed that he had written the very book
anti-Semites had hoped to write themselves for years. Scholem's acidic comments did not go unnoticed, and one of his colleagues from the Hebrew University challenged his criticism by calling attention to Roth's gifts as a writer.
In response, Scholem conceded that his criticism had nothing to do with Roth's
literary abilities and that he had read the book as a historian seeking to ascer-
tain its social significance. He maintained that the Jewish community would
be forced to pay a price for such a book, but he rejected any attempt to con-
strue his own review as an attempt at self-censorship. He concluded: "True: we
should not conceal anything out of fear of what the gentiles might say, and I
myself have emphasized this simple truth in a number of my articles con-
demning Jewish apologetics. But we also need to understand and recognize
that the declaration of this kind of truth, even a 'truth from America,' exacts a

51. Biale, *Gershom Scholem*, 155.
52. Bloom, "Scholem," 208–9.

price, and there is no need to be angry with the person who says so."[53] Roth's profanity, Scholem insisted, was bad for the Jews. Scholem associated Roth's truth—the young Jewish man's fascination with the *shiksa*—as a "truth from America."

A year later Scholem published an article first delivered as a lecture in memory of his recently deceased student Joseph Weiss. "The Neutralization of the Messianic Element in Early Hasidism" argued that the Jewish pietism in eighteenth-century Poland and Lithuania known as Hasidism had transformed classical Jewish teachings about the doctrine of the Messiah. For Scholem, the early Hasidim had stripped the messianic teachings of Lurianic kabbalists of their acute apocalyptic sting by emphasizing the communion with God on a strictly personal level. They replaced collective messianism with a personal and mystical concept of salvation. Scholem had written the essay largely as a response to the claim made by Tishby, his former student and colleague, about the messianic character of early Hasidism. Scholem's dispute with Tishby on this score was sharp but conducted well within the confines of normal scholarly disagreement. The tone of one of Scholem's later footnotes, by contrast, was extremely, even aggressively, polemical. In the essay's final section Scholem had called for an examination of the links between Sabbatianism and Hasidism: "Not only ideas stemming from the heretical theology of the sectarians, but also customs, which were destined to occupy a vital place in Hasidic group life[,] would have to be investigated in this connection." In a note to this call for research he remarked:

> This holds true for such customs as dancing, violent gestures during prayer, and probably also for the Sabbath meal. The extraordinary statements of Yafa [*sic*] Eliach in this connection, maintaining that these things, as well as the substance of Hasidic teaching, came originally from the Russian sect of the Khlysti, are entirely without foundation. Cf. *Proceedings, American Academy for Jewish Research* xxxvi (1968), 53–83.

Had Scholem stopped there, it would have been a harsh remark, but not much different in tenor from the character of his remarks about Tishby earlier in the article. But he continued: "This paper and all its hypotheses are a deplorable example of scholarly irresponsibility, leaving the reader wondering about the state of Jewish studies."[54] From the misspelling of Yaffa Eliach's first name to

---

53. Scholem's review had appeared in *Ha-aretz* on April 7, 1969, and his letter to the editor on June 6, 1969. See Scholem, *Devarim be-go*, 537.

54. Scholem, "Neutralization of the Messianic Element in Early Hasidism," 196n37.

the generalizing comment about the state of the discipline, Scholem's statement bristles with rage.

One might dismiss each of these comments as momentary lapses of scholarly etiquette or the temporary venting of intellectual bile. Nearly a decade later, however, Scholem reviewed a biography of Harry Wolfson in the *Times Literary Supplement*. Born a decade earlier than Scholem and trained in the Lithuanian Yeshiva of Slobodka, Wolfson had emigrated to the United States in 1903. He attended Harvard as an undergraduate, and, except for two brief interludes—one to travel in Europe prior to World War I and another for military service—he never left Harvard. Wolfson held the first chair in Jewish studies at a secular American university and wrote on an astonishing range of subjects in medieval Jewish philosophy. Moreover, he wrote in limpid English. Wolfson had died in 1974. Four years later a biography by Leo Schwarz, a student of Wolfson's who had predeceased him, appeared.[55] Scholem's review of this biography was anything but generous, either to Schwarz's portrayal of his teacher or to Wolfson as a scholar. Early on, Scholem had this to say about his late colleague from Lithuania:

> That the first professor of Jewish studies at Harvard should be a *Yeshiva Bocher*, a pupil of one of the most famous places in Talmudic learning in Lithuania, the Yeshiva of Slobodka, may not be so surprising, given the background of most Jewish scholars who came to America. What is surprising is that after having gone through the school of Harvard and bearing the imprint of his education, he remained essentially a *Yeshiva Bocher* and transplanted the mind of a remarkably gifted exemplar of this species into the august halls of Harvard and into a method and language that could be given a modernist name: in his words, the "hypothetico-deductive method of text-interpretation."

A bit later he continued:

> Fully aware of his sovereign standing as a Jewish scholar of the first rank, he hankered after Gentile praise. The eulogy of a Jesuit Father, I was flabbergasted to witness, meant more to him than the admiration of his most distinguished Jewish colleagues. There was always about him something of the air of an unfinished personality, a personality who had paid for his ambitions by sacrificing the fullness of his life for something that, in his last years, he came to disparage and to decry.[56]

55. Schwarz, *Wolfson of Harvard.*
56. Scholem, "Sleuth from Slobodka," 16.

The barely implicit contrast was with Scholem himself, who had come to Hebrew and Jewish studies through Zionism rather than through the Talmudic Yeshiva of Slobodka, who had emigrated to Palestine rather than to New York, who wrote in Hebrew and German rather than in English, who taught at the Hebrew University rather than at Harvard, and who did not hanker after gentile praise.

Of course, this was all nonsense. Moreover, Wolfson was neither Eliach nor Roth. But by 1979 he had already been dead for five years. Scholem's review would in all likelihood have gone unanswered, and his vicious portrayal of Wolfson would have endured in the hallowed pages of the *Times Literary Supplement*, had it not been for Judah Goldin. In an article in the *American Scholar* the following summer, "On the Sleuth of Slobodka and the Cortez of Kabbalah," Goldin parted company with nearly every other American intellectual, Jewish or otherwise, who had written about Scholem. Rather than take Scholem at face value and offer worthless praise, Goldin took him to task. Goldin described Wolfson's love affair with Harvard and with the English language, provided a description of his scholarly achievement, and responded head-on to Scholem's indictment of his person:

> Nor is it particularly instructive to be informed "of the air of an unfinished individual," of paying "for his ambitions by sacrificing the fullness of life" (is there another form of payment?), every word of which is true. Who is a finished individual? The man who never marries but devotes his whole long life to creative study and teaching is doubtless unfinished. How about the man who marries a madwoman and in humiliation scurries to collect a hundred rabbinical signatures to be granted release to remarry, yet all the time produces important papers? Or the scientist who can no longer satisfy even his mistress? Or the lady classicist who has never married because she has been too busy classifying artifacts from excavations? Everyone is unfinished, and very likely everyone is saved from insanity or meaningless existence by being fragmentary, being consumed by the work he gives himself over to— which is to our profit also.[57]

Goldin was withering in his final sentences: "As Milton Anastos put it when he began his address on Wolfson's eighty-fifth birthday celebration in the Rare Book Room of the Widener Library, he was 'Magister Noster.' There aren't that many around in the halls of ivy or on adjacent greenswards. And in its own way Scholem's review also attests to this."[58] Scholem was very much alive

---

57. Goldin, "On the Sleuth of Slobodka and the Cortez of Kabbalah," 402.
58. Ibid., 404.

when this response appeared, which had all the marks of "intellectual honesty and personal integrity" for which Goldin had praised Wolfson.

To sum up: Gershom Scholem and America is a story of profound ambivalence. Scholem understood the importance of America early on and in a way that none of his colleagues at the Hebrew University did. He used it as a site of patronage for his work, as a means of reprieve from the stresses of Jerusalem, and as a continued source of validation. With great skill he played on the fact that he came to America as a German intellectual who taught in Jerusalem. But Scholem was appalled at the vulgarity of American life and the ignorance of its Jews. America, or its Jews and its intellectuals, by contrast, could not get enough of him. Scholem, like many other German intellectuals, became an icon abroad, whether abroad meant New York or Frankfurt, before he became one in his adopted homeland of Jerusalem.

References

Abrams, Daniel. 2000. "Defining Modern Academic Scholarship: Gershom Scholem and the Establishment of a New (?) Discipline." *Journal of Jewish Thought and Philosophy* 9, no. 2: 267–302.

Adorno, Theodor W., and Gershom Scholem. 2015. *Der Briefwechsel, 1939–1969*, edited by Asaf Angermann. Frankfurt am Main: Suhrkamp.

Alter, Robert. 1991. *Necessary Angels: Tradition and Modernity in Kafka, Benjamin, and Scholem*. Cambridge, MA: Harvard University Press.

Anidjar, Gil. 2002. *"Our Place in al-Andalus": Kabbalah, Philosophy, Literature in Arab Jewish Letters*. Stanford, CA: Stanford University Press.

Arendt, Hannah, and Gershom Scholem. 1964. *"Eichmann in Jerusalem*: An Exchange of Letters." *Encounter*, January 22, 51–56.

———. 2010. *Der Briefwechsel*, edited by Marie Luise-Knott. Berlin: Suhrkamp.

Aschheim, Steven E. 2004. "The Metaphysical Psychologist: On the Life and Letters of Gershom Scholem." *Journal of Modern History* 76, no. 4: 903–33.

———. 2007. *Beyond the Border: The German Jewish Legacy Abroad*. Princeton, NJ: Princeton University Press.

Biale, David. 1979. *Gershom Scholem: Kabbalah and Counter-history*. Cambridge, MA: Harvard University Press.

Bloom, Harold. 1975. *Kabbalah and Criticism*. New York: Seabury.

———. 1987. "Scholem: Unhistorical or Jewish Gnosticism." In *Gershom Scholem: Modern Critical Views*, edited by Harold Bloom, 207–20. New York: Chelsea House.

Campanini, Saverio. 2005. "A Case for Sainte-Beuve: Some Remarks on Gershom Scholem's Autobiography." In *Creation and Re-creation in Jewish Thought: Festschrift in Honor of Joseph Dan on the Occasion of His Seventieth Birthday*, edited by Rachel Elior and Peter Schäfer, 363–400. Tübingen: Mohr Siebeck.

Dan, Joseph. 2010. "Gershom Scholem, *Eranos*, and *Religion after Religion*." In *On Gershom Scholem: Twelve Studies* (in Hebrew), 133–73. Jerusalem: Zalman Shazar Center.

Dweck, Yaacob. 2016. "Introduction to the Princeton Classics Edition." In *Sabbetai Sevi: The Mystical Messiah, 1626–1676*, by Gershom Scholem. Princeton. NJ: Princeton University Press.

Goldin, Judah. 1980. "On the Sleuth of Slobodka and the Cortez of Kabbalah." *American Scholar* 49, no. 3: 391–404.

———. 1988. "About Shalom Spiegel." In *Studies in Midrash and Related Literature*, edited by Barry L. Eichler and Jeffrey H. Tigay, 393–400. Philadelphia: Jewish Publication Society.

Herman, Dana. 2008. "*Hashavat Avedah*: A History of Jewish Cultural Reconstruction, Inc." PhD diss., McGill University.

Howe, Irving. 1990. "The New York Intellectuals." In *Selected Writings, 1950–1990*, 240–80. New York: Harcourt Brace Jovanovich.

King, Richard H. 2015. *Arendt and America*. Chicago: University of Chicago Press.

Kriegel, Maurice. 2009. *Gershom Scholem*. Paris: Herne.

Kurzweil, Baruch. 1957. "Notes on 'Sabbetai Sevi' by Gershom Scholem" (in Hebrew). *Ha-aretz*, September 25–October 2.

Laqueur, Walter. 1973. "George Lichtheim." *Commentary* 56, no. 2: 45–52.

Lazier, Benjamin. 2008. *God Interrupted: Heresy and the European Imagination between the World Wars*. Princeton, NJ: Princeton University Press.

Lieberman, Saul. 1963. "How Much Greek in Jewish Palestine?" In *Biblical and Other Studies*, edited by Alexander Altmann, 123–41. Cambridge, MA: Harvard University Press.

Maciejko, Paweł. 2011. *The Mixed Multitude: Jacob Frank and the Frankist Movement, 1755–1816*. Philadelphia: University of Pennsylvania Press.

McGuire, William. 1982. *Bollingen: An Adventure in Collecting the Past*. Princeton, NJ: Princeton University Press.

Meir, Yonatan. 2009. "From Scholem's Archive" (in Hebrew). *Tarbiz* 78, no. 2: 255–70.

Mosse, George L. 1993. "Gershom Scholem as a German Jew." In *Confronting the Nation: Jewish and Western Nationalism*, 176–92. Hanover, NH: Brandeis University Press.

Myers, David N. 1986. "The Scholem-Kurzweil Debate and Modern Jewish Historiography." *Modern Judaism* 6, no. 3: 261–86.

———. 1995. *Re-inventing the Jewish Past: European Jewish Intellectuals and the Zionist Return to History*. New York: Oxford University Press.

Necker, Gerold, Elke Morlok, and Matthias Morgenstern. 2014. *Gershom Scholem in Deutschland: Zwischen Seelenverwandtschaft und Sprachlosigkeit*. Tübingen: Mohr Siebeck.

Ozick, Cynthia.1974. "Slouching toward Smyrna." *New York Times Book Review*, February 24, 27.

Pynchon, Thomas. 1973. *Gravity's Rainbow*. New York: Viking.

Rabinbach, Anson. 2004. "Eichmann in New York: The New York Intellectuals and the Hannah Arendt Controversy." *October*, no. 108: 97–111.

Raz-Krakotzkin, Amnon. 2001. "Binationalism and Jewish Identity: Hannah Arendt and the Question of Palestine." In *Hannah Arendt in Jerusalem*, edited by Steven E. Aschheim, 165–81. Berkeley: University of California Press.

Schäfer, Peter. 1995. "Gershom Scholem und die 'Wissenschaft des Judentums.'" In *Gershom Scholem zwischen den Disziplinen*, edited by Peter Schäfer and Gary Smith, 122–56. Frankfurt am Main: Suhrkamp.

Scholem, Gershom. 1927. *Bibliographia Kabbalistica: Verzeichnis der gedruckten die jüdischen Mystik (Gnosos, Kabbala, Sabbatianismus, Frankismus, Chassidismus) behandelnden Bücher und Aufsätze von Reuchlin bis zur Gegenwart*. Leipzig: Drugulin.

———. 1928. *Hebrew Manuscripts in the National Library in Jerusalem* (in Hebrew). Jerusalem: Hebrew University.

———. 1941. *Major Trends in Jewish Mysticism*. Jerusalem: Schocken.

———. 1944. "Reflections on Jewish Studies" (in Hebrew). *Luah ha-aretz*, 94–112.

———. 1959. "Zum Verständnis der messianischen Idee im Judentum." *Eranos Jahrbuch* 28: 193–239.

———. 1960. *Jewish Gnosticism, Merkabah Mysticism, and Talmudic Tradition*. New York: Jewish Theological Seminary of America.

———. 1960. *Zur Kabbala und ihrer Symbolik*. Zürich: Rhein.

———. 1965. *On the Kabbalah and Its Symbolism*. New York: Schocken.

———. 1971. *The Messianic Idea in Judaism and Other Essays on Jewish Spirituality*. New York: Schocken.

———. 1971. "The Neutralization of the Messianic Element in Early Hasidism." In *The Messianic Idea in Judaism and Other Essays on Jewish Spirituality*, 176–202. New York: Schocken.

———. 1971. "Redemption through Sin." In *The Messianic Idea in Judaism and Other Essays on Jewish Spirituality*, 78–141. New York: Schocken.

———. 1971. "Towards an Understanding of the Messianic Idea in Judaism." In *The Messianic Idea in Judaism and Other Essays on Jewish Spirituality*, 1–36. New York: Schocken.

———. 1973. *Sabbatai Sevi: The Mystical Messiah, 1626–1676*, translated by R. J. Zwi Werblowsky. Princeton, NJ: Princeton University Press.

———. 1975. *Devarim be-go*. Tel Aviv: Am Oved.

———. 1979. "The Sleuth from Slobodka." *Times Literary Supplement*, November 23, 16.

———. 1994. *Briefe*. Vol. 1, *1914–1947*, edited by Itta Shedletzky. Munich: Beck.

———. 2008. *The Final Phase: Studies on Hasidism* (in Hebrew), edited by David Assaf and Esther Liebes. Jerusalem: Magnes and Am Oved.

———. 2012. *From Berlin to Jerusalem: Memories of My Youth*, translated by Harry Zohn. Philadelphia: Dry.

Scholem, Gershom, and Walter Benjamin. 1989. *The Complete Correspondence of Walter Benjamin and Gershom Scholem, 1932–1940*, edited by Gershom Scholem, translated by Gary Smith and Andre Lefevere. New York: Schocken.

Scholem, Gershom, and Morton Smith. 2008. *Morton Smith and Gershom Scholem: Correspondence, 1945–1982*, edited by Guy G. Stroumsa. Leiden: Brill.

Schwarz, Leo. 1978. *Wolfson of Harvard: Portrait of a Scholar*. Philadelphia: Jewish Publication Society.

Spiegel, Shalom. 1967. *The Last Trial*, translated by Judah Goldin. Philadelphia: Jewish Publication Society.

Steiner, George. 1973. "Inner Lights." *New Yorker*, October 22, 152–74.

Tishby, Isaiah. 1958. "On Gershom Scholem's Approach to the Study of Sabbatianism" (in Hebrew). *Tarbiz* 28, no. 1: 101–33.

Walker, D. P. 1973. "Mystery in History." *New York Review of Books*, October 4.

Wasserstrom, Steven M. 1999. *Religion after Religion: Gershom Scholem, Mircea Eliade, and Henry Corbin at Eranos*. Princeton, NJ: Princeton University Press.

Weidener, Daniel. 2003. *Gershom Scholem: Politisches, esoterisches und historiographisches Schreiben*. Munich: Fink.

Weisenburger, Steven C. 2006. *A "Gravity's Rainbow" Companion: Sources and Contexts for Pynchon's Novel*. Athens: University of Georgia Press.

Werblowsky, R. J. Zwi. 1957. "Reflections on 'Sabbatai Sevi' by G. Scholem" (in Hebrew). *Molad* 112: 539–46.

Wieseltier, Leon. 1976. "Response to Justus George Lawler." *New York Review of Books*, April 15.

———. 1976. "Summoning Up the Kabbalah." *New York Review of Books*, February 19.

———. 2004. "Sidney." *New Republic*, August 16–23, 34.

Zadoff, Noam. 2007. "The Debate between Baruch Kurzweil and Gershom Scholem on the Study of Sabbatianism" (in Hebrew). *Kabbalah* 16: 299–360.

———. 2015. *From Berlin to Jerusalem and Back: Gershom Scholem between Israel and Germany* (in Hebrew). Jerusalem: Carmel.

The Anonymity of Siegfried Kracauer

Johannes von Moltke

In his obituary for Siegfried Kracauer, Theodor W. Adorno offers a striking assessment of his friend's lifelong work as a film critic and theorist. By the time of his death, Adorno claims, Kracauer's approach to film had "long since become anonymous."[1] As he is quick to qualify, the line is intended as a compliment on one of Kracauer's principal accomplishments (*Errungenschaften*)—a recognition of the pervasive influence of his way of thinking. In this view, Kracauer's writings on cinema from the 1920s through the 1960s have receded into the very fabric of film theory and criticism, woven into its DNA as the "self-evident condition . . . for all reflection on the medium."[2]

Today film and media studies have indeed integrated into their disciplinary protocols Kracauer's original insights on the task of the film critic and on the relationship between the social and aesthetic dimensions of cinema. If we have become somewhat more skeptical about the specificity of film's relation to reality, we do take for granted the central argument of Kracauer's film theory on the relation between media and experience.[3] Exaggerating only slightly, we might agree with Adorno that the symptomatic reading of national

This article is based on a talk first delivered at the conference "Transatlantic Theory Transfer— Missed Encounters" at Columbia University's Deutsches Haus, March 27–28, 2015. It condenses and expands on arguments I make in *The Curious Humanist* (2016). I thank the editors of *New German Critique* for the invitation both to present at the conference and to contribute to this issue.

1. Adorno, "Nach Kracauer's Tod," 195.

2. Ibid.

3. See Kracauer, "The Task of the Film Critic"; von Moltke, "2 February, 1956"; and Kracauer, *Theory of Film.*

New German Critique 132, Vol. 44, No. 3, November 2017
DOI 10.1215/0094033X-4162250   © 2017 by New German Critique, Inc.

cinema in terms of hidden social tendencies, which Kracauer pioneered in
From Caligari to Hitler and which Adorno considered one of Kracauer's two
signal contributions at the time of his death, has become the lingua franca of
film journalism—even if it no longer serves as the "master narrative for the
study of film in a national context," as it did during the 1970s and 1980s.[4] Both
canonized and criticized, occasionally even reviled in the comparatively short
history of film studies as a discipline,[5] Kracauer's methodological premises
remain operative whenever a critic proposes that Steven Spielberg's films tell
us something about masculinity or the fixations of American popular culture
at large; that Filipino cinema speaks to a postcolonial struggle; or that Jean
Rouch's *Chronique d'un été* "could only have been made in France."[6] In this
regard as well as in other respects to which I return, it would be wrong to
speak of a "missed encounter" in the same sense applied to other theorists
discussed in this special issue: Kracauer's name is now well recognized on
both sides of the Atlantic (though one might certainly qualify aspects of Kracauer's American reception as *belated*—particularly his Weimar writings,
many of which remain untranslated and unknown in this country). By the
same token, in the case of Kracauer, theory transfer may involve forms of anonymity as much as explicit reference: theoretical legacies can become influential by shedding their origins and entering discourse detached from any particular theorist's name—anonymous.

But Adorno's tribute, like his more (in)famous portrait of the "Critical
Realist" on the occasion of Kracauer's seventy-fifth birthday only two years
earlier, remains ambivalent: it fails fully to rein in the implication that, having
become anonymous, Kracauer is invisible.[7] In this reading, the polarities are
reversed, and anonymity does imply a failed theory transfer. From this perspective, Adorno's presumably well-intentioned remark suggests that Kracauer's work on film dissipated into the ether of cultural criticism, lacking any
consequence that would attach to an authorial name. Even though Kracauer
indisputably helped bring film theory and criticism into its own, and although

4. Kaes, "German Cultural History and the Study of Film," 49.

5. See, among others, Leonardo Quaresima's highly informative introduction to the recent reissue
of *From Caligari to Hitler*; more specifically, see Kaes's useful reflections in "German Cultural History and the Study of Film."

6. Kidel, "DVD: Chronicle of a Summer."

7. In speaking of Kracauer's anonymity, Adorno inevitably (and perhaps wittingly) also taps into
a discourse on assimilation that for him was largely anathema, but with which Kracauer—who
decided to remain in the United States for the rest of his life after fleeing the Nazis in 1933—arguably
entertained a more ambivalent relationship. For Adorno's biting remarks on the "adjustment"
demanded of exiles, see "Scientific Experiences."

in his early essays he may have outlined a "proleptic physiognomics of [the] culture industry" (as Adorno somewhat self-servingly admits), by the time of Kracauer's death the world had moved on to find itself occupied with other issues and discourses. An exile forced out of Germany within days of Hitler's assumption of power, Kracauer shared the posthumous fate of countless other émigré intellectuals whose work would not be fully rediscovered in their home country until after Germany decided to face the legacy of the Third Reich in earnest—a process arguably only in its very early stages in 1966. Nor did Kracauer's name at the time rank among the most recognized members of the intellectual emigration in the United States, where he had become a naturalized citizen at the first opportunity in the mid-1940s and settled in New York for the last quarter century of his life. Though his death did not escape notice (obituaries ran in the *New York Times* and in the organ of cinema studies' fledgling professional organization, *Cinema Journal*), compared with towering figures as different as Hannah Arendt, Herbert Marcuse, or Adorno himself, "Friedel" Kracauer (as he was known to his friends) was virtually anonymous indeed. And although he contributed not one but two tomes that were quickly considered classics in the developing field of film theory, these were also the object of often vociferous critique from the outset. By the 1970s, to Anglo-American critics at least, they appeared dated: in the wake of 1968, the realist position articulated in *Theory of Film* was overtaken by the psychoanalytic and social critique of so-called *Screen* theory, and the reflectionist and teleological assumptions underpinning *From Caligari to Hitler* would soon be superseded by the methodological innovations of the New Film History in the wake of a 1978 FIAF conference in Brighton.[8]

Curiously, both assessments that resonate in Adorno's description of Kracauer's anonymity capture something important about the latter's work. Particularly when viewed from the American side of the Atlantic, his work at times has receded into a picture puzzle where its impact appears alternately invisible and "self-evident," to adopt Adorno's term. Viewed from within the premises, the guiding motifs, and the salient arguments of Kracauer's work itself, however, both of these forms of anonymity carry the weight of a theoretical motif in their own right. For they both open up a gap between identity and the subject, a gap that Kracauer explored throughout his writings as a critic, as a theorist, and as a novelist. Indeed, it is arguably in the guise of fiction that Kracauer's own discourse on anonymity finds its most intriguing form.

---

8. Elsaesser, "'New' Film History"; see also Rentschler, "Kracauer, Spectatorship, and the Seventies," 62–63. FIAF is the acronym for the International Federation of Film Archives.

"Incognito": Ginster, Georg, Friedel

If there is any one figure Kracauer theorized consistently from his early Weimar writings through the posthumous book on historiography, it is the figure of a vanishing subject. From his film criticism of the 1920s, where we find him enthusiastically embracing the endless malleability of Charlie Chaplin's literally self-less Tramp, through the productive absent-mindedness of the historian in the posthumous *History: The Last Things before the Last*, we find Kracauer locating and valorizing forms of self-effacing subjectivity.[9] This motif similarly connects the semiautobiographical novels to Kracauer's curious reluctance to confront or publicize his own biography. From his correspondence with Adorno, we know how jealously Kracauer guarded against any public reference to his age, preferring instead to remain in a state of "chronological anonymity."[10] Conceding this idiosyncrasy on his part, Kracauer ties this desire to "a deeply rooted need to live exterritorially—both as regards the intellectual climate and with respect to chronological time."[11] When "Teddie" Adorno first informs "Friedel" Kracauer of his intention to deliver a major radio address on the occasion of his friend and mentor's seventy-fifth birthday, the latter is at once pleased and "deeply frightened": "My very mode of existence would literally be threatened should the dates be startled into action [*aufgeschreckt*] and accost me from the outside."[12]

The psychic energy that Kracauer invests in this issue, not to mention the space that he devotes to it in his correspondence with Adorno, is striking—but so is the literariness of the formulation that imagines calendar dates banding together like so many predators to attack the hapless subject. This turn to literary imagery is far from accidental, not only because Kracauer had long proved himself a consummate stylist in his essays and reviews for the *Frankfurter Zeitung* during the 1920s, but also because he had previously fashioned a similar subject in Ginster, the quasi-autobiographical antihero of his eponymous 1928 novel. Still too little known on this side of the Atlantic, the yet-to-be-translated *Ginster* and its sequel of sorts, *Georg* (completed in French exile and only recently rendered into English by Carl Skoggard), are central to our appraisal of Kracauer, not simply in view of a more complete picture of the author's many writerly pursuits but as a crucial facet of his theoretical legacy

---

9. In his review of Chaplin's *Gold Rush*, Kracauer describes the protagonist as a figure whose "I has gone astray" (ihm ist das Ich abhanden gekommen) ("Chaplin," 269). Elsewhere he calls for the historian to "blot out his self" (Kracauer, *History*, 81).

10. Letter to Adorno, November 8, 1963, in Adorno and Kracauer, *Briefwechsel*, 621.

11. Ibid.

12. Letter to Adorno, October 25, 1963, ibid., 611.

as well.[13] *Ginster* and *Georg* are of a piece with Kracauer's lifelong exploration of modern subjectivity and a certain condition of anonymity, to whose theorization the novels contribute as literature.

Ginster begins by insisting on its protagonist's anonymity: not only do we learn at the outset that Ginster is not really our hero's name (even though the subtitle indicates that it is "written by himself"),[14] but we are also told that he hopes to live "incognito, so to speak."[15] The subject of Ginster's name—and by extension the question of anonymity—remains a concern throughout the novel. Besides the prominent discussion in the opening paragraph of *Ginster* as a misnomer, a fascinating encounter with naming and anonymity occurs during Ginster's first roll call at the military. Waiting for his name to be called, he becomes distracted by the responses ("Here—Here—Here") of the other soldiers. As a result, the "string of syllables" constituted by the jumble of names comes to a halt:

> Suddenly torn right in half, the Heres also ceased. A void, and in this void a single name, alone. The name seemed foreign to Ginster, but it did awaken in him some memory; as if he had encountered this name repeatedly in the past. It took quite a while until he grasped that it was his own. Helplessly, he stared at the name that occupied the entire courtyard and made demands that he, Ginster, could not possibly meet, for after all, he was nothing and could not make any claims to being named individually with such power in the courtyard. He hesitated for a long time whether he should not rather repudiate himself. In the end, it occurred to him that he belonged externally to the name and might commit a legal infraction by withdrawing from it.[16]

Not exactly nameless, Ginster makes for a reticent subject. Kracauer's protagonist is uneasy with being named, if not with the notion of identity itself. He prefers to remain anonymous in the sense that he keeps his name somehow external to his subjectivity, a faint memory that leaves him helpless. What might it mean, then, for a protagonist to live incognito, to refuse his name and remain unknown? For all its autobiographical reference and historical specificity, *Ginster* might also be read as a sustained meditation on this question. The answer that the novel construes certainly suggests a need to blend in, if not the kind of "deliberate head-in-the-sand policy" that Adorno attests to

---

13. Kracauer, *Ginster*; Kracauer, *Georg*.

14. Kracauer, *Ginster*, 145. For an extended discussion of *Ginster* and its implications for Kracauer's film theory, see von Moltke, "Theory of the Novel."

15. Kracauer, *Ginster*, 7, 11.

16. Ibid., 145.

Kracauer himself in the underhanded tribute he delivered on the radio in 1964.[17] But there is far more to this "incognito," an aspiration that Ginster shares with other modern antiheroes we might encounter in the writings of Franz Kafka and Robert Musil or in the films of Chaplin and Buster Keaton.[18] If *Ginster* imputes a certain degree of conformism to its eponymous subject, this is tempered by the naggingly ironic narrative voice and the poignancy of the protagonist's reflections. Of himself Ginster says that "after all, he was nothing" (eigentlich war er ja nichts),[19] insisting that "he would have preferred not to become anything" (am liebsten wäre er gar nichts geworden),[20] but rather dreams repeatedly of somehow vanishing from the scene altogether. "For my part," Ginster insists, "I want nothing. You probably can't understand this, but I'd rather trickle away" (Ich selbst will nichts. Sie werden mich nicht verstehen, aber am liebsten zerrieselte ich).[21] In the novel Kracauer finds several formulations for his protagonist's "precarious selfhood,"[22] his impulse to vanish: on a purely physical level, he tries to avoid the draft by eating less and losing weight, but Ginster's maxim to "hunger himself away, just away" (weghungern, nur weg) betrays broader metaphysical—or at least metafictional—implications.[23] So does his desire to flee into a place beyond space ("gerne wäre Ginster ins Raumlose geflüchtet"),[24] or to replace his bodily existence with a different aggregate state altogether: "For his part, [Ginster] . . . would have liked to be gaseous" (Er selbst wäre gerne gasförmig gewesen).[25] To put this in the cinematic terms that hover just below the surface of this text: Ginster dreams of the dissolve.

Consequently, when the character Ginster dissolves into Georg in Kracauer's second novel, the same reticence to identify fully as a subject characterizes the new protagonist. As his peregrinations through the late Weimar Republic come to a temporary stop in a moment of postcoital introspection, Georg finds that "he wanted to throw himself away. . . . He always discovered the same thing: when he tried to engage his whole self, reality slipped away from him and the words turned false in his mouth."[26] Musing about the inade-

---

17. Adorno, "Curious Realist," 172.
18. See Ryan, *Vanishing Subject.*
19. Kracauer, *Ginster,* 145.
20. Ibid., 24.
21. Ibid., 132.
22. Ryan's term for Kafka in *Vanishing Subject,* 109.
23. Kracauer, *Ginster,* 181.
24. Ibid., 117.
25. Ibid., 140.
26. Kracauer, *Georg,* 264.

quacy of elevated notions such as the soul, ideas, and experience for capturing the essential elusiveness of subjectivity, Georg decides: "No, this higher existence sprang from dubious roots and became a nearly intolerable burden. Better to cast it off and be a nobody."[27] Neither a mere sign of alienation nor quite the clever ruse of Odysseus, this gesture toward self-effacement is one that the novel's narrative then enacts in various forms, whether through other observations conveyed by Georg's free indirect discourse ("Ah, one was always being blended into the doings of the world—an ingredient for a dish") or by the way in which the protagonist simply vanishes from the scene, to be replaced by the anonymous masses and an ominous storm blowing down the Kurfürstendamm from Berlin's Gedächtniskirche at the novel's end.[28]

As I suggested above, we can trace the figure of a vanishing subject and escape into invisibility throughout Kracauer's work.[29] From the imaginative investigation of this desire for anonymity in the form of Kracauer's two novels, we might draw a line to *Theory of Film*'s description of cinematic spectatorship as "self-unconscious like an amoeba," or to Kracauer's posthumous theorization of the historian as an exilic subject working in a "state of self-effacement"; successful historiography, Kracauer avers, requires a paradoxical subject-position akin to the "active passivity" of the photographer, the filmmaker, and the film spectator—an attitude of receptivity, for which the self has been "put to sleep," if not "blotted out" entirely.[30] As I show elsewhere, in the context of Kracauer's own American exile, this idiosyncratic notion of subjectivity responds in compelling ways both to the effacement of subjectivity by totalitarianism and to the enthronement of a liberal humanist subject in the Cold War era.[31] Indeed, we may consider this Kracauer's seminal theoretical contribution, above and beyond any specific aspects of his film theory.

However, like Adorno's obituary, Kracauer's own theorization of modern subjectivity is double-edged—a powerful figure that simultaneously establishes the importance of the nonsovereign subject as a response to ideological interpellation, on the one hand, and reduces it to invisibility, on the other. Kracauer's own ambivalent figuration of anonymity colors the image we hold of Friedel himself. It is against this backdrop that we should chart Kracauer's explicit and countervailing efforts at networking, establishing himself, and, to

27. Ibid.
28. Ibid., 265.
29. See Mülder-Bach, "History as Autobiography."
30. See Kracauer, *Theory of Film*, 165; and Kracauer, *History*, 81–85.
31. See von Moltke, *Curious Humanist*.

a degree, organizing his own legacy.[32] It is a legacy that followed distinct paths of reception in the German and Anglo-American contexts. As not only Kracauer himself but also his German- and English-language writings crisscrossed the Atlantic, some nuances lost in translation and others unduly amplified, there remains ample room for reconsidering the encounter—whether missed or successful—with his writings on both sides of the Atlantic.

Networks and Name Recognition: Transatlantic Reception

Scholars for a long time relied on a largely anecdotal account of Kracauer not only as anonymous but also as a somewhat sad, isolated figure cut off from the social and intellectual life of the city in which he spent the last quarter century of his life. Unfamiliar with the breadth of Kracauer's writings and activities during the 1940s and 1950s, American readers of *From Caligari to Hitler* in particular like to imagine him ensconced in the film library of the Museum of Modern Art (MoMA), where he allegedly surrounded himself with piles of books, as if to stave off communications with others. From scattered evidence and from anecdotes told and retold in New York until they found their permanent place in secondary literature, we have acquired an image of Kracauer as the émigré scholar toiling away at MoMA and otherwise out of touch with his Manhattan surroundings.[33] Kracauer's "problem," Peter Harcourt noted in *Cinema Journal* two years after his death, was that he did not interact with his cultural context. Unlike his contemporary André Bazin, whom we easily locate in the Paris film scene of the 1940s and 1950s, Kracauer "gives us the sense more of a man alone," a position that Harcourt finds both noble and "a little sad."[34] Some years later Dudley Andrew seized on this portrait of the critic as a lone intellectual in an influential overview of *The Major Film Theories*, where he describes Kracauer as "the kind of man who decided after forty years of viewing film that he ought to work out and write down his ideas about the medium; so he went straight to a library and locked himself in. There, reading widely, thinking endlessly, and working always alone, always cut off from the buzz of film talk and film production, he slowly and painstakingly

---

32. In a letter to the publisher Siegfried Unseld from 1963, Kracauer writes, "Brecht once told me: 'you have to work for your reputation! [Man muss seinen Ruhm organisieren!]' But I have neither the talent nor the desire" (original in Deutsches Literaturarchiv Marbach). However, from his well-organized archive we know that Kracauer did invest a fair amount of energy in securing and organizing his legacy.

33. Gertrud Koch retells the anecdote of Kracauer's self-constructed isolation behind a "veritable tower of books," which she attributes to Annette Michelson, in *Siegfried Kracauer*.

34. Harcourt, "What, Indeed, Is Cinema?"

gave birth to his theory."[35] Andrew concedes this portrait to be "imaginary" (for one thing, it melds the story of *Caligari* with that of the later *Theory of Film*), but it remained influential nonetheless for our understanding of how Kracauer's American writings were produced and received.[36]

In my own work I have attempted to put these anecdotal accounts into perspective and to reconstruct also some of the networks in which Kracauer moved and thought—networks that emerge clearly not only from his voluminous correspondence and his notebooks but also in the urban fabric of Manhattan. Moving between MoMA, film theaters, foundation offices, and research projects, Kracauer sought to settle in as the New York intellectual that he ultimately had become. As such, he plainly longed for recognition—including that of his name: as at the beginning of the Weimar Republic, when he had started out as a freelancer, his livelihood in exile depended on it.[37] Because of a speech impediment, he never held an academic appointment; after losing his position as editor at the *Frankfurter Zeitung* within days of Adolf Hitler's seizure of power in 1933, he had to earn his living by publishing books and articles, occasionally supported by government grants and later supplemented by consulting jobs for various agencies. Consequently, first in Paris and then in New York, Kracauer's first order of business was to network, introduce, and make a name for himself—activities hardly designed to achieve anonymity. As for his contributions to film criticism and theory, Kracauer's own hopes were hardly that they would recede from view, even if only to furnish the nascent discipline with generally accepted premises; rather, as he wrote to his friend Leo Löwenthal shortly before publication of his summa, *Theory of Film*, he fully expected it to "become a classic" (ein classic werden).[38]

Thus it would be wrong to think of Kracauer as dissolving into the ether like Ginster or merging with the city like Georg. For the reception of his work has been energized periodically by new materials, translations, and rediscoveries that have now firmly established Kracauer as one of the twentieth century's critical voices on media, mass culture, and modernity. This renewed reception, however, has often followed distinct trajectories on opposite sides of the

35. Andrew, *Major Film Theories*, 107. Harcourt freely admits that he deduces his impressionn entirely from Kracauer's writing, "for I know nothing at all about his personal life" ("What, Indeed, Is Cinema?," 25).

36. Andrew, "Core and the Flow," 908.

37. See Isenberg, "This Pen for Hire."

38. Letter to Leo Löwenthal, February 16, 1957, in Löwenthal and Kracauer, *In steter Freundschaft*, 188.

Atlantic, where it has been beset by various disparities and nonsynchronicities, as Eric Rentschler has pointed out.[39] Thanks first to Adorno's efforts on Kracauer's behalf and then in Karsten Witte's uncompleted edition of *Schriften*, German readers from the 1960s on encountered the considerable power of Kracauer's prose miniatures from the 1920s. Only in the mid-1990s was a subset of these writings translated for an English-language readership in Tom Levin's influential edition of *The Mass Ornament*.[40] Conversely, in a missed encounter of a different sort, one might argue that both *From Caligari to Hitler* and *Theory of Film* became influential in Germany during the 1960s and 1970s just as their impact appeared to wane in the United States. In recent decades, on the other hand, both volumes have been reissued in newly introduced, revised, and expanded versions. With increasing momentum in the wake of the hundredth anniversary of his birth in 1989, Kracauer's works have drawn renewed attention from scholars across the disciplines. His collected writings have now been issued by Suhrkamp in a project of stunning editorial and critical proportions; by comparison, the set of texts on which the Anglo-American reception of Kracauer tends to draw remains small, further reduced by the easy dismissal of both *Theory of Film* and *From Caligari to Hitler*. Simply put, multiple volumes of Kracauer's earlier writings, and his film and cultural criticism in particular, still remain to be translated and integrated into the intellectual image of Kracauer that English-language reception has generated. On the other hand, even the posthumous *History: The Last Things before the Last*, long disregarded by the field to which it had hoped to speak, has been gaining traction in recent years, with international conferences and anthologies devoted to Kracauer as a "thinker of history."[41]

The "Other" Frankfurt School

To be sure, this reputation has grown in the shadow of other theorists affiliated with the Frankfurt School. Löwenthal, the sole surviving member of the group on Kracauer's hundredth anniversary, quipped that his late friend had in fact been "a super-member of our school of critical thinking"—an ardently committed thinker yet a relentless critic of absolutes[42]—but it seems obvious that other members were more super as far as reputation and impact at the time

---

39. Rentschler, "Kracauer, Spectatorship, and the Seventies."

40. Kracauer, *Mass Ornament*; on the role of these texts as "miniatures," see Huyssen, *Miniature Metropolis*.

41. See Baumann, *Im Vorraum der Geschichte*; Despoix and Schöttler, *Siegfried Kracauer*; Robnik, Kerikes, and Teller, *Film als Loch in der Wand*; and Ginzburg, *Threads and Traces*.

42. Löwenthal, "As I Remember Friedel," 10.

were concerned, whether Walter Benjamin, who, like Kracauer, was never actually a member of the Frankfurt School; Marcuse, who had risen to prominence in the American Left of the 1960s; or Adorno, whose "troubled friendship" with Kracauer was the object of an early and influential set of portraits by Martin Jay.[43] Interestingly, it would remain for Adorno's students to redress this imbalance and underline the specificity and importance of Kracauer's contributions. In doing so, they cemented his place in a revised image of an "other" Frankfurt School: through numerous essays and monographs, Heide Schlüpmann, Gertrud Koch, and Miriam Hansen have, each in her own way, made a case for how Critical Theory would have been "unthinkable without Kracauer."[44] Thus it was Koch who provided the wide-ranging introduction to Kracauer's thought that was designed explicitly to move him out of the shadow cast by his friends from the Frankfurt School. She picks up the connection with the Frankfurt School to test its limits and show the productive contradictions and heterogeneity even in Kracauer's own work, which fail to amount to any sort of "membership" in the group. But the lasting power of the Frankfurt connections manifests in Koch's approach as well. Schlüpmann, in turn, has emphasized the importance of Kracauer's earlier work from the 1920s for any reading of his American writings, even as she also reads the latter more explicitly than anyone else as a response to the Holocaust. What animates Schlüpmann's work on Kracauer at its core, though, is an argument with the Frankfurt School—and her teacher Adorno, in particular—about the place of cinema in Critical Theory. Taking the high road of cinephilia, she turns to Kracauer as her guide in moving from Adorno's seminar room to the cinema in pursuit of the meaning of aesthetic objects and forms. Hansen, finally, demonstrated in many articles and in her synoptic *Cinema and Experience* how Kracauer's critique of modernity and its media helped generate a discourse that Adorno would join with his writings on music, the culture industry, and aesthetics and that Benjamin would reshape in different ways through his discussions of photography, film, aura, and experience.[45] A tireless champion of Kracauer's place in these discussions all her life, Hansen emphasized the untapped riches of Kracauer's work prior to his arrival in the United States, from the daily and often brilliant journalistic pieces to the extensive notebooks in which he began

43. Jay, *Permanent Exiles*.

44. Miriam Hansen, quoted in Rentschler, "Cinema and the Legacies of Critical Theory," 20.

45. In a discussion of Hansen's *Cinema and Experience*, Bill Brown remarks that "the accomplishment of the book was to put Kracauer into the conversation so that he becomes a critical theorist of equal standing. That she went through the feuilleton bits and pieces and produced a Kracauer argument to begin with, and then said, 'Kracauer belongs with *these* guys,' is essential to that rhetorical strategy." Rentschler, "Cinema and the Legacies of Critical Theory," 21.

conceptualizing his later film theory. While she pointed to the "curious Americanism" of those early writings, however, she was comparatively silent on the American writings that emerged out of those notes, reading the 1960 *Theory of Film* largely for the traces of the Marseille notebooks from 1941, and having little to say about *From Caligari to Hitler*. Instead, her project was to bring Kracauer into cultural and film theory as a critical theorist of that "other Frankfurt School" that could help us better understand spectatorship and reception in silent cinema, the global power of film as a form of "vernacular modernism," and the place of media in modernity up to our digital present.[46]

Whereas Hansen had to rely for her work on untranslated, if not unpublished, texts from the 1920s on, German reception was more attuned to the importance of Kracauer's early work thanks to Witte's (truncated) edition of *Schriften* during the 1970s, Inka Mülder-Bach's critical dissertation from the mid-1980s, and then her tireless work on the comprehensive *Werke* for Suhrkamp. As a result, Kracauer's work has begun to take on a new shape that has moved him out of the shadow of the Frankfurt School—even as we can now trace some of the most influential motifs of Critical Theory back to his earliest writings.

A somewhat different trajectory for Kracauer's work and its relevance opens up if we adopt the vantage point of Anglo-American film and media studies. Here Kracauer certainly owes much of his renewed currency to the notable interest in rethinking the history of film theory, a project that motivates some of my own ongoing work on Kracauer as well. Whether as confirmation of, or in opposition to, post-theoretical turns and elegies for theory, we have begun to see a concerted return to some of the central texts and authors of classical film theory.[47] This return comes in the wake of psychoanalytic and poststructuralist theories of the 1970s and 1980s, after the ostensible "end" to that mode of theoriz-

46. Hansen, *Babel and Babylon*, x, 377; Hansen, "Mass Production of the Senses."

47. See Bordwell and Carroll, *Post-Theory*; and Rodowick, *Elegy for Theory*. Over the past decade conferences and symposia in London, Paris, and Vienna and at Harvard and Yale Universities, the University of Chicago, and Dartmouth College, among other institutions, have led to anthologies taking up "Arnheim for Film and Media Studies," "Opening Bazin" for reconsideration, investigating the works of Jean Epstein, and probing the legacies of Kracauer. See Higgins, *Arnheim for Film and Media Studies*; Andrew and Joubert-Laurencin, *Opening Bazin*; Keller and Paul, *Jean Epstein*; Gemünden and von Moltke, *Culture in the Anteroom*; and Ahrens et al., *Doch ist das Wirkliche auch vergessen*. Just as important, and doubtless prompting some of these new reflections, the archive has been expanding, and many texts and fresh translations have become newly available: thanks to Erica Carter and Rodney Livingstone, Béla Balázs's early film theory—the subject of a 2009 *Screen* symposium—became available in a new and complete English translation (Balázs, *Early Film Theory*); Keller and Paul's Epstein anthology includes a substantial section of new translations of Epstein's own writings; and Kracauer's American writings are now available in a single volume (*American Writings*).

ing proclaimed by David Bordwell and Noël Carroll in *Post-Theory*. In this sense, we might think of the return to classical texts as a rethinking of the place of theory itself—its methodological implications, its politics, its very definition *as* theory.[48] But the renewed attention to classical ways of conceptualizing cinema and film comes also after the digital turn, the explosion of media platforms, new media theories, and the apparent dissolution of film as a concrete, clearly delimited object of study in the age of convergence: developments that virtually seem to mandate rethinking the ontological premises of earlier work. After all these seismic shifts, the field is looking back to early theorizations of film, including Kracauer's, as a way to reorient itself and gain its bearings in a shifting discursive and technological landscape; in keeping with an image that Béla Balázs coined for film theory back in 1924, the field seems to be recalibrating its "compass." Dudley Andrew, who by his own admission contributed to a prolonged period in which Kracauer's work was largely neglected, has recently offered the compelling suggestion that his impact, like that of Critical Theory more generally, could "perhaps . . . only be felt when American film studies began to realize that media was integral to a discipline no longer bounded by dates or by specific technologies": perhaps, in other words, the tradition of classical film theory harbors still-untapped resources for media theory.[49]

In the final analysis, then, to speak of Kracauer's anonymity is at once flattering and flawed. It is flattering because it is sensitive to an avowedly idiosyncratic trait of Kracauer's character and indexes the degree to which some of his pioneering insights now appear to us as received wisdom. It is flawed because to speak of Kracauer's anonymity today is somewhat disingenuous, given that his name is by now firmly established in pantheons of intellectual history alongside (depending on the angle from which you consider his work) Adorno and Benjamin;[50] Rudolf Arnheim, André Bazin, and Christian Metz;[51] Aby Warburg and Erwin Panofsky;[52] or, as I argue in *The Curious Realist*, the key figures on the New York scene in the 1940s and 1950s—from the members of the Institute for Social Research uptown to Arendt, to the New York intellectuals and their "little magazines" downtown.

Accordingly, to consider Kracauer in the context of a German-American theory transfer requires a twofold approach: to rescue Kracauer from anonymity and restore him to it. To the degree that Kracauer's work has become routinized, assimilated by film criticism and cultural theory whose unexamined

48. On this last point, see esp. Rodowick, *Elegy for Theory*.
49. Andrew, "Core and the Flow," 909.
50. Hansen, *Cinema and Experience*.
51. Andrew, *Major Film Theories*.
52. Kracauer and Panofsky, *Siegfried Kracauer, Erwin Panofsky*.

premises it informs, we should continue to elucidate the logic, the contradic-tions, and the specificity of his many contributions. Here the task remains to reconstruct the coherence of Kracauer's cultural critique and to outline the politics of subjectivity that underpin it.[53] But to shore up this authorial signa-ture is simultaneously to dissolve its contours and return to it the contextual, historical energies that coursed through the conception of Kracauer's works.[54] If Adorno is right to speak of Kracauer's anonymity, then we must specify the curious forms it takes: it is the influential anonymity of a transatlantic media-tor between Frankfurt and New York, between (film) criticism and (cultural) theory, between high and low culture, between differing intellectual tradi-tions—none of which bear his name but all of which might be imagined coun-terfactually to communicate through Kracauer's oeuvre.

Postscript: Adorno's Dream

On October 10, 1960, a few weeks before *Theory of Film* finally appeared in print, Adorno awoke to record his previous night's dream: "Kracauer appeared to me: My dear chap [*mein Lieber*], it is a matter of indifference [*gleichgültig*] whether we write books and whether they are good or bad. They will be read for a year. Then they will be put in the library. Then the headmaster will come along and distribute them among the kids [*an die Kinner*]."[55]

Adorno's dream followed on the heels of a heated personal exchange between the two friends in Switzerland some weeks earlier. From Kracauer's extensive notes we know that the two men touched on fundamental philosoph-ical issues of dialectics, ontology, ideology, and their respective conceptions of utopia (triangulated, over the discussion, with Benjamin's thoughts on the mat-ter). Significantly, Kracauer's notes read at times like the description of a spar-ring match, in which the interlocutors take jabs, look for weaknesses, and rec-ognize openings. When Kracauer imprudently invokes G. W. F. Hegel, Adorno immediately "exploits the situation"; Kracauer fights back, "explores further

---

53. For a discussion that distinguishes Kracauer's "critique" from the proximate projects of criti-cism and theory, see our introduction, "Kracauer's Legacies," in Gemünden and von Moltke, *Culture in the Anteroom*, 1–25.

54. To adopt a motif that Adorno uses in a letter critiquing Kracauer's book on Offenbach, the goal here would be to "dissolve the figure-ground dualism." See letter to Kracauer, May 13, 1937, in Adorno and Kracauer, *Briefwechsel*, 355.

55. Adorno, *Dream Notes*, 65. "Kracauer erschien mir: Mein Lieber, ob wir Bücher schreiben, ob sie gut oder schlecht sind, ist doch ganz gleichgültig. Gelesen werden sie ein Jahr. Dann kommen sie in die Bibliothek. Dann kommt der Rektor und verteilt sie an die Kinner."

[his] advantage," and mounts "new attacks" until "I had Teddie trapped" and "at the end of his rope." In view of these notes, Kracauer's assertion—in a letter written during the week in which he appeared to Adorno in his dreams—that "it was good to have found the opportunity to clarify things between us" (es war gut sich einmal ausgesprochen zu haben) sounds rather like an embellishment;[56] and his almost sheepish question to Adorno, "Don't you believe so as well?," betrays lingering uncertainty about the final result of the "match."[57]

Like Kracauer's notes on the "Talk with Teddie," but in a completely different textual register, Adorno's "dream note" condenses a lifelong, erotically charged but troubled friendship between Teddie and Friedel into verbal form;[58] but whereas Kracauer's notes foreground the figural language of a fight, the dream image is more ambiguous. Kracauer, Adorno's erstwhile mentor, visits the dreamer in the manner of a *Geist*—a genie or spirit: "Kracauer appeared to me." Like a biblical apparition or a ghost in a fairy tale, Kracauer haunts Adorno with a message that remains unmarked as belonging to the former and which consequently could also be attributed to the dreamer himself. It is a message about the impact of intellectual work, about influence and legacy, about *Theorietransfer*: whether as a threat or to absolve Adorno of his unrelenting work, he draws into question the use value of the books that both men published. On one level, then, the dream encapsulates the anxiety on the dreamer's part that his work should be in vain (*gleichgültig*), its one-year public half-life shorter than its shelf life in the anonymity of some library stacks (occasional borrowings by faithful patrons notwithstanding, in the logic of the short dream sequence the library becomes charged with the specter of forgetting). On another level, though, the dream opens up, somewhat cryptically, on the books' afterlives. Having specified the duration of their brief stint among readers, the dream traces their subsequent journey both into, and back out of, the library—whence the headmaster (re)distributes them to the *Kinner*.

Though the earlier conversation in Switzerland arguably provides both the dream material and a context for the competitive undertone of Kracauer's

56. Adorno and Kracauer, *Briefwechsel*, 514.

57. See ibid., 513. For more on the troubled friendship, see Jay, *Permanent Exiles*; and von Moltke, "Teddie and Friedel."

58. On the erotics of this friendship, see von Moltke, "Teddie and Friedel"; an earlier dream that Adorno recorded in 1937 has Kracauer lending his friend two hundred francs to visit a "particularly elegant brothel" in Paris—under the condition that Adorno spend it only on the excellent food at the establishment in question. Adorno eats an excellent steak, served with a white sauce, "that made me so happy that I forgot about everything else." See Adorno, *Dream Notes*, 2.

notes on his "Talk with Teddie," the interpretation of the dream manifestly hinges on the meaning we give to its final word, which one would seek in vain in any German dictionary. It has been rendered into English as "kids," following the phonetics that, in some dialectal variations, might approximate the plural *Kinder*. On this reading, the fate of the books ends on a hopeful, future-oriented note, as their readership multiplies with a new generation after a library hiatus of unspecified length. Such a deciphering of the dream would coincide closely, moreover, with Adorno's well-known description of his own writings as so many messages in a bottle, tossed into the sea of European barbarism to be retrieved by the "kids" of a future generation around 1968. Whereas Kracauer did not live to see a similar reception in Germany, his writings, too, would be taken up by successive generations of young cinephiles and critics who latched on to the politics of *From Caligari to Hitler* and then on to the ostensibly more subject-centered and depoliticized aesthetics of *Theory of Film*.[59]

Kinner also permits other decodings, however, if we allow not the consonants but its stressed vowel to morph into meaning. Phonetically, it is but a minor shift to *Kenner*—experts or cognoscenti—which would preserve the readership for the books but limit their reach to a specialized in-group rather than a new generation. A less proximate (because agrammatical) displacement would produce *Keiner*: nobody.[60] In this reading, of course, the indifference that attaches to the writing of books according to Kracauer's apparition only initiates the downward spiral toward oblivion. If, in the end, *Keiner*/nobody reads Adorno's and Kracauer's books a year after their completion, then the message in the bottle remains adrift, the meaningfulness of its authors' intellectual pursuits thrown into question.

Dreams are, according to Sigmund Freud, wish fulfillments whose subject is always the dreamer. Although Kracauer literally appears at the beginning of the dream as its *spiritus rector*, whatever anxieties and wishes (whether for fame or for anonymity) it encodes and fulfills would have to be Adorno's:

---

59. See Rentschler, "Kracauer, Spectatorship, and the Seventies."

60. Although "an die Kinner" necessitates a plural accusative where the singular "nobody" would have to form "verteilt sie an *Keinen*," there is a circumstantial and somewhat circuitous (dreamlike) route that links "Kinner" to "nobody": Bertolt Brecht, Adorno's and Kracauer's fellow exile in the United States during the 1940s, had used Karl Kinner as a pseudonym in his correspondence with his publisher; this was a variation on his own figure of "Keuner"—the name under which Brecht himself also published his play *Der aufhaltsame Aufstieg des Arturo Ui* (*The Resistible Rise of Arturo Ui*)— which, in turn, was designed, among other things, to evoke precisely the anonymity of *Keiner* as the precondition for universalizable thinking (in drafts and manuscripts, Brecht had also apostrophized Keuner as "der Denkende"). See *Werke*, 461.

does the shared fate of the two men's books signify a leveling of the relation-ship where Adorno—at this point by far the more outwardly successful of the two men—still senses competition and a lingering hierarchy vis-à-vis his older friend? Or does the dream's tripartite structure enact a (negative) dialectic of reading/nonreading/redistribution that materializes and worries at the exchange value of thinking—anathema for Adorno's theory?

On the other hand, again according to Freud, few if any details in dreams can be considered coincidental, and none are inconsequential. Long periods of estrangement notwithstanding, and despite—or because of—their tussle over dialectics and ontology a few weeks earlier, Adorno knew his friend well enough to summon Kracauer, of all people, in a dream about publishing, books, and their impact.[61] In their lifelong correspondence, Kracauer had often voiced open admiration for Adorno's productivity and remarked on his own, comparatively slow working tempo. During his American years especially, Kracauer struggled hard to make a living out of writing books, the subject of Adorno's dream. In a very material sense, his livelihood depended on the life of his books in public, their distribution and lasting value. In this sense, the dream is perhaps after all about Kracauer as much as about Adorno. It encodes both the subjective anxiety of the intellectual and an objective historical pat-tern of reception in which recognition and anonymity, readers and nonreaders, *Kinder/Kenner/Keiner* alternate. Articulated by a ghostlike apparition, it is a pattern that extends beyond the life of either the dreamer or the dreamed. In the weeks after Kracauer's death, Adorno made a waking pronouncement about the latter's works in a letter to Gershom Scholem. Branding Kracauer's wife, Lili, a "protective devil," he ventures the prediction that "almost noth-ing" will remain of his admittedly talented but fatally self-satisfied friend's (today we might say: frenemy's) intellectual output.

> During the second half of his life Kracauer was truly dominated by a protec-tive devil who knew how to direct him in ways that prevented any criticism, including self-criticism, from reaching him. Consequently, he harbored an all but complete self-satisfaction, and that ruined him mentally [*geistig*]. Nothing will remain of his later works, and almost nothing of his earlier ones—as I had to discover when trying to facilitate at least this or that publication. He

---

61. However condescending and mean he could be toward his older friend at times, one should add that Adorno became an active champion of Kracauer in postwar Germany, facilitating contacts and ultimately contracts with major publishers for Kracauer's collected essays and his translated monographs on film.

was in fact extremely talented by nature, and I owe him a level of gratitude that alone remains as I swallow all the troubles I had with him over decades and which occasionally took on grotesque dimensions.[62]

The passage has all the hallmarks of a dream, condensing the troubled male friendship in the figure of the devilish wife, and ending on an all but physical image of repression that puts the lie to the gratitude Adorno alleges. And like a dream, it is retrospective even in its self-assured prediction. While it thus provides further documentation of Adorno and Kracauer's fraught lifelong—even posthumous—relationship, it misses its mark in assessing the shape of the Kracauer reception to come. Writing from Frankfurt to Scholem in Jerusalem about Kracauer in New York, Adorno remains unable to project the vagaries of transatlantic theory transfers that, as I have suggested, followed other pathways in addition to those paved by the Frankfurt School. What he misses in his characterization of Kracauer as self-satisfied is the latter's characteristic hesitancy, his constitutive aversion—encoded in literary figures such as Ginster and Georg as well as in the essential motifs of his criticism and theory—to laying claim to any self that could be satisfied in the first place. Though he would coin the term and knowingly incur its ambiguity in his obituary, Adorno perhaps never quite grasped the theoretical import of anonymity for Kracauer's work. At our greater remove, however, half a century after Kracauer's death, we may begin fully to assess the pivotal role of anonymity for his rethinking of subjectivity between Cold War humanism and our own posthumanist present.

References

Adorno, Theodor W. 1986. "Nach Kracauers Tod." In *Vermischte Schriften I: Theorien und Theoretiker, Gesellschaft, Unterricht, Politik*. Vol. 20.1 of *Gesammelte Schriften*, edited by Rolf Tiedemann, 194–96. Frankfurt am Main: Suhrkamp.
———. 1991. "The Curious Realist." *New German Critique*, no. 54: 172.
———. 1998. "Scientific Experiences of a European Scholar in America." In *Critical Models: Interventions and Catchwords*, translated by Henry W. Pickford, 215–42. New York: Columbia University Press.

62. "Kracauer ist wahrhaft, während der zweiten Hälfte seines Lebens, von einem Schutzteufel beherrscht worden, der es vermochte, ihn so zu lenken, daß keine Kritik, auch keine Selbstkritik, an ihn herangelangen konnte. Infolgedessen hatte er fast vollkommene Zufriedenheit mit sich, und die hat ihn, geistig, ins Verderben gerissen. Aus seiner späteren Produktion wird nichts bleiben, und aus seiner früheren—davon mußte ich mich überzeugen bei dem Versuch, doch noch die eine oder andere Publikation zu ermöglichen—fast nichts. Dabei war er wirklich von Haus aus höchst begabt, und ich bin ihm zu einer Dankbarkeit verpflichtet, die jetzt allein übrigbleibt, während ich all den Ärger, den ich Dezennien lang mit hatte, und der zuweilen groteske Formen annahm, friedlich herunterschlucke." Letter to Scholem, December 16, 1966, in Adorno and Scholem, *Briefwechsel*, 399. I am grateful to Matthew Handelmann for pointing me to this letter.

———. 2007. *Dream Notes*, edited by Christoph Gödde and Henri Lonitz, translated by Rodney Livingstone. Cambridge: Polity.

Adorno, Theodor W., and Siegfried Kracauer. 2008. *Briefwechsel*, edited by Wolfgang Schopf. Frankfurt am Main: Suhrkamp.

Adorno, Theodor W., and Gershom Scholem. 2015. *Briefwechsel*, edited by Asaf Angermann. Frankfurt am Main: Suhrkamp.

Ahrens, Jörn, Paul Fleming, S. Martin, and Ulrike Vedder, eds. 2016. *"Doch ist das Wirkliche auch vergessen, so ist es darum nicht getilgt": Beiträge zum Werk Siegfried Kracauers*. New York: Springer.

Andrew, Dudley. 1976. *The Major Film Theories: An Introduction*. London: Oxford University Press.

———. 2009. "The Core and the Flow of Film Studies." *Critical Inquiry* 35, no. 4: 879–915.

Andrew, Dudley, and Hervé Joubert-Laurencin, eds. 2011. *Opening Bazin: Postwar Film Theory and Its Afterlife*. Oxford: Oxford University Press.

Balázs, Béla. 2010. *Early Film Theory: "Visible Men" and "The Spirit of Film,"* edited by Erica Carter, translated by Rodney Livingstone. New York: Berghahn.

Baumann, Stephanie. 2014. *Im Vorraum der Geschichte*. Konstanz: Konstanz University Press.

Bordwell, David, and Noel Carroll. 1996. *Post-Theory: Reconstructing Film Studies*. Madison: University of Wisconsin Press.

Brecht, Bertolt. 1988. *Werke*. Vol. 18. Frankfurt am Main: Suhrkamp.

Despoix, Philippe, and Peter Schöttler, eds. 2006. *Siegfried Kracauer, penseur de l'histoire*. Paris: Edition de la Maison des Sciences de l'Homme.

Elsaesser, Thomas. 1986. "The 'New' Film History." *Sight and Sound* 55, no. 4: 246–51.

Gemünden, Gerd, and Johannes von Moltke, eds. 2012. *Culture in the Anteroom: The Legacies of Siegfried Kracauer*. Ann Arbor: University of Michigan Press.

Ginzburg, Carlo. 2012. *Threads and Traces: True, False, Fictive*. Berkeley: University of California Press.

Hansen, Miriam. 1991. *Babel and Babylon: Spectatorship in American Silent Film*. Cambridge, MA: Harvard University Press.

———. 1999. "The Mass Production of the Senses: Classical Cinema as Vernacular Modernism." *Modernism/Modernity* 6, no. 2: 59–77.

———. 2012. *Cinema and Experience: Siegfried Kracauer, Walter Benjamin, and Theodor W. Adorno*. Berkeley: University of California Press.

Harcourt, Peter. 1968. "What, Indeed, Is Cinema?" *Cinema Journal* 8, no. 1: 22–28.

Higgins, Scott, ed. 2010. *Arnheim for Film and Media Studies*. New York: Routledge.

Huyssen, Andreas. 2015. *Miniature Metropolis: Literature in the Age of Photography and Film*. Cambridge, MA: Harvard University Press.

Isenberg, Noah. 2012. "This Pen for Hire: Siegfried Kracauer as American Cultural Critic." In *Culture in the Anteroom: The Legacies of Siegfried Kracauer*, edited by Gerd Gemünden and Johannes von Moltke, 29–41. Ann Arbor: University of Michigan Press.

Jay, Martin. 1986. *Permanent Exiles: Essays on the Intellectual Migration from Germany to America*. New York: Columbia University Press.

Kaes, Anton. 1995. "German Cultural History and the Study of Film: Ten Theses and a Postscript." *New German Critique*, no. 65: 47–58.

Keller, Sarah, and Jason N. Paul, eds. 2012. *Jean Epstein: Critical Essays and New Translations*. Amsterdam: Amsterdam University Press.

Kidel, Mark. 2013. "DVD: Chronicle of a Summer; BFI Reissue of the Mother of All Vérité Docs." Arts Desk.com, May 20. www.theartsdesk.com/film/dvd-chronicle -summer.

Koch, Gertrud. 2000. *Siegfried Kracauer: An Introduction*, translated by Jeremy Gaines. Princeton, NJ: Princeton University Press.

Kracauer, Siegfried. 1969. *History: The Last Things before the Last*. New York: Oxford University Press.

———. 1994. "The Task of the Film Critic." In *The Weimar Republic Sourcebook*, edited by Anton Kaes, Martin Jay, and Edward Dimendberg, 634–35. Berkeley: University of California Press.

———. 1995. *The Mass Ornament: Weimar Essays*, edited and translated by Thomas Y. Levin. Cambridge, MA: Harvard University Press.

———. 1997. *Theory of Film: The Redemption of Physical Reality*. Princeton, NJ: Princeton University Press.

———. 2004 (1926). "Chaplin." In *Kleine Schriften zum Film*, edited by Inka Mülder-Bach. Vol. 6.1 of *Werke*, 269–70. Frankfurt am Main: Suhrkamp.

———. 2004. *Ginster: Von ihm selbst geschrieben*. In *Romane und Erzählungen*, edited by Inka Mülder-Bach and Sabine Biebl. Vol. 7 of *Werke*, 9–256. Frankfurt am Main: Suhrkamp.

———. 2012. *American Writings: Essays on Film and Popular Culture*, edited by Johannes von Moltke and Kristy Rawson. Berkeley: University of California Press.

———. 2016. *Georg*, translated by Carl Skoggard. Troy, NY: Publication Studio Hudson.

Kracauer, Siegfried, and Erwin Panofsky. 1996. *Siegfried Kracauer, Erwin Panofsky: Briefwechsel, 1941–1966*, edited by Volker Breidecker. Berlin: Akademie.

Löwenthal, Leo. 1991. "As I Remember Friedel." *New German Critique*, no. 54: 5–17.

Löwenthal, Leo, and Siegfried Kracauer. 2003. *In steter Freundschaft: Leo Löwenthal— Siegfried Kracauer, Briefwechsel, 1921–1966*. Springe: Klampen.

Mülder-Bach, Inka. 1991. "History as Autobiography: *The Last Things before the Last*." *New German Critique*, no. 52: 139–57.

Quaresima, Leonardo. 2004. Introduction to *From Caligari to Hitler: A Psychological History of the German Film*, by Siegfried Kracauer. Princeton, NJ: Princeton University Press.

Rentschler, Eric. 2012. "Kracauer, Spectatorship, and the Seventies." In *Culture in the Anteroom: The Legacies of Siegfried Kracauer*, edited by Gerd Gemünden and Johannes von Moltke, 61–75. Ann Arbor: University of Michigan Press.

Rentschler, Eric, moderator. 2014. "Cinema and the Legacies of Critical Theory: Roundtable Discussion." *New German Critique*, no. 122: 20–28.

Robnik, Drehli, Amália Kerekes, and Katalin Teller, eds. 2013. *Film als Loch in der Wand: Kino und Geschichte bei Siegfried Kracauer*. Vienna: Turia + Kant.

Rodowick, David Norman. 2014. *Elegy for Theory*. Cambridge, MA: Harvard University Press.

Ryan, Judith. 1991. *The Vanishing Subject: Early Psychology and Literary Modernism*. Chicago: University of Chicago Press.

von Moltke, Johannes. 2010. "Teddie and Friedel: Theodor W. Adorno, Siegfried Kracauer, and the Erotics of Friendship." *Criticism* 51, no. 4: 683–94.

———. 2012. "2 February, 1956: Siegfried Kracauer Advocates a Socio-aesthetic Approach to Film in a Letter to Enno Patalas." In *A New History of German Cinema*, edited by Jennifer M. Kapczynski and Michael David Richardson, 359–64. Rochester, NY: Camden House.

———. 2013. "Theory of the Novel: The Literary Imagination of Classical Film Theory." *October*, no. 144: 49–72.

———. 2016. *The Curious Humanist: Siegfried Kracauer in America*. Berkeley: University of California Press.

Verfehlungen: *Hans Blumenberg and the United States*

Paul Fleming

When it comes to missed encounters, it just so happens that Hans Blumenberg has, if not a theory, then a set of anecdotes that stages precisely this phenomenon. In *Care Crosses the River*, Blumenberg titles a section "Verfehlungen," a word that technically means "misdemeanors" or "transgressions" but that in this context draws its semantic energy from the verb *verfehlen*: to miss, mistake, fail. Blumenberg's "Verfehlungen" consists of anecdotes relating "missed encounters" in which two people meet, an encounter takes place, but something goes wrong—yet in this very going awry (and this is Blumenberg's point) something essential takes place: something important is revealed in the missed encounter. A simple example is "In Jena" (all the anecdotes are named for places, creating a topography of going astray): in 1912 the young student Ludwig Wittgenstein, on his way home to see his parents for the holidays, stops in Jena to seek out Gottlob Frege, one of the few stars in his philosophical pantheon. He rings Frege's doorbell, a gentleman answers, Wittgenstein

I wish to thank the many people who eagerly shared ideas and insights into Blumenberg's fate in the United States, especially Hannes Bajohr, Eva Geulen, Peter Uwe Hohendahl, Andreas Huyssen, Niklaus Largier, Steffen Martus, Ethel Matala de Mazza, Helmut Müller-Sievers, Anson Rabinbach, William Rasch, Carlos Spoerhase, Nathan Taylor, and all the engaged participants and audience members at the "Missed Encounters" conference at Columbia University as well as the "Theory Transfer" conference at Cornell University and the "Theoriegeschichte" conference at the Zentrum für Literatur- und Kulturforschung in Berlin.

New German Critique 132, Vol. 44, No. 3, November 2017
DOI 10.1215/0094033X-4162262   © 2017 by New German Critique, Inc.

asks if Professor Frege is at home, the man says: "I am he." Wittgenstein blurts out uncontrollably: "Impossible!"[1] A "Verfehlung" in every sense. Wittgenstein is, however, according to Blumenberg, *right*. The Frege who met Wittgenstein at the door turned out, in fact, to not be *his* Frege—the Frege that he imagined and needed. Wittgenstein's Frege, the one whom he sought in 1912, would have been a philosopher who could have understood the *Tractatus* when it appeared a few years later. Instead, the person who met him at the door was truly "impossible." Six years later, in 1918, Wittgenstein writes to Russell with exasperation: "Frege doesn't understand a word of my work; I am already completely exhausted from explaining it all the time."[2] And thus does a missed encounter express something essential: in blurting out "Impossible!" Wittgenstein already revealed the truth of their intellectual relationship.[3]

Blumenberg never set out for the United States, which probably did not help his reception here, nor did he have an American Frege in his pantheon to seek out. Yet he did arrive in the English-speaking world only to "miss the mark"—from 1983 to 1987 he was translated, and very well, by Robert M. Wallace in a herculean effort that produced some twenty-five hundred pages and three massive tomes over four years: *The Legitimacy of the Modern Age* (1983), *Work on Myth* (1985), and *The Genesis of the Copernican World* (1987). All these books were published by MIT Press in the prestigious series Studies in Contemporary German Social Thought, where translations of works by Theodor W. Adorno, Hans-Georg Gadamer, Jürgen Habermas, Ernst Bloch, Carl Schmitt, and Reinhart Koselleck appeared in the same time frame. The condition of his reception seemed right—good translations, the proper context, an excellent press, and a rich diversity of material cutting across intellectual history, the history of science, myth, and literary studies. There was even a prepublication of an excerpt and related essays in *New German Critique*. In short, Blumenberg's arrival in the United States was a coordinated, concentrated effort.[4] Yet one cannot shake the sense of something missing the mark, a disjunctive *and* between Blumenberg *and* the United States.

1. Blumenberg, *Care Crosses the River*, 126. The series of "Missed Encounters" can be found on pp. 117–35.

2. Blumenberg, *Care Crosses the River*, 127.

3. On "Verfehlungen"/missed encounters in Blumenberg, see also my essay "The Perfect Story."

4. *New German Critique*, no. 32 (1984), prepublished a chapter from *Work on Myth* titled "To Bring Myth to an End," and Robert M. Wallace provided a preview of Blumenberg's argument in the forthcoming *Legitimacy of the Modern Age* with his 1981 essay "Progress, Secularization, and Modernity: The Löwith-Blumenberg Debate," as well as a 1984 "Introduction to Blumenberg," both in *New German Critique*. In the fall of 1987 the journal *Annals of Scholarship* (vol. 5, no. 1) dedicated an entire issue to him, "Symposium: Hans Blumenberg."

The question therefore arises: is Blumenberg's missed encounter in the United States simply contingent—that is, could it have been otherwise—or is there something about his thought, method, and materials that makes his transfer from a German to an American or Anglophone context particularly difficult? There is clearly no *one* reason or even an easily discernible set of reasons as to why Blumenberg (or many of the other theorists under discussion in this special issue) have not really "made it" in the English-speaking world. And I do think Blumenberg's presence in American theoretical debates could have, should have been—*should be*—stronger. Nevertheless, I am not sure if he ever could have really caught on like, for example, Michel Foucault, Jacques Derrida, or Gilles Deleuze for reasons I hope to indicate. But then again—and this, I fear, is the real specter looming over this special issue of *New German Critique*—other than Habermas (who profited enormously from the legacy of the Frankfurt School and the time he himself spent in the United States) and Friedrich Kittler in media studies, what German intellectual whose career clearly comes after World War II did make it in the English-speaking world? The missed encounter here is almost total.[5]

The Timing of Translation

The initial title of this article was "Missed Metaphors," which is now abandoned, since much more than metaphors have been missed. Originally, I was referring to the lamentable fifty-year delay in translating *Paradigms for a Metaphorology*, which first appeared in German in 1960,[6] and only in 2010 was

---

5. One can, of course, debate what it means to have an impact, whether book sales or popularity is equal to success, as well as many other factors. I am admittedly arguing with broad brushstrokes to encourage debate. So, too, I am referring largely to intellectuals writing exclusively in German (i.e., where literal translation is imperative) and whose careers begin after World War II (which is why I exclude the two great pillars of German thought in the United States, Martin Heidegger and the first generation of the Frankfurt School widely conceived, that is, including Walter Benjamin). Hannah Arendt, for example, clearly has had an important, ongoing impact in the United States for many reasons, but her writing in English and living here were certainly factors; the same applies to Siegfried Kracauer and Herbert Marcuse.

6. The reception history of *Paradigms* in both German and English is complicated. The German original appeared in the journal *Archiv für Begriffsgeschichte* and in a Bonn Bouvier edition, both in 1960, but only appeared in a Suhrkamp edition in 1998, two years after Blumenberg's death. In 1983 Anselm Haverkamp published excerpts (the introduction, the first paragraph of chapter 6, as well as chapters 7 and 8) from *Paradigms* in the essay collection *Theorie der Metapher*. This excerpt may have been the most readily available "version" of *Paradigms* in Germany in the 1980s. At the end of the 1970s and in the early 1980s Suhrkamp wanted to reprint the entire volume, but Blumenberg decided against it, since he thought it outdated and was working on an updated version, now expanded to a "theory of nonconceptuality," whose elements are contained in *Lesbarkeit der Welt, Shipwreck with Spectator: Paradigm of a Metaphor for Existence* (especially the appendix "Prospect for a Theory of

brilliantly translated by Robert Savage—and brilliantly I mean three essential features: (1) an elegant and fluid translation (far from easy with Blumenberg); (2) the translation of all quotations, some a half page, from Latin, Greek, and French, while keeping the originals (the German version did not translate the quotations until the reissue of *Paradigms* in 2013, along with providing copious footnotes and essays); and (3) a strong introduction or afterword that not only situates Blumenberg's project in its German context but also expands the scope to include more timely and relevant points of contact in French and American theory.

In *Paradigms*, this foundational work from 1960—which I note was published before Derrida's "White Mythology" (1971; English 1974), Paul de Man's "Rhetoric of Temporality" (1969), much less *Allegories of Reading* (1979), and Paul Ricoeur's *Rule of Metaphor* (1975; English 1977)—Blumenberg already articulates a theory of metaphor, in which essential aspects of thought withdraw from or cannot be captured by the domain of the concept. One could call it a "tropology" or a "reading of rhetoric" at work in the heart of philosophy; Blumenberg himself called it a theory of "absolute metaphor," which he later expanded into a "theory of nonconceptuality." For Blumenberg, certain metaphors are "absolute" to the extent that they are not residual elements of thought on the way from mythos to logos but "foundational elements of philosophical language, 'translations' that resist being converted back into . . . logicality."[7] This resistance of metaphor to logos (its nonlogocentrism, one might say) is neither arbitrary nor provisional but necessary, part of an expanded philosophical language. Blumenberg's metaphorology (again, we are talking 1960) posits rhetoric not as a counterproject to epistemology but as integral to it, which therefore both expands and problematizes a classical notion of knowledge, since it now must include discursive realms that can be expressed only figuratively. His central insight—that absolute metaphors "in a more radical sense than concepts" bring to light "the metakinetics of the historical horizons of meaning" (i.e., that the movement and withdrawal of epochal meaning is most clearly traced by metaphorology)[8]—would have been a crucial, theoretical

---

Nonconceptuality," also included in the Haverkamp volume), and the essay "Beobachtungen an Metaphern" as well as the posthumous volumes *Theorie der Unbegrifflichkeit* and *Quellen, Ströme, Eisberge*. For a brief overview of the history of Blumenberg's plan to rewrite a metaphorology (as Unseld reports in a letter from December 1977), see von Bülow and Krusche's afterword to *Quellen, Ströme, Eisberge*, 283–85. Blumenberg was approached in 1985 to translate *Paradigms* into English, but since he decided against a republication in Suhrkamp, he felt that his refusal of the text to Unseld prevented him from publishing it elsewhere. I want to thank Hannes Bajohr for this information.

7. Blumenberg, *Paradigms*, 4.

8. Ibid., 5.

intervention into the rhetoric debates of the 1980s. None of this took place, not in the United States, and hardly in Germany.[9]

There are, of course, important differences between Blumenberg and Derrida or de Man and Blumenberg; his metaphorology from 1960 is not a simple anticipation of the rhetorical readings to come, and some theorists might consider Blumenberg to be not radical enough by limiting himself to a subset of metaphor (i.e., "absolute metaphors"), and thus ultimately too acquiescent to conceptuality (it still exists), too stable in his historical formations (there are metaphoric regimes that come into being and fade away), too reliant on notions of "ground," and thus perhaps too metaphysical, too ontological, too phenomenological, and so on and so forth. These differences would have needed to be elaborated and fought out, work that Anselm Haverkamp started in German (but, since Derrida and de Man had such a small audience there, without sweeping effects) and that never really took place in the United States,[10] because the translation of *Paradigms* did not exist as the basis for a wider discussion, despite the centrality of Derrida, de Man, and rhetorical readings for several generations of literary scholars.

There is, then, a double loss in this missed encounter: the translation of *Paradigms* in 2010 came far too late to play a defining role in a major methodological question of literary theory—the role of rhetoric and metaphor—in the 1980s and 1990s; at this point, 2017, such belated arrivals mostly tell us what hypothetically could have happened and what may have been possible and how it may have been different; it helps us assess what was, but this does not affect the debates themselves, which have already achieved their contours and whose passionate negotiations are (for now) over.[11] The second, and perhaps more critical, loss in the delayed translation of *Paradigms* was the

9. There are, however, two Blumenberg essays translated in the late 1980s and early 1990s that directly address the centrality of rhetoric and metaphor: "An Anthropological Approach to the Contemporary Significance of Rhetoric," first published in Italian in 1971 (German in 1981), was translated by Robert M. Wallace in 1987, and "Light as a Metaphor for Truth: At the Preliminary Stage of Philosophical Concept Formation," which was published in German in 1957 and forms a foundation of *Paradigms*. Joel Anderson translated this essay into English in 1993. As an early scholarly intervention, David Adams published the essay "Metaphors for Mankind: The Development of Hans Blumenberg's Anthropological Metaphorology" in 1991.

10. For example, in the Darmstadt volume *Theorie der Metapher* (1983), Haverkamp juxtaposes the work of Blumenberg, Ricoeur, Lacan, and de Man, among others.

11. This raises a related question that cannot be addressed here: Is it the case that as soon as we start to historicize "theory," its days of efficacy are over? Is the urgency of theory tied to its actuality? This question belongs to the tension between literary theory and literary history that emerged in the wake of theory's ascendancy. The Zentrum für Literaturforschung in Berlin is dedicating one of its research foci to the question of "Theoriegeschichte" (history of theory).

chance for Blumenberg to be read by a much larger set of readers beyond intellectual historians and a few scholars in the history of science, that is, by the wide range of literary scholars performing rhetorical readings. This did not happen, which probably hindered literary scholars' access to *Legitimacy* and *Work on Myth*.

Belatedness

In the case of Blumenberg, however, such belatedness is actually his fate in the English-speaking world. From the very beginning, Blumenberg arrived in the English-speaking world after the debates he could have helped shape had already assumed clear form. It began with the first book publication *The Legitimacy of the Modern Age* and the immediate review essay by no less than Richard Rorty, both appearing in 1983. Rorty concludes his aptly titled review "Against Belatedness" with the lament (July 7, 1983):

> The first edition of Blumenberg's book [*Legitimacy*, 1966] was published four years after Kuhn's *Structure of Scientific Revolutions* [1962] and one year before Foucault's *Les Mots et les Choses*. But the latter book waited only six years to be translated into English. Ever since it has stood side by side with Kuhn's on many bookshelves, profoundly affecting the way we English-speakers think about intellectual history. It is a pity that Blumenberg's book went untranslated for 17 years.[12]

Rorty names precisely the right book ends for contextualizing Blumenberg's thought in *Legitimacy*; yes, Blumenberg famously takes as his starting point and point of contention the secularization theses of Karl Löwith and Schmitt, and does so for over one hundred pages, but on the level of theory and method, his intellectual peers are Thomas S. Kuhn and Foucault, the "paradigm shift" and the "episteme," where Blumenberg's "reoccupation" (*Umbesetzung*) and "epochal threshold" (*Epochenschwelle*) should have formed the correlative terms.[13] Here, too, differences naturally obtain, with Foucault tracing more "striking discontinuities" and "abjuring 'totalising' stories,"[14] whereas Blumenberg straddles an almost imperceptible space between continuity and dis-

---

12. Rorty, "Against Belatedness." I note that Foucault's *Order of Things* was actually published in 1966 in France, the same year as Blumenberg's *Legitimacy*, and in 1970 in its English translation.

13. The case was different in Germany: immediately before Löwith's and Gadamer's famous, lengthy double review of Blumenberg's *Legitimacy* book in *Philosophischer Rundschau* (vol. 15, no. 3, 1968), one finds an equally substantial review of Kuhn's *Structure of Scientific Revolutions* by Kurt Hübner, placing the works quite literally side by side.

14. Rorty, "Against Belatedness."

continuity; he rejects the persistence of "transfigured substances"[15] and thus Schmitt's insistence of modern political theory merely being secularized theological concepts while maintaining that certain questions persist and demand, often blindly, answers that then reoccupy the space of the now vacated position. The structure of reoccupation consists, then, in a simultaneous continuity and discontinuity, a rupture that partly overlays a persistence, and in this suture of the incongruent, history limps forward, at once genuinely new (hence the *legitimacy* of the modern age) and subtended by persistent problems in need of ever-new responses.

Creating a Context

Like Rorty, Martin Jay emphasizes Blumenberg's proximity to Foucault and Kuhn in intellectual history in his 1985 review in *History and Theory*. Taking Rorty and Jay together, one can read between the lines a slight but important critique of or supplement to Wallace's translated volume viewed as a whole. While Wallace's introductions are enormously helpful in guiding the reader through the ensuing Blumenberg text—doing the signposting that Blumenberg generally does not—they do not additionally place him in a wider theoretical context, particularly one that exceeds the rather internal debates of Germany (e.g., Schmitt and Löwith in the case of *Legitimacy*).[16] Given that Kuhn and Foucault had both been available in English, for twenty-one and thirteen years, respectively, Rorty and Jay rightfully try to place him in this theoretical context.[17]

Placing Blumenberg between Kuhn and Foucault is not only faithful to their respective projects but also reflects a simple fact: from the 1970s forward, the theory superhighway to the United States leads through either France (predominantly)[18] or the Frankfurt School (in the wide sense, including Walter Benjamin—hence the presence of Habermas). Both Rorty and Jay, I sense,

15. Jay, review of *Legitimacy of the Modern Age*, 185.

16. Alasdair MacIntyre, for example, complains in his rather critical review of *Legitimacy* that the secularization debates opened by Schmitt have "parallels in other modern cultures, but which in Germany [have] been conducted with almost exclusive reference to German thought" (924).

17. I want to emphasize that this should not be read as overly critical of Wallace's introductions; they are excellent and enormously helpful. In fact, my translation of *Care Crosses the River* had no introduction. In his double review of *Paradigms* and *Care*, David Adams underscores the importance of such introductions and contextualizations, particularly in the case of Blumenberg.

18. The notion of "French theory" possesses a complex and rich history, precisely because what now goes by this name never existed in France (and certainly not under such a unified nomenclature) and thus was largely invented in the United States. For a history of the reception of "French theory" in the United States, see Cusset, *French Theory*.

grasped this need in their 1983 and 1985 essay-length reviews of *Legitimacy*, since both go to great lengths in discussing Blumenberg in the context of not only Kuhn and Foucault but also Derrida, Martin Heidegger, Jean-François Lyotard, Marxism, postmodernism, and so on. Absent this context and situating his thought within it, Blumenberg had a much harder road to finding relevance in the United States at the time.[19]

One also has to acknowledge that Rorty, writing for a much larger audience in the *London Review of Books* than Jay in the academic journal *History and Theory*, probably did Blumenberg no favors in celebrating him rather simplistically and wrongly as the antidote to the postmodern rejection of the grand récit, centered subjectivity, continuity, progress, optimism, and all other liberal-Enlightenment hopes. "He gives us good old-fashioned *Geistesgeschichte*," Rorty writes, "but without the teleology and purported inevitability characteristic of the genre," and shortly thereafter postulates: "Those of us . . . whose highest hopes are still those of Mill, now have a champion."[20] Bestowed with such "praise" in 1983, Blumenberg also needed to be defended partly against his devotees. Alasdair MacIntyre, for one, does not fail to pick up Rorty's belief that Blumenberg announces a return to a Whiggish notion of history—only to write his epitaph. The final line of Macintyre's review of *Legitimacy* from 1985 reads: "Lastly, Blumenberg's whole approach to his task suggests strongly that when the Whig interpretation of history finally died in the English-speaking world, it went to Germany."[21] Whether MacIntyre—with a silent nod to Marx—is ironic in claiming that theories of historical progress take a last stand in Germany before dying as farce remains unclear.

Nevertheless, while Rorty's and Jay's reviews certainly tried to make the case for Blumenberg—to varying degrees of success—neither was part of the book itself, and Jay's came two years after the fact. Since Blumenberg throughout his work was not wont to follow Foucault's example, who provides his own foreword to the English translation of *The Order of Things* (which Foucault himself describes as "directions for use") as well as his original French preface

---

19. One sees the failure of this attempt to shift the context of Blumenberg's thought beyond Germany—for instance, to Italy, France, and the United States—in the case of Giorgio Agamben, who knows the German tradition very well (including, e.g., Max Kommerell) but in a 2008 essay, "What Is a Paradigm?," discusses at length the intimate relation between Kuhn's and Foucault's notions of paradigm/episteme as mediated not only by Aristotle, Kant, and Plato but also by lesser-known authors such as Enzo Melandri and Victor Goldschmidt, and Blumenberg is not mentioned. See Agamben, "What Is a Paradigm?"

20. Rorty, "Against Belatedness."

21. MacIntyre, "Review," 926.

with the famous anecdote of laughing in the face of Jorge Luis Borges's ordering of animals in a "certain Chinese encyclopedia," followed by the exemplary exegesis of "Las Meninas"—a true tour de force in framing one's own project—in lieu of this, what Blumenberg may have needed (and again, I write this with the benefit of much hindsight) was something done with the same intensity and capaciousness as Gayatri Spivak's introduction to her translation of Derrida's *Of Grammatology*, his first book published in the United States (1967; English 1976). Nearly one hundred pages long—a small book in its own right—Spivak's introduction situates Derrida in the United States (where he had been a guest professor), briefly outlines his earlier work, and then delineates Derrida's thought simultaneously in the context of and as the absolute radicalization of the Continental tradition from Immanuel Kant and G. W. F. Hegel to Friedrich Nietzsche, Sigmund Freud, Edmund Husserl, and Heidegger. Spivak, in short, did everything to put Derrida's thought not only in a larger European context but also, frankly, into a German intellectual context—as the ineluctable cutting edge of the German tradition. The inverse work of situating Blumenberg in the larger theoretical contexts in France and the United States was and still is necessary.[22]

But this almost anecdotal set of *Verfehlungen*—belated translations, insufficient introductions to wider intellectual interlocutors, and missed contextualizations—is merely a speculative history of what could have been done, should have been done, and then (maybe!) it would have been different. That is not enough. The grounds for the missed encounter, in the case of Blumenberg, also lie deeper.

The Archive of the Inconspicuous

Blumenberg, for one, does not make his own reception easy. He does not help his own cause, nor (quite honestly) does he seem interested in it. This is where we begin to approach the real possibility that Blumenberg's missed encounter is not entirely contingent but also partly inheres in the infrastructure of his thought, both its material and its method. (And one can justifiably ask, despite the sales numbers, to what extent he really has had an influence yet in Germany—but that is another topic.) To put it bluntly, it is not easy to

---

22. I note that Paul de Man's introduction to the translation of Hans Robert Jauss's *Toward an Aesthetic of Reception* (1982) famously performed the exact opposite task as Spivak: effectively demolishing the author it introduces by pitting Jauss against Benjamin on allegory, with Jauss representing "the classical tradition" and Benjamin "a tradition that undoes it, and that includes in the wake of Kant, among others Hamann, Friedrich Schlegel, and Nietzsche" (xxiii).

meet Blumenberg where he reads, writes, and thinks. While he did write a short essay on Kuhn ("paradigma, grammatisch," 1971), contemporary French thinkers—from Foucault to Ricoeur to Derrida—played no role in his writings. Even Adorno is rarely mentioned, despite shared concerns about the relation between myth and logos. The same applies to Benjamin. Blumenberg, in short, did not openly, much less polemically, position himself vis-à-vis the debates and schools of his age: certainly not in relation to the Frankfurt School (not to mention "French theory") and surprisingly little in relation to Heidegger, a critique indicated in *Lebenszeit und Weltzeit* (*Lifetime and Worldtime*) and *Care Crosses the River*, but that only becomes clearer in the posthumous work, especially *Beschreibung des Menschen* (*Description of Man*).[23]

It is not simply the case that Blumenberg is difficult—which applies equally to Derrida, Foucault, Deleuze, Lacan, and the like, and is, indeed, part of their attraction—but also that Blumenberg does not make it easy for the reader, which is related to but not the same as being difficult. It begins in the classroom: Blumenberg is not easy to teach—particularly with undergraduates, where much theoretical work begins—because few of his texts lend themselves easily to the classroom, even among the untranslated work. (I note that this is in sharp contradistinction to contemporary French theorists as well as the Frankfurt School.) That is, Blumenberg is not an essay writer (which has become the genre of the day), nor are there readily extractable segments from his big books,[24] nor does he provide many exemplary methodological statements through a preface or introduction along the lines of Foucault's "Las Meninas." Jay, for one, describes *Legitimacy* as "600 extremely subtle, dense and, alas, often maddeningly difficult pages."[25] One could add to this density the fact that Blumenberg's theoretical lexicon generally lacks dynamic new words or phrases (such as *differánce, paradigm shift, episteme, dialectical image*), much less the punchy one-liner (e.g., "Only for the sake of the hopeless ones have we been given hope" [Benjamin]; "There is no correct life in a false one" [Adorno]). "The second overcoming of Gnosticism," while fascinating in Blumenberg's detailed delineation as the origin and legitimacy of modernity, is not exactly a barn burner as a programmatic statement.

23. For a partial examination of Blumenberg's relation to Heidegger (and Husserl), see my entry "Sorge" in *Blumenberg Lesen: Ein Glossar.*

24. The more recently translated works offer a bit of a respite, especially *Paradigms* and *The Laughter of the Thracian Woman*, both of which are thoroughly articulated books constructed as a series of exemplary cases. With *Paradigms*, for example, one can easily use the introduction and one short paradigm in the classroom. But again, the major methodological debates about metaphor and rhetorical readings have subsided for now at least.

25. Jay, "Review," 185.

The deeper "Blumenberg problem," however, and perhaps the main obstacle to accessing his thought, is the authors and texts he engages in pursuing his method of "burrowing down to the substructure of thought."[26] Blumenberg's erudition plumbs the margins of Western thought to an unprecedented degree among theorists with grand ambitions concerning modernity, metaphor, myth, and the history of science. His intellectual heroes are not foremost Nietzsche, Freud, Heidegger, and the like (though he gives them due attention) or the usual suspects from antiquity, Plato, Aristotle, and the pre-Socratics (though they too play an important role). Rather, most of Blumenberg's arguments in *Legitimacy of the Modern Age*, *Genesis of the Copernican World*, and even *Paradigms for a Metaphorology* are drawn from much-less-known philosopher-theologians from late antiquity to the late Middle Ages: Marcion, William of Ockham, Nicholas of Cusa, Giordano Bruno. That is, the names that populate and determine the trajectory of Blumenberg's thought are often, from today's perspective, smaller players in world history, the horses and not Napoléon on their backs—one could call it the "archive of the inconspicuous," people such as Lactantius, the early Christina theologian and adviser to Constantine I, who plays an essential role in *Paradigms* and whom Blumenberg gives one of the greatest introductions to the stage of high theory. Regarding the choice of Lactantius, Blumenberg defends his exemplarity as follows:

> Precisely the fact that he is not a thinker of the first order [*kein Stern erster Ordnung*] makes him a suitable case study for our investigations into epochal (not epoch-making) historical structures. . . . Minds like Lactantius's have enough "suction power" to soak up the nutrient solution of the historical current; yet because they also stand authentically in relation to the new crystallizations that, in the horizon of meaning of their age, correspond to its problems and needs, they can actively participate in the historical current without changing its course [*ohne ihm eine Wendung zu geben*].[27]

Lactantius is exemplary for Blumenberg's project precisely because of his middling status in early Christian thought. In determining what constitutes an epoch as an epoch or, more precisely here, a metaphorical regime (which is what he is tracing in paradigms), Blumenberg necessarily emphasizes not the stars who mark a change in course but the sponges with maximal "suction power" who stand in the middle of the stream, only to be washed away by the

---

26. Blumenberg, *Paradigms*, 5.
27. Ibid., 32; translation slightly modified.

torrent of time. Therefore the "Blumenberg problem" is that the material he mobilizes to make his theoretical claims often relies on inconspicuous, unspectacular thinkers. To make matters worse, because Blumenberg pushes the origins of modernity back to the return of an early Christian problem (the first failed overcoming of gnosticism via Augustine) in the fifteenth and sixteenth centuries (as opposed to the more familiar ground of the seventeenth and eighteenth centuries), it also demands incredible command of the nuances of early Christian, medieval, and Renaissance theology. In short, Blumenberg's notion of intellectual history in its relation to modernity—the question of modernity, when it begins, how it is defined, what determines the break—is much more capacious and invested in theological questions (and necessarily so) than one often finds in the world of academic "theory."

In this respect, Foucault's *Order of Things* provides an excellent point of comparison to *Legitimacy*, both as a contemporaneous work (each first appearing in 1966) and as one whose foundational archive is often equally obscure. A quick glance at the authors cited in the first chapter (after "Las Meninas"), "The Prose of the World," underscores this issue: with the exception of the last reference to Montaigne, few if any of the sources will be familiar to the nonspecialist. While more canonical thinkers, such as René Descartes, Francis Bacon, George Berkeley, Denis Diderot, and Adam Smith, appear throughout the study, much of the work is built from an archive of much less canonical scientists and thinkers. As Didier Eribon points out, *The Order of Things* "was an extremely difficult work, meant for a limited audience interested in the history of science."[28] Nevertheless, when released in France, *The Order of Things* was immediately a "huge success," going through multiple printings per year during the 1960s and accompanying people to beaches and cafés to show others that they "were not ignorant of such a major event."[29] Why this particular book struck such a chord in mid-1960s France is difficult to discern. Eribon comments on Foucault's late decision to include the analysis of Diego Velázquez's *Las Meninas*: "This bit of bravura, undoubtedly added at the last minute, played a large part in the book's success."[30] The same certainly holds true in the United States (given how often "Las Meninas" is republished and taught), and I would add the systematic lucidity of the original preface and new one for the English edition. Nevertheless: despite the "buzz" surrounding the work in France and the dynamic, tripartite setup that Foucault offers the

28. Eribon, *Michel Foucault*, 156.
29. Ibid.
30. Ibid., 155.

English reader, *The Order of Things*—like *Legitimacy*—relies on less-known historical figures to chart its course, to produce its archaeology, and this poses equal problems to the reader. One crucial difference, however, is the preponderance of much earlier, genuinely theological thought in Blumenberg's work, and thus an emphasis on the importance of theology from early Christianity to the Renaissance in understanding modernity—in an unparalleled fashion, Blumenberg insists on a "theological imperative" for engaging the questions (not the answers) defining Western thought.

This is where Blumenberg's erudition runs into equal doses of amazement and embarrassment even among his admirers (and indifference among others). Put simply, many of Blumenberg's arguments in the first two translated books that commenced and largely determined his "reception" in the English-speaking world (e.g., a full three-quarters of the *Legitimacy* book, or five hundred pages) are genuinely theological arguments that secular, theory-hungry, Continent-inflected academics (i.e., Blumenberg's ideal audience) are largely ill equipped to engage.[31] Therefore the difficulty that the 1983 translation of *Legitimacy* (again, rather early in the theory decades) had in finding its place alongside Kuhn and Foucault is not just due to belatedness, as Rorty suggests, but also because its theory is being drawn from a very foreign archive. For Blumenberg, the only way to discern modernity is via the juxtaposition of Nicholas of Cusa and Bruno on either side of the epochal threshold. Neither constitutes the break; for Blumenberg, the rupture or threshold is a gray zone that can only be read negatively, from the careful reconstruction of two thinkers responding to the same questions in radically different ways. Or as Blumenberg puts it: "There are no witnesses to changes of epoch. The epochal turning is an imperceptible frontier, bound to no crucial date or event."[32]

31. An interesting comparative case would be the reception of Agamben's most recent work, particularly the four volumes on Christian theology and history from early Christianity to the Middle Ages, replete with theologians who normally do not belong to the theory canon often at the core of argumentation: *The Sacrament of Language: An Archaeology of the Oath* (2010), *The Kingdom and the Glory: For a Theological Genealogy of Economy and Government* (2011), *Opus Dei: An Archaeology of Duty* (2013), and *The Highest Poverty: Monastic Rules and Form-of-Life* (2013). These recent works, particularly their genealogy of modern economy and government as anchored in theological questions of the early church, show clear affinities to both the sweeping erudition and the reception problems of Blumenberg (though the longest are half the length of *Legitimacy*, most are one-quarter or less); it is probably too early to assess their influence on subsequent thought (though it seems they will not have the same impact of, e.g., *Homo Sacer*). Moreover, unlike Blumenberg, these recent books by Agamben come after the success of much shorter, straightforward theoretical works that built on canonical authors (e.g., Aristotle) and addressed well-specified, even theoretical-political, structures and concerns: *Homo Sacer: Sovereign Power and Bare Life* (1998), *Remnants of Auschwitz: The Witness and the Archive* (2002), *The Open: Man and Animal* (2003).

32. Blumenberg, *Legitimacy*, 469.

This means that not only is Blumenberg's major "archive" defined by rather arcane theological debates from early Christianity onward, but his method consists in meticulous, detailed reconstructions of epochal situations where answers explicitly precede the questions, and thus one needs to elaborate the stakes, what is really being said, in the unsaid (and this, I note, in texts that are often available only in Latin). Only in this often imperceptible movement (especially when it happens that two otherwise radically different theories are, in fact, addressing the same question) can one begin to trace the outline, but only the outline, of an "epochal threshold"—the event itself is absent, blurred, and one needs two witnesses (and lot of erudition and theoretical work) to circumnavigate it. The hermeneutic task is to take all the "assertions, doctrines and dogmas, speculations and postulates" and figure out what are the real questions, the driving issues that motivated them in the first place.[33] Or, to cite an anecdote that Blumenberg uses to illustrate the logic of what he calls "reoccupation": "In a cartoon . . . De Gaulle was pictured opening a press conference with the remark, 'Gentlemen! Now will you please give me the questions to my answers!' Something along these lines would serve to describe the procedure that would have to be employed in interpreting the logic of a historical epoch in relation to the one preceding it."[34] In privileging not the answer but the question, and asserting the belatedness of the question (first the answers, then the reconstruction of the questions that incited them), Blumenberg again finds allies in the contemporary theory, such as Derrida writing on Heidegger in *Of Spirit*. But because this is worked out in loving detail over hundreds of pages via two unsung heroes, Nicholas of Cusa and Bruno, one effect is that even Blumenberg's dedicated readers, who are often not as well acquainted with the fine details of theological history, can admire the fireworks of erudition without being able to fully assess the results it leaves behind. Insofar as the theoretical argument for Blumenberg is inextricably also a historical one, the theory reader all too often has to take the historical reconstruction on good faith. And the philosopher in the philosophy department tends to view him as a "mere" intellectual historian, and not a thinker.[35]

---

33. Ibid., 483.

34. Ibid., 379.

35. As Bajohr writes in his review of Angus Nicholls's *Myth and the Human Sciences*: "But already Blumenberg's characterization as an intellectual historian rather than a philosopher showed how unprepared the American academic public was for him. The strict separation between both disciplines was at odds with a German tradition that often practiced philosophy by way of the history of ideas, so that *Legitimacy* and *Genesis* were received as 'mere' works of intellectual historiography, which, although impressively erudite, inevitably lowered expectations as to Blumenberg's philosophical originality" (358–59).

Therefore, as much as a Blumenberg renaissance is taking place in the United States (eight books have now been translated with three more under contract, with certainly more to come),[36] and as much as I sense that Blumenberg, akin to Foucault, ages very well via his posthumous work (which is not insignificant, since the afterlife can take on a life of its own), and while Angus Nicholls, who knows Blumenberg exceptionally well, has just published the first book-length study on Blumenberg in English: *Myth and the Human Sciences: Hans Blumenberg's Theory of Myth*—despite all this, I am not sure that Blumenberg will suddenly become a theoretical phenomenon in the United States, a "best seller" in the theory charts, for all the reasons outlined above.[37] Success, however, can be measured many ways, and Blumenberg's importance and influence will certainly continue to grow in the English-speaking world (as it already has since the translations of *Paradigms for a Metaphorology* and *Care Crosses the River*), as more of his remarkably diverse body of work is translated, quoted, critically engaged, and placed in its proper interdisciplinary intellectual contexts; success, in other words, can also be found slowly, driven by a cumulative effect, the persistence of certain questions, and the resulting staying power. In fact, the capacious reflection and erudite depths of his thought certainly offer the possibility that Blumenberg achieves the esteemed status of a "thinker's thinker," a treasure trove of theoretical engagement for those with the fortitude and curiosity to make their way through his work. For the average theory reader, which is where sales numbers come from, he may remain a tougher sell. But while this may be part of the "Blumenberg problem," it is not his alone, for as I suggested at the beginning, what German theorist since the war has avoided the fate of a missed encounter?

References

Adams, David. 1991. "Metaphors for Mankind: The Development of Hans Blumenberg's Anthropological Metaphorology." *Journal of the History of Ideas* 52, no. 1: 152–66.
———. 2011. "Review of *Paradigms for a Metaphorology* and *Care Crosses the River*." *Notre Dame Philosophical Reviews*, August 23. ndpr.nd.edu/news/25580-paradigms -for-a-metaphorology-and-care-crosses-the-river.

36. As of March 2017, *The Legitimacy of the Modern Age*, *The Genesis of the Copernican World*, *Work on Myth*, *Shipwreck with Spectator*, *Paradigms for a Metaphorology*, *Care Crosses the River*, and *The Laughter of the Thracian Woman* have all appeared, with *Lions* slated for late 2017. *Rigorismus der Wahrheit*, *Matthäuspassion*, and a Blumenberg reader are forthcoming from Cornell University Press.

37. Presses could, however, be more creative in publishing Blumenberg and other German theorists, using, for example, the enormously successful *Semiotext(e)* model (or, in Germany, Merve model) that mobilizes short, provocative texts, even excerpts, that aim to prod, motivate thinking, even and especially at the expense of a "truncated" version of the whole work.

Agamben, Giorgio. 2009. "What Is a Paradigm?" In *The Signature of All Things: On Method*, translated by Luca D'Isanto with Kevin Atell, 9–32. New York: Zone.

Bajohr, Hannes. 2015. "Review of Angus Nicholls' *Myth and the Human Sciences.*" *Germanic Review* 90, no. 4: 358–70.

Blumenberg, Hans. 1971. "Beobachtungen an Metaphern." *Archiv für Begriffsgeschichte* 15: 161–214.

———. 1981. *Lesbarkeit der Welt*. Frankfurt am Main: Suhrkamp.

———. 1983. *The Legitimacy of the Modern Age*, translated by Robert M. Wallace. Cambridge, MA: MIT Press.

———. 1984. "To Bring Myth to an End," translated by Robert M. Wallace. *New German Critique*, no. 32: 109–40.

———. 1985. *Work on Myth*, translated by Robert M. Wallace. Cambridge, MA: MIT Press.

———. 1987. "An Anthropological Approach to the Contemporary Significance of Rhetoric," translated by Robert M. Wallace. In *After Philosophy: End or Transformation?*, edited by Kenneth Baynes, James Bohman, and Thomas McCarthy, 423–58. Cambridge, MA: MIT Press.

———. 1987. *The Genesis of the Copernican World*, translated by Robert M. Wallace. Cambridge, MA: MIT Press.

———. 1993. "Light as a Metaphor for Truth: At the Preliminary Stage of Philosophical Concept Formation," translated by Joel Anderson. In *Modernity and the Hegemony of Vision*, edited by David Michael Levin, 30–62. Berkeley: University of California Press.

———. 1997. *Shipwreck with Spectator: Paradigm of a Metaphor for Existence*, translated by Steven Randall. Cambridge, MA: MIT Press.

———. 2007. *Theorie der Unbegrifflichkeit*, edited by Anselm Haverkamp. Frankfurt am Main: Suhrkamp.

———. 2010. *Care Crosses the River*, translated by Paul Fleming. Stanford, CA: Stanford University Press.

———. 2010. *Paradigms for a Metaphorology*, translated by Robert Savage. Ithaca, NY: Cornell University Press.

———. 2012. *Quellen, Ströme, Eisberge*, edited by Dorit Krusche and Ulrich von Bülow. Berlin: Suhrkamp.

———. 2015. *The Laughter of the Thracian Woman: A Protohistory of Theory*, translated by Spencer Hawkins. New York: Bloomsbury Academic.

———. 2017. *Lions*, translated by Kári Driscoll. New York: Seagull.

Cusset, François. 2008. *French Theory: How Foucault, Derrida, Deleuze, & Co. Transformed the Intellectual Life of the United States*, translated by Jeff Fort. Minneapolis: University of Minnesota Press.

de Man, Paul. 1982. Introduction to *Toward an Aesthetic of Reception*, by Hans Robert Jauss, translated by Timothy Bahti, vii–xxv. Minneapolis: University of Minnesota Press.

Eribon, Didier. 1991. *Michel Foucault*, translated by Betsy Wing. Cambridge, MA: Harvard University Press.

Fleming, Paul. 2011. "The Perfect Story: Anecdote and Exemplarity in Linnaeus and Blumenberg." *Thesis 11* 104, no. 1: 72–86.

———. 2014. "Sorge." In *Blumenberg Lesen: Ein Glossar*, edited by Robert Buch and Daniel Weidner, 291–305. Berlin: Suhrkamp.

Gadamer, Hans-Georg. 1968. "Review of Hans Blumenberg, *Die Legitimität der Neuzeit.*" *Philosophische Rundschau* 15, no. 3: 201–9.

Haverkamp, Anselm, ed. 1983. *Theorie der Metapher.* Darmstadt: Wissenschaftliche Buchgesellschaft.

Hübner, Kurt. 1968. "Review of T. S. Kuhn, *The Structure of Scientific Revolutions.*" *Philosophische Rundschau* 15, no. 3: 185–95.

Jay, Martin. 1985. "Review of *Legitimacy of the Modern Age.*" *History and Theory* 24, no. 2: 183–96.

Löwith, Karl. 1968. "Review of Hans Blumenberg, *Die Legitimität der Neuzeit.*" *Philosophische Rundschau* 15, no. 3: 195–201.

MacIntyre, Alasdair. 1985. "Review of *Legitimacy of the Modern Age.*" *American Journal of Sociology* 90, no. 4: 924–26.

Rorty, Richard. 1983. "Against Belatedness." *London Review of Books*, June 16, 3–5. www.lrb.co.uk/v05/n11/richard-rorty/against-belatedness.

Wallace, Robert M. 1981. "Progress, Secularization, and Modernity: The Löwith-Blumenberg Debate." *New German Critique*, no. 22: 63–79.

———. 1984. "Introduction to Blumenberg." *New German Critique*, no. 32: 93–108.

Against Rigor: Hans Blumenberg on Freud and Arendt

Martin Jay

In his wrenching memoir of surviving Auschwitz, *If This Is a Man*, the Italian writer Primo Levi recalls a moment when he learned a bitter lesson about the vanity of seeking the meaning of his suffering: "Driven by thirst, I eyed a fine icicle outside the window, within reach of my hand. I opened the window and broke off the icicle, but at once a large, heavy guard prowling outside brutally snatched it away. '*Warum?*' I asked in my poor German. '*Hier ist kein warum*' (There is no why here), he replied, shoving me back inside."[1] The guard's chilling candor about the utter gratuity of his cruel gesture has become an emblematic moment in the unending struggle to explain, interpret, and represent the bafflingly savage rupture in civilization we have come to call "the Holocaust" or "the Shoah." It is the moment when all our intellectual resources seem to fail us and we are confronted with the unyielding absurdity of actions and events that resist any attempt to provide a plausible answer to the questions of why they happened or what they signify. Like the icicle that melts in the guard's hand

This essay is published on the occasion of the appearance of the English-language edition of Hans Blumenberg's posthumous work, *Rigorism of Truth*: *"Moses the Egyptian" and Other Writings on Freud and Arendt*, translated by Joe Paul Kroll. Originally published in German in 2015 as *Rigorismus der Wahrheit: "Moses der Ägypter" und weitere Texte zu Freud und Arendt*, the English edition is anticipated in December 2017 as the inaugural book in Signale|TRANSFER, a component of Cornell's series Signale: Modern German Letters, Culture and Thought. All translations in this essay of quotations from *Rigorismus der Wahrheit* are taken from this forthcoming English edition.

1. Levi, *If This Is a Man*, 25.

New German Critique 132, Vol. 44, No. 3, November 2017
DOI 10.1215/0094033X-4162274 © 2017 by New German Critique, Inc.

before it can slake Levi's thirst, reasons for the horror vanish into the air before they satisfy our yearning to find meaning in an indifferent universe bereft of it.[2]

It is as if Job in the Hebrew Bible were confronted not with an ineffable God but with God's satanic opposite, who tortures Job for reasons that he refuses to divulge.[3] The conventional rhetoric of tragedy, sacrifice, and martyrdom all reveal themselves to be woefully inadequate to characterize, let alone justify, the slaughter of so many innocents. Not surprisingly, for some survivors like Elie Wiesel in his searing fictionalized memoir *Night*, the consoling balm of religion could no longer provide comfort for an affliction that could find no conceivable justification. Although God may move in a mysterious way, "his wonders to perform," he does not get a pass when it comes to performing unaccountable horrors. But for other survivors, precisely because it is the devil and not God whose unjust cruelty is inexplicable, the victim should never renounce the search for meaning and withdraw in the end, as does Job in the Bible, his seemingly hubristic demand for a reason for his suffering. Instead, they continue to press for an answer to "Warum?" Failing to do so, they fear, would be to grant a posthumous victory to the tormentors whose arrogant retort must not be allowed to serve as the last word.

For the intellectuals among those personally touched by the Holocaust, the imperative to deny that victory to the devil must have seemed especially overwhelming. Intellectuals, after all, are people defined by their need to explain and interpret the world, no matter how opaque it may appear, and then to justify their answers to others. To be in the midst of an unfolding catastrophe the likes of which even the long-suffering Jewish people could never have imagined must have compelled intellectuals identified, however tenuously, as Jews to explain or find deeper meaning in the cataclysmic events that menaced their existence. Inevitably, such unprecedented and unexpected horrors demanded all the imaginative resources at their command.

But what if the dogged quest for intelligibility might produce unintended consequences? If slaking one's thirst means ingesting an icicle of tainted water, is it perhaps better to accept that no "Warum" can be conclusively answered, to acknowledge that even if he were willing to do so, neither God nor the devil could provide a plausible explanation, let alone justification, for so dreadful an event? Refusing to concede this inability may, after all, lead to crediting false answers, with all their attendant dangers. Or at least such was the worry that motivated one survivor of the Holocaust, the distinguished phi-

---

2. It can, of course, be asked if the cruel absurdity of "L'univers concentrationnaire," to cite the title of David Rousset's famous 1946 book, was a microcosm of the universe at large or only an island of malign insanity within it.

3. For a thoughtful analysis of the book of Job and Levi, see Alford, *After the Holocaust.*

losopher and historian of ideas Hans Blumenberg, to compose an impassioned reflection on the previous attempts made by two of the twentieth century's most prominent Jewish intellectuals, Sigmund Freud and Hannah Arendt, to answer Levi's desperate question.

Unpublished in his lifetime, ostensibly because he feared that it would offend his close friend the philosopher Hans Jonas, *Rigorism of Truth: "Moses the Egyptian"* was completed over a long period of intermittent rumination, which seems to have ended, according to the reckoning of the volume's German editor and Blumenberg's last assistant, Ahlrich Meyer, in the late 1980s.[4] As the trail of notecards left in Blumenberg's voluminous *Nachlass* shows, he was already troubled by the implications of Freud's *Moses and Monotheism* (1939) as early as 1947, and invoked it in *The Legitimacy of the Modern Age* a few years later as a cautionary example of the dubious practice of "working through" past circumstances as a cure for present ills.[5] Although Blumenberg had a marginal interest in Arendt's work before *Eichmann in Jerusalem*—they even had a brief correspondence and one unproductive meeting—it was apparently his reading of it in 1978, some fifteen years after its original publication, that stimulated Blumenberg to bring her together with the father of psychoanalysis.

Linking Freud and Arendt, as Blumenberg knew full well, was itself an audacious move, unprecedented in the voluminous literature on either of them, as was a fortiori the parallel he drew between Moses and Adolf Eichmann as the targets of their debunking. Arendt, after all, was never an admirer of psychoanalysis, even if she was awarded the Sigmund Freud Prize of the Deutsche Akademie für Sprache und Dichtung in 1969.[6] Their approaches to politics radically differed, with Arendt extolling its intrinsic virtues and Freud reducing it to allegedly deeper psychological causes.[7] Her classic work *The Origins of Totalitarianism* contains no insights from the psychoanalytic tradition, which set her apart from other exiles such as Erich Fromm, Wilhelm Reich, or Erik Erikson, who sought to interpret Nazism in terms of collective psychological pathologies. Yet, on the basic issue of relentlessly seeking the true causes of genocidal anti-Semitism no matter the consequences, so Blumenberg came to believe, Freud and Arendt were united.

4. Blumenberg, *Rigorismus der Wahrheit*; *Rigorism of Truth*.

5. Blumenberg, *Legitimacy of the Modern Age*, 117–18. The controversy over Freud's book still rages. For a sampling of recent entries, see Ginsburg and Pardes, *New Perspectives on Freud's "Moses and Monotheism."*

6. According to her biographer Elizabeth Young-Brühl, she received the award "to her great surprise" (*Hannah Arendt*, 392). As far as I can tell, Arendt never seriously addressed psychoanalysis in her work. For an attempt to discern some common ground, despite her antipathy, see Whitebook, "Omnipotence and Radical Evil."

7. For an attempt to discern hidden similarities nonetheless, see Brunner, "Eichmann, Arendt, and Freud in Jerusalem."

Freud, it might be objected, died in London in 1939, before the Holocaust's full fury was unleashed, in an exile forced on him by the annexation of his native Austria by the Nazis a year earlier. He was thus spared knowing the fate of his people, including his four sisters, one of whom died in Theresienstadt, the other three in Auschwitz. Yet *Moses and Monotheism*, his controversial final book, was clearly written in the anticipatory shadow of the horrors to follow. It was, among many other things, an attempt to understand why the Jewish people were so often in their long history the target of hatred and bigotry. Rueful that his answer might be construed as blaming the victims, he nonetheless pointed to the very promulgation of Mosaic law, which, to make matters worse, he claimed was actually the work of a son of Egypt mistakenly understood to be a Jew and then killed by "his people."

Tumbling the pantheon of pagan gods from their various pedestals, prohibiting idolatrous images, discrediting the tricks of magicians and their ilk, the Jews, Freud speculated, had turned the monotheistic message of that wayward Egyptian Moses into the elevation of spirituality—*Geistigkeit*—over the body and the senses.[8] In so doing, they unwittingly unleashed a seemingly never-ending struggle in human history between higher and lower, internal and external, paternal and maternal forces, a struggle responsible for both the glorious achievements of human culture and the smoldering resentment of its repressed victims, who mourned what they had lost in terms of more direct corporeal gratification. It was, Freud now tacitly acknowledged, not simply civilization *tout court* that brought with it discontents, but one civilization in particular that was grounded in the ethical rigor, sensual constraints, and rejection of matriarchal warmth that accompanied the triumph of Mosaic law.

But in a way, so Blumenberg argued, Freud had gone beyond merely exposing the resented costs of Jewish spirituality. For he also discredited the myth of Moses the messenger of God, and in so doing undermined his foundational role as charismatic lawgiver for a people newly freed from bondage. That is, Freud had extended the rigorous spiritual logic of monotheistic lawgiving to discredit the very figure who was its alleged source. Freud, moreover, knew that his scandalous debunking of the "legend of Moses," the acclaimed liberator of the Jewish people, combined with his exposure of the costs of renouncing the flesh in the service of spirit, might be seen as a betrayal of solidarity with his fellow Jews at the moment of their greatest danger. In the very opening sentences of his book, he felt compelled to defend his decision in

---

8. Often the continuing temptations of sensuality are identified with the appeal of Aaron, Moses's brother, and the worship of the golden calf, for example, in Arnold Schoenberg's uncompleted opera *Moses und Aron*. However, Freud did not foreground this dualism in *Moses and Monotheism*.

terms that Blumenberg would ponder with increasing disquiet: "To deny a people the man whom it praises as the greatest of its sons is not a deed to be undertaken lightheartedly—especially by one belonging to that people. No consideration, however, will move me to set aside truth in favor of supposed national interests."[9] In other words, Freud felt that he had no choice but to follow the celebrated Latin imperative "Fiat justitia, et pereat mundus" (Let justice be done, though the world perish),[10] albeit with truth substituted for justice.

This imperative, so Blumenberg claimed, likewise seized Arendt a generation later. She too was driven by an intransigent passion for the truth, the consequences be damned. Her "rigorism is very much like that of Sigmund Freud," he argued. "She believes in the truth—that is her truth, she can neither change nor prevent."[11] Also exiled by the Nazis but fortunate enough to survive well after their defeat, she often returned to the vexed question of how their regime, and that of their "totalitarian" counterparts, could have emerged in the heart of "civilized" Europe. Her most sustained confrontation with the specificity of the German case was in her response to the trial in Israel of Eichmann, *Eichmann in Jerusalem: A Report on the Banality of Evil*, which generated a storm of criticism that has scarcely abated in the half century since it appeared.

Blumenberg shared many of the standard criticisms of her book: its problematic case against the "collaboration" of Jewish councils in the smooth running of the annihilation machinery; its dubious reduction of Eichmann to a thoughtless bureaucrat—or even feckless "clown"—rather than an ideologically committed Nazi; its disdain for the Zionist project in the service of a universalist internationalism; and its preference for charging Eichmann with a "crime against humanity" rather than a specific one against the Jewish people. But the most fundamental of Blumenberg's charges was against Arendt's alleged truth-telling absolutism, which was symptomatic of a moral rigidity as well: "Her book is a document of rigorism, the definition of which is the refusal to acknowledge an ultimate and inexorable dilemma in human action."[12] As in the case of Freud, Blumenberg charged, her insistence on the truth despite everything, an insistence that bespeaks moral intransigence, produced lamentable consequences for the Jews. "As Freud took Moses the man from his people, so Hannah Arendt took Adolf Eichmann from the State of Israel. Some states

9. Freud, *Moses and Monotheism*, 3.

10. The same sentiment is contained in the similar phrase "Fiat justitia ruat caelum" (Let justice be done, though the heavens fall), with the fall of heaven replacing the perishing of the world. Although sometimes attributed to classical authors, the phrases seem to have been introduced in early modern jurisprudence.

11. Blumenberg, *Rigorismus der Wahrheit*, 13.

12. Ibid., 18.

are founded on their enemies."[13] In short, "a negative hero," as Arendt called Eichmann in one of her preparatory notes, was as necessary as a "positive hero" like Moses in the imaginary of a people striving for its full realization in the world. Both were mythic figures, one appearing when the Jewish people achieved its first political embodiment, the other when it reestablished it with the realization of the Zionist dream of a Jewish state.

In his careful annotations and the judicious afterword he prepared for the original German edition, Meyer addresses the plausibility of many of Blumenberg's specific charges and helps us see how the essay emerged from the voluminous card files left behind in his extensive *Nachlass*, a rich quarry still mined for new publications two decades after his death. What I want to add here is some context for this little text by looking at Blumenberg's career as a whole, as well as casting a glance at his own relationship to the Holocaust and the challenge of its ineffability.

Blumenberg (1920–96) is certainly a less celebrated figure than either Freud or Arendt, but he has steadily earned a reputation as one of the towering presences in twentieth-century German thought, a unique combination of philosophical depth and historical erudition. The son of a Catholic father, a dealer in devotional objects, and a Jewish mother, who had converted to Protestantism in 1935 to avoid persecution, he toyed with a career in the church and spent a semester studying Catholic theology. But he was classified as a "half-Jew" by the Nazis, forced to suspend his education during the war and take shelter with the family of his future wife. In February 1945 he was interned in a labor camp of the Organization Todt in Zerbst in Saxony-Anhalt.[14] After the war he studied with Ludwig Landgrebe, a student of Edmund Husserl, in Kiel, and taught philosophy at universities in Hamburg, Giessen, and Bochum. His last and most extended position was in Münster, where he taught from 1970 to 1986, distant from the center of intellectual life in the Federal Republic. Whereas Freud and Arendt were quintessentially "public intellectuals,"[15] often commenting on the most pressing issues of the day, Blumenberg was the very model of a private scholar, not only eschewing pronouncements on current events but also disdaining the normal whirl of academic conferences, public lectures, and interviews, both in Germany and abroad. Although he was involved for a while with

---

13. Ibid., 13.

14. The Organization Todt was primarily an engineering enterprise using forced labor, which had helped build the autobahns and after 1943 was incorporated into Albert Speer's Armaments and War Production.

15. For Arendt's role as a public intellectual, see Wurgaft, *Thinking in Public*; for a recent consideration of Freud's interventions, direct and indirect, in public matters, see Zaretsky, *Political Freud*.

the research group "Poetics and Hermeneutics," including leading postwar figures like Hans Robert Jauss, Wolfgang Iser, Jacob Taubes, Reinhart Koselleck, and Odo Marquard, he was essentially an intellectual lone wolf. Explaining his self-imposed isolation, he liked to say that he had to make up for the eight years of scholarly productivity he lost during the Nazi period.[16]

Blumenberg kept his distance as well from the political cacophony of the 1960s and 1970s, avoiding the controversies in which, for example, members of the Frankfurt School were so often embroiled. If he held strong political opinions, they were only indirectly expressed in his esoteric writings.[17] He founded no new school of thought with eager disciples spreading his gospel and was himself very hard to place in any tradition. Although his own forays into the history of metaphor—or more capaciously, "non-conceptuality"[18]—did find an appreciative, if modest audience, they have not been as influential as the "Begriffsgeschichte" (history of concepts) developed by Koselleck, Otto Brunner, and Erich Rothacker.[19]

Yet Blumenberg has earned enormous respect among serious students of Western thought from its inception in classical times to the present. His astonishing command of primary sources, it is widely acknowledged, was unmatched, while it never supported self-indulgent pedantry. His confident mastery of theological and scientific as well as philosophical traditions was unparalleled. In the 1980s the heroic translation by Robert M. Wallace in rapid succession of three of Blumenberg's earliest major books, *Legitimacy of the Modern Age*, *The Genesis of the Copernican World*, and *Work on Myth*, introduced the richness of his scholarship and the subtlety of his thinking to an English-speaking public.[20] Despite their merciless demands on readers lacking

16. According to Marquard, Blumenberg also slept only six nights a week to make up for lost time. See Marquard, "Entlastung vom Absoluten," 26.

17. See Heidenreich, "Political Aspects in Hans Blumenberg's Philosophy"; and Nicholls, "Hans Blumenberg on Political Myth."

18. Blumenberg, "Prospect for a Theory of Non-conceptuality." For more accounts, see Zill, "'Substrukturen des Denkens'"; Recki, "Der praktische Sinn der Metapher"; and Savage, "Laughter from the Lifeworld."

19. For one account, see Müller, "On Conceptual History."

20. Unfortunately, most of his other major works, including *Die Lesbarkeit der Welt* (1981); *Lebenzeit und Weltzeit* (1986); *Das Lachen der Thrakerin: Eine Urgeschichte der Theorie* (1987); *Matthäuspassion* (1988); and *Höhlenausgänge* (1989) have yet to find their Wallace. In addition to *Shipwreck with Spectator* and *Paradigms for a Metaphorology*, the only other English translation is *Care Crosses the River*, translated by Fleming in 2010. For a bibliography of his work and the responses it generated before 1999, see the appendix to Timm and Wetz, *Die Kunst des Überlebens*. There have been several special issues of English-language journals devoted to his legacy, for instance, *Annals of Scholarship* 5, no. 1 (1987); *Qui Parle* 12, no. 1 (2000); and *Telos*, no. 158 (2012).

his range of reference, and the challenges of Blumenberg's often turgid prose, they stimulated novel ways of thinking about the most profound questions of the human condition, questions whose historically evolving answers Blumenberg skillfully traced. In particular, he offered arresting new ways to make sense of the continuities and discontinuities between historical epochs, especially the transition from the Middle Ages to modernity, and the unending search for meaning in a world that consistently thwarts it.

Against the reduction of ideas to their social functions as mere ideologies, Blumenberg honored what might be called the functional dignity of both concepts and their metaphorical counterparts, at least as temporary consolations for the challenges of an intractable reality. Metaphors can guide us through the unfamiliar and distant by a salutary detour through the familiar and proximate, while concepts organize the inscrutable particularities of the here and now through broader spatial and temporal categories enabling some predictive control over a future that appears not entirely contingent. Along with other nonconceptual cultural expedients, such as myth and the telling of anecdotes, they allow us to orient ourselves without the hardwired adaptive responses of other species, who need no cultural supplement to compensate for their lack of instinctual guidance.

Because Blumenberg was a critic of the claim made by Karl Löwith, Carl Schmitt, and others that the modern world was a pale, secularized version of what went before, a claim evident, for example, in the discourse of what has come to be called "political theology,"[21] he was often seen as a defender of modernity, even a champion of the Enlightenment project. If compared with the influential critique of modernity generated by, say, Martin Heidegger, from whom Blumenberg distanced himself throughout his career, his careful argument for modernity's inherent "legitimacy" certainly earned that reputation.[22] But if a defense, it was a nuanced one, without illusions about the capacity of reason and the scientific method to solve the perennial problems facing humanity, thus overcoming the legacy of magic and myth. As Robert Pippen

21. In one prominent iteration, political theology argues that modern concepts of sovereignty are derived from secularized versions of earlier theological notions of divine will. For two useful compilations that treat this issue, see Davis, Milbank, and Žižek, *Theology and the Political*; and de Vries and Sullivan, *Political Theologies*. Blumenberg's alternative to the secularization thesis was what he called "reoccupation," in which external forms were retained from earlier periods but were filled with new content as perennial questions demanded new answers. These answers were no less "legitimate" than the ones offered before.

22. Blumenberg's critique of Heidegger was apparent in his unpublished *Habilitationsschrift*, "Die ontologische Distanz" (1950).

has pointed out, Blumenberg's was a modernity without a radical "disenchantment" of the type famously posited by Max Weber.[23]

Behind the intricate historical narratives spun out by Blumenberg was a fundamental belief in an essential human condition that owed a great deal to his training in Husserl's phenomenology and interest in the anthropology of Arnold Gehlen.[24] From Husserl, or more precisely the later Husserl who authored *The Crisis of European Sciences and Transcendental Phenomenology*, Blumenberg gained an awareness that the discursive world of concepts is rooted in a preconceptual, prereflective "lifeworld," the realm of everyday experience, in which the role of rhetoric in general and of metaphor in particular is key. From Gehlen, he learned that our fecund cultural imagination allows humans to compensate as best they can for their lack of the biologically determined, instinctual preprogramming that orients other animals in the world.

In what is sometimes designated as his implicit "negative anthropology," Blumenberg contended that the recalcitrant opacity of the world, a world of irreducible contingency rather than necessity, presents never-ending challenges to fill the void left by previous failures to provide enduring answers to insoluble questions.[25] What he came to call the "absoluteness of reality" means that the world can never be fully explained by human intellectual projections;[26] it is always in excess of the most advanced interpretations of natural or social being. This is just as true, pace Freud, of the inner world of the subject as of the outer world of objects. It, too, stubbornly resists our best efforts to render it transparent.

23. Pippen, "Eine Moderne ohne radikale Entzauberung."

24. Gehlen, *Der Mensch*. The term *human condition*, which needs to be distinguished from the stronger, often normative notion of "human nature," shows a certain commonality with Arendt, whose book with that title was perhaps her most singular achievement. In other respects as well, their arguments invite positive comparisons. See, e.g., Brient, "Hans Blumenberg and Hannah Arendt on the 'Unworldly Worldliness' of the Modern Age." For a discussion of Blumenberg's development of Husserl's concept of "Lebenswelt" and Gehlen's "Mängelwesen," see Merker, "Bedürfnis nach Bedeutsamkeit."

25. For a discussion of his negative anthropology, which compares his approach with Arendt's, see Bajohr, "Unity of the World." See also Müller, *Sorge um die Vernunft*. In *The Legitimacy of the Modern Age* Blumenberg had emphasized the importance of the nominalist undermining of medieval realism, which led to a contingent world open to the capricious will of an omnipotent God. Abandoning the nominalists' faith in that God, he nonetheless retained their skepticism about the reality of inherent order in the world.

26. *Absoluteness* was one of Blumenberg's key terms, which he used to designate an uncompromising position resisting relativization, for example, the "theological absolutism" of the late Middle Ages in which God's arbitrary and willful omnipotence was posited. Although he normally used it in a negative sense, Blumenberg also spoke approvingly of "absolute metaphors," which resisted translation into concepts.

But because that absolute reality is also one that relentlessly threatens our survival, we are compelled to find ways to cope and orient ourselves, both practically and theoretically, to domesticate and distance ourselves from the relentless indifference of the real. Escape from the world—the temptation of world-denying gnosticism—is fruitless, although the temptation to do so always remains. Thus modernity, Blumenberg argued, could be understood as entailing "the second overcoming of Gnosticism," after the first attempt by the early Christians failed in the late Middle Ages.[27] Later comparable efforts, he implied, would likely follow, as the pragmatic struggle to replace ultimately unsuccessful cultural responses to the unforgiving "absoluteness of reality" would continue without resolution.[28] Despite the relief provided by technological antidotes to the indifference of "absolute reality"—Blumenberg was never inclined to disdain technology in the manner of, say, Heidegger—the precariousness of the human condition remained.

Because Blumenberg assumed that the deepest secrets of reality would always elude human attempts to reveal them, he concluded that there was more of a continuity between mythos and logos than a radical caesura.[29] Both were stratagems for managing the anxieties unleashed by the elusiveness of reality. Believers in a break between them usually advanced an exorbitant notion of reason—Blumenberg liked to call it "rigorous," with a nod to the early Husserl's dubious attempt to make phenomenology a "strenge Wissenschaft"— that sought clear and distinct ideas and unequivocally defined concepts. Blumenberg was by no means an enemy of logos, but he thought it wise to recognize as well the value of the more imprecise and flexible alternatives that the exponents of the rigorous view had so disdainfully rejected. For example, in rhetoric, which rationalists ever since Plato had scorned, Blumenberg saw an imperfect but still functional way to compensate for the "poverty of our instincts" and the limits of our intelligence. It is based on what he called, with a sly twist on Gottfried Leibniz's famous formula, "the principle of insufficient reason (*principium rationis insufficientis*). It is the correlate of the anthropol-

27. Blumenberg, *Legitimacy of the Modern Age*, 127–36.
28. The affinity between Blumenberg and pragmatism was noted approvingly by Richard Rorty. For a discussion, see Reynolds, "Unfamiliar Methods."
29. The once widespread assumption that such a break had occurred with the Greeks has not fared well in recent scholarship. See, e.g., Buxton, *From Myth to Reason?*; and Morgan, *Myth and Philosophy from the Presocratics to Plato*. Blumenberg's argument invites comparison with that made by Max Horkheimer and Theodor W. Adorno in *Dialectic of Enlightenment*. They too argue for the imbrication of myth and logos, but with a far more critical and pessimistic analysis of the implications than Blumenberg's.

ogy of a creature who is deficient in essential respects."[30] This is not, he emphasized, the same thing as an irrationalist abdication of the need for justifications or giving reasons, just a recognition that the rules of logic and the scientific method do not exhaust the full repertoire of human attempts to make sense of their world. Indeed, rhetoric is "a form of rationality itself—a rational way of coming to terms with the provisionality of reason."[31] Sophistry was not the antithesis of reason but a more supple and effective form of it than its enemies had contended.

Metaphor in particular is a tool that humans, *animals symbolicum*, have forged to cope with a world—both external and internal—that they cannot fully understand or master. It seeks to replace something frightening and uncanny with something familiar and comforting, taking an indirect and often lengthy route to assuage the fears generated by the disorienting blockage of the more direct route provided by unthinking instinct. It inevitably retains a trace of the affect that generated it, in opposition to the development of rational concepts, which claim to transcend feeling.[32] Not only does it operate on the level of language, but it also functions in actions that substitute one thing for another. "If history teaches us anything at all," Blumenberg argued,

> it is this, that without this capacity to use substitutes for actions not much would be left of mankind. The ritualized replacement of a human sacrifice by an animal sacrifice, which is still visible through the story of Abraham and Isaac, may have been a beginning. Christianity, through two millennia, has regarded it as quite understandable that the death of one can compensate for the mischief for which all are responsible.[33]

When such metaphorical displacements coalesce into full-fledged stories, myth emerges as a way to orient ourselves in a baffling world of natural forces beyond our control.[34] By anthropomorphizing those forces, giving them names and identifying them with personalities, mythic narratives allayed fears,

30. Blumenberg, "Anthropological Approach to the Contemporary Significance of Rhetoric," 447.

31. Ibid., 452.

32. For a discussion of the importance of affect for metaphor in Blumenberg, see Zill, "Wie die Vernunft es macht."

33. Blumenberg, "Anthropological Approach to the Contemporary Significance of Rhetoric," 440.

34. For the most substantial account of Blumenberg's discussion of myth, including its relation to earlier theories, such as those of Ernst Cassirer, and the responses engendered by *Work on Myth*, see Nicholls, *Myth and the Human Sciences*.

allowing humans to propitiate gods through sacrifices, rituals, and prayer. In particular, the myths of polytheism in which humanized gods struggle for power avoided the potential for dogmatic rigor that emerged with the monotheistic ideal of a transcendent and distant God—a conclusion, ironically, not so far from that reached by Freud in *Moses and Monotheism*, as Blumenberg had acknowledged in his earliest discussion of myth in 1968.[35] Even when myths are debunked, as inevitably they are, and lose their power to console us, they are not always replaced by rigorous scientific thinking or conceptual reason, for "demythicization is in large measure nothing more than remetaphorization."[36] These new metaphors then can become the foundation of new myths, as well as serve as the irreducible kernel of rational concepts. Moses, in other words, may have unleashed the spiritual revolution of monotheism and the law, which dethroned polytheistic mythic gods, but as the charismatic messenger of God, he was also the embodiment of a new myth. Although it was precisely Freud's great transgression to undermine Moses's mythic status as the founding father of the Jews in the name of disinterested science, he ironically set himself up as the mythic founder or primal father of psychoanalysis, a new attempt to break through the inherent opacity of "absolute reality."

Blumenberg's ruminations on the enduring function of myth, which have earned him a comparison with Giambattista Vico, place him somewhere on a spectrum between Friedrich Nietzsche, who urged that it replace logos, and Ernst Cassirer, who hoped for the opposite.[37] Inevitably, they have generated considerable controversy. Not only have defenders of monotheism, such as Jacob Taubes, been troubled by the relativizing moral implications of polytheism, but other commentators have also wondered how Blumenberg could ignore the political costs of mythmaking so soon after the disaster of Nazism.[38] Although it has come to light since the original publication of *Work on Myth* in 1979 that he left out a final chapter that did touch on the Nazi case, at least obliquely,[39] he never really confronted head-on the dangers of mythic thinking in the political realm.

---

35. Blumenberg, "Wirklichkeitsbegriff und Wirkungspotential des Mythos." In *Moses and Monotheism* Freud argued that "religious intolerance, which was foreign to antiquity before this and for long after, was inevitably born with the belief in one God" (21).

36. Blumenberg, "Prospect for a Theory of Nonconceptuality," 94.

37. See Moyn, "Metaphorically Speaking"; Pippen, "Modern Mythic Meaning"; and Barash, "Myth in History."

38. Blumenberg and Taubes, *Briefwechsel*; Müller, "Hans Blumenberg, *Arbeit am Mythos*."

39. Blumenberg, *Präfiguration*. The chapter deals with the effects on Hitler's military plans of his belief in putative prefigurations of the battles he waged. Blumenberg replied to Götz Müller's critique in this volume.

All the more surprising, therefore, is his critique of the debunking of myth in Freud and Arendt. It appears motivated by an unexpected allegiance to the Zionist project of a Jewish homeland, based on the belief in the unique destiny of the Jewish people challenged by Freud and the persistent threat of radically evil anti-Semitism undermined by Arendt. Blumenberg's Jewish identity, such as it was, seems derived as much from Nazi racial categorizations as from anything more deeply felt (although one can conjecture that his mother's strategic conversion when he was fifteen is likely to have left residues of guilt). Rarely if ever included in discussions of Jewish philosophers, he does not seem to have drawn much sustenance from explicitly Jewish cultural traditions.[40] He contributed nothing of note to postwar debates about "working through" the Nazi past or Germany's responsibility to compensate the survivors of its crimes. Nor did he weigh in publicly on the touchy subject of the Israeli-Palestinian conflict.[41] Significantly, in his last letter, he acknowledged his intellectual debts to the early training he had received in Catholic theology.[42]

Yet, in the notes rescued from *Nachlass*, we find several brief but clearly heartfelt ruminations on the challenges of being Jewish in a hostile world. In one, he speculates that anti-Semitism has engendered two basic responses, which he calls "the cloven consciousness of Jewry": anarchic opposition to and resentment of the dominant social order, on the one hand, and self-abnegation, on the other. Ironically, the latter can be redescribed in the Freudian terms he so vigorously resisted as "identification with the aggressor."[43] Blumenberg may perhaps have recognized it as a temptation to which he had himself succumbed. If so, in now bemoaning Freud's and Arendt's alleged demolitions of a necessary myth for the Jewish people in the name of disinterested intellectual rigor, was he trying indirectly to distance himself from Jewish self-abnegation? And if he was, did he fully succeed?

A clue might be found in another notecard in his file, which recounts one of those telling anecdotes he was so fond of citing to make a larger theoretical point. Titled "Ambiguity without Comprehension," it recalls an episode during

40. There is no mention of him, for example, in Morgan and Gordon, *Cambridge Companion to Modern Jewish Philosophy*.

41. In May 2015 a conference was held at the Van Leer Foundation in Jerusalem on the theme "Hans Blumenberg in Jerusalem," but from the topics of the papers it is not clear that any significant time was spent on his thoughts on Israel or the conflict with the Palestinians (www.vanleer.org.il/sites/files/HansBlumberg_0.pdf).

42. The letter, sent to the Catholic theologian Uwe Wolff, is published in *Communio: Internationale Katholische Zeitschrift* (2014).

43. The term was first developed by Anna Freud and often invoked by Adorno in his critique of individual and collective phenomena.

the war in which Thomas Mann reflected on the reactions to Hitler he encountered at a party at Max Horkheimer's house in Pacific Palisades. Mann was apparently uncomfortable with what he saw as their inflated sense of the Nazis' importance. "These Jews have a sense of Hitler's greatness," he confessed, "that I cannot bear." Noting that Mann's reaction anticipated Arendt's dismissive characterization of Eichmann two decades later in Jerusalem as a "buffoon of pathetic insignificance," Blumenberg contrasted it with the need of Horkheimer's friends—"these open or disguised Hegelians"—to find deep meanings in the events unfolding before them, even a manifestation of "the cunning of reason." Blumenberg, however, confessed that he identified with Mann, not Horkheimer: "No, he too, to whom this was unbearable, was right." Blumenberg, in short, sided not with the Jewish detractors of a demonic Hitler, desperately trying to address the unanswered "Warum?" posed by Nazism, but with the gentile who was unable to share their full sense of Hitler's monstrosity and who resisted fishing for deeper answers, at least on the level of rational explanations.[44]

Such a choice suggests Blumenberg's own struggle to come to grips with both his own conflicted identity and the challenge of explaining Nazism and the Holocaust—or accepting that they cannot be satisfactorily explained. For in siding with Mann, and explicitly linking his position with Arendt's, Blumenberg was admitting that from an objective viewpoint—one, in other words, that sidestepped the pragmatic implications of the positions taken—she was actually right in denying the demonic monstrosity of Eichmann. Her argument about the "banality of evil" was thus problematic not because it trivialized what required a deeper explanation but because it eroded the function that myth played in the founding of a Jewish state. When he got around to addressing Arendt's argument in *The Rigorism of Truth*, Blumenberg embraced the pragmatic necessity of myth as an alternative to both deep explanations and impotent skepticism. That is, he applied his general lesson in *Work on Myth* that the impenetrable "absolutism of reality," and a fortiori a reality where one can boast that "hier ist kein Warum," needs some sort of myth to console and orient those who are beset by it.

However, in so doing, Blumenberg unwittingly subjected Arendt herself to a certain mythic reconstruction as the latter-day Platonic defender of truth at all costs and a moral rigorist, a deontologist with no sympathy for the consequentialist implications of her actions. For in building his image of her, Blu-

44. Whether this was fair to Mann, who did in fact often try to make sense of Nazism by looking into the tangled history of German culture and politics, is less important than his positioning in this anecdote as the non-Jewish critic of excessive theorizing.

menberg ignored the fact that Arendt was deeply suspicious of the fetish of truth, at least when it came to politics, explicitly claiming that the assumption of a single correct view of the world contradicted the pluralism and contest of opinions necessary for freedom in the political sphere. Although the shoe fashioned by Blumenberg may have fit Freud, who often did seek to pierce the fabric of self-delusions and the armor of defense mechanisms to uncover occluded truths, it was far less comfortable in the case of Arendt.[45] In an essay written after the controversy over *Eichmann in Jerusalem*, Arendt addressed the wisdom of "Fiat justitia, et pereat mundus" and its correlate "Fiat veritas, et pereat mundus" (Let truth be done, though the world perish).[46] Although skeptical of the former, she acknowledged that the latter was worth heeding, at least in general, for "the sacrifice of truth for the survival of the world would be more futile than the sacrifice of any other principle or virtue."[47] But, and this was a point Blumenberg missed, when it came to the specifically political realm, the lesson was different. Whether in what Arendt called its "factual" or "rational" guise, truth telling was inherently antipolitical, for "seen from the viewpoint of politics, truth has a despotic character. . . . The modes of thought and communication that deal with truth, if seen from the political perspective, are necessarily domineering; they don't take into account other people's opinions, and taking these into account is the hallmark of all strictly political thinking."[48] Although never specifically sanctioning myth as an antidote to the dubious imperative to tell the truth no matter the cost, she understood the virtues of rhetoric, metaphor, and even mendacity, at least when it came to politics.[49]

It was thus problematic to associate her, as did Blumenberg, with a Platonic hostility to sophistic rhetoric. In a posthumously published essay on Socrates, originally written in the 1950s, Arendt explicitly condemned Plato's elevation of truth over doxa (opinion) as inherently hostile to politics.[50] The world of politics, moreover, is the world of appearances, not essences. In general,

45. Freud's own partiality for the truth may well have been more complicated than appears at first glance. It might be said that he was far more interested in the subjective truths—including fantasies—of the patient than the objective truths of what had actually happened in reality. The debate over his revision of seduction theory from an account of real seductions to their role in the psychic imaginary of patients focuses on this distinction. See, e.g., Masson, *Assault on Truth*. For subtle discussions of the complexities of the role of truth in psychoanalysis, see Weber, "Blindness of the Seeing Eye"; and Forrester, *Truth Games*. It also should also be remembered that Freud originally called *Moses and Monotheism* "an historical novel."

46. See, in particular, Arendt, "Truth and Politics," 546.

47. Ibid. For a discussion of the various places in which she interrogated the implications of the motto, see Bajohr, "Der Preis der Wahrheit," 56.

48. Arendt, "Truth and Politics," 546.

49. For a discussion of her thoughts on lying in politics, see Jay, *Virtues of Mendacity*.

50. Arendt, "Socrates."

Arendt defended the importance of phenomenal reality, the reality of surfaces rather than depths, including the deeper psychological interiority posited by Freud. As she put it in *The Life of the Mind*: "Our habitual standards of judgment, so firmly rooted in metaphysical assumptions and prejudices—according to which the essential lies beneath the surface and the surface is 'superficial'—are wrong. . . . Our common conviction that what is inside ourselves our 'inner life,' is more relevant to what we 'are' than what appears on the outside is an illusion."[51] Later in that work, moreover, she approvingly drew on Blumenberg's metaphorology in a longer argument against Plato that stressed the inevitability of metaphors in metaphysical language, many of which are based on the body and produce unintended consequences.[52]

Blumenberg was also on unsteady ground in characterizing her as a moral rigorist, a deontological thinker in the absolutist mold of Immanuel Kant. In fact, her essay celebrating Gotthold Lessing's sacrifice of truth to the value of friendship explicitly argues that "the inhumanity of Kant's moral philosophy is undeniable. And this is so because the categorical imperative is postulated as absolute, and in its absoluteness introduces into the interhuman realm—which by its nature consists of relationships—something that runs counter to its fundamental relativity."[53] In *Eichmann in Jerusalem* she mulled over Eichmann's startling defense, which on the surface seemed outrageous, that he was observing Kant's categorical imperative. Although admitting that in most respects the defense was dubious, she concluded that "there is not the slightest doubt that in one respect Eichmann did indeed follow Kant's precepts: a law was a law, there could be no exceptions."[54]

Still, on the larger issue raised by his essay, Blumenberg was right to include Arendt along with Freud as a theorist who could not rest content with the cynical answer "Hier ist kein warum" when it came to explaining the centuries of anti-Semitism that culminated in the Holocaust. *Eichmann in Jerusalem*, for all its flaws, can be understood as an attempt, to cite the Finnish political theorist Tuija Parvikko, to resist the conventional wisdom that tends to "absolutize and depoliticize the Holocaust by claiming that it was an indecipherable and incomparable phenomenon" in which the victims were denied their role "as active contributors to their own history."[55]

51. Arendt, *Thinking*, 30. She is paraphrasing Adolph Portmann, with whose argument she is agreeing.

52. Ibid., 113. She did not, however, cite him with full accuracy, as Blumenberg himself later noted. See the discussion in Bajohr, "Unity of the World," 58.

53. Arendt, "On Humanity in Dark Times," 27.

54. Arendt, *Eichmann in Jerusalem*, 137.

55. Parvikko, *Arendt, Eichmann, and the Politics of the Past*, 20.

It was, of course, that latter claim regarding Jewish complicity in their own destruction that most rankled, as it seemed to be a case not only of blaming the victim but also of insisting on the truth no matter the consequences.[56] Blumenberg was deeply suspicious of the ideal of truth telling at all costs, or indeed the faith that truth can ever finally be established. As he put it in one of the notecards in *Nachlass*, ironically titled "The Power of Truth": "Among the intimate convictions of European history is that the truth will triumph. That is as little self-evident as can be, considering what measure of description and polemic was deployed in order to represent and warn against rhetorical distractions up to the possibilities of demagogy."[57]

Yet the hope that the truth will triumph is so powerful that we can see it operating in the case of Blumenberg himself. For he was no less a compulsive truth teller than his two targets, no less reluctant than they to risk the world's doom in the name of intellectual honesty. Tacitly echoing Freud's confession at the beginning of *Moses and Monotheism*, Blumenberg tells us in *Rigorism of Truth* that he was "prepared to court indignation" but could not draw back from his inflammatory comparison, even if he were "aghast by the deep-rooted similarities" he discerned in Freud's and Arendt's most controversial works.[58] Moreover, despite his suspicion of exorbitant rationalism and defense of the enduring role of mythos even after the emergence of logos, he rejected their binary status as mutually exclusive. Thus he could promote an "ology" of metaphors and generally refrain from presenting his thoughts in an aesthetic form rather than in a traditional scholarly fashion.[59] For all his hostility to ahistorical Platonic universalism, the never-ending challenges of the human condition posited by his negative anthropology have earned him the label of an "immanent Platonist," uncomfortable with a radically historicist denial of any constants in history.[60]

But it was perhaps most in his treatment of myth itself that Blumenberg showed his unexpected affinity to his two targets in *Rigorism of Truth*. That is, contrary to other recent exponents of mythic thought, such as Joseph Campbell and Mircea Eliade, he did not claim that myths represented eternal wisdom or enduring archetypes of the human mind.[61] His own stance was that of

---

56. The issue of whether the charge of complicity was itself correct, not only from a factual but also from a moral point of view, is addressed with finesse in Diner, *Beyond the Conceivable*.

57. Blumenberg, *Rigorismus der Wahrheit*, 91.

58. Ibid., 13.

59. One exception would be the aphorisms collected in *Care Crosses the River*, which invite comparison with the *Denkbilder* of Benjamin, Kracauer, and Adorno.

60. See Carchia, "Platonismus der Immanenz." It should also be remembered that Arendt never talked of human nature but only of the human condition.

61. For a recent comparison of theories of myth, see Segal, *Theorizing about Myth*.

someone investigating its functions from afar, a cultural anthropologist of a tribe to which he did not fully belong, a metatheorist of both mythos and logos in their pure forms. He was, more precisely, a forgiving analyst of myth from the outside, but a more ambivalent critic of reason from within. Thus, when he accused Freud and Arendt of robbing the Jewish people of their enabling myths, it is not at all clear that he ever believed in them himself. There is little evidence, in fact, that he shared the Zionist dream of a Jewish homeland, at least one to which he was personally drawn.[62] Nor, as his concluding remark in the notecard devoted to Mann and Horkheimer shows, did he really believe that Eichmann was a nonbanal "negative hero," whose symbolic role was crucial in justifying the existence of the new state.

If anything, by the very act of exposing that role as grounded in myth rather than reality, and arguing that the pragmatic function of myth was necessary as a way for humans to cope with the contingent "absoluteness of reality," Blumenberg revealed that he too could not rest content with mythical consolations for both the general "Hier ist kein Warum" of "absolute reality" and the specific lack of a justification for the Holocaust. Although he eschewed deontological rigorism, he showed himself to be an ethical consequentialist, fully aware of the practical implications of beliefs whose compelling power he did not himself feel. For all his fury at the damaging effects of compulsive truth telling, for all his pessimism about conceptual precision replacing metaphorical play, for all his insistence that logos cannot emerge from the shadow of mythos, Blumenberg reveals himself in the end to be one of those insistent intellectuals *malgré lui*, Jewish, half-Jewish, or otherwise, who cannot entirely relinquish the need to seek a nonmythic answer to Levi's desperate question: "Warum?"

References

Alford, C. Fred. 2009. *After the Holocaust: The Book of Job, Primo Levi, and the Path to Affliction.* New York: Cambridge University Press.

Arendt, Hannah. 1968. "On Humanity in Dark Times: Thoughts about Lessing." In *Men in Dark Times*, 3–31. New York: Harcourt.

———. 1978. *Thinking.* Vol. 1 of *The Life of the Mind.* New York: Harcourt.

---

62. In fact, in one sense by exposing the latent function of the Eichmann trial as a founding myth of the Israeli state, Blumenberg was tacitly giving ammunition to those who would point out that Zionism excluded players besides Germans and Jews, in particular the Palestinians, who are absent from this particular story. The controversial slogan "a land without people for a people without a land" exemplifies the power of this myth, in which the only "people" are the Jews escaping from the demonic anti-Semitism of a hostile world that had led to the Holocaust. For an illuminating discussion of other Zionist myths and countermyths, see Ohana, *Origins of Israeli Mythology.*

———. 2000. "Truth and Politics." In *The Portable Hannah Arendt*, edited by Peter Baehr, 545–75. New York: Penguin.

———. 2005. "Socrates." In *The Promise of Politics*, edited by Jerome Kohn, 5–39. New York: Schocken.

Bajohr, Hannes. 2015. "Der Preis der Wahrheit: Hans Blumenberg über Hannah Arendts 'Eichmann in Jerusalem.'" *Merkur*, no. 792: 52–59.

———. 2015. "The Unity of the World: Arendt and Blumenberg on the Anthropology of Metaphor." *Germanic Review* 90, no. 1: 42–59.

Barash, Jeffrey Andrew. 2011. "Myth in History: Philosophy of History as Myth; On the Ambivalence of Hans Blumenberg's Interpretation of Ernst Cassirer's Theory of Myth." *History and Theory* 50, no. 3: 328–40.

Blumenberg, Hans. 1950. "Die ontologische Distanz: Eine Untersuchung über die Krisis der Phänomenologie Husserls." *Habilitationsschrift*, University of Kiel.

———. 1971. "Wirklichkeitsbegriff und Wirkungspotential des Mythos." In *Terror und Spiel: Problem der Mythenrezeption*, edited by Manfred Fuhrmann, 11–66. Munich: Fink.

———. 1981. *Die Lesbarkeit der Welt*. Frankfurt am Main: Suhrkamp.

———. 1983. *The Legitimacy of the Modern Age*, translated by Robert M. Wallace. Cambridge, MA: MIT Press.

———. 1985. *Work on Myth*, translated by Robert M. Wallace. Cambridge, MA: MIT Press.

———. 1986. *Lebenszeit und Weltzeit*. Frankfurt am Main: Suhrkamp.

———. 1987. "An Anthropological Approach to the Contemporary Significance of Rhetoric." In *After Philosophy: End or Transformation?*, edited by Kenneth Baynes, James Bohman, and Thomas McCarthy, 429–58. Cambridge, MA: MIT Press.

———. 1987. *Das Lachen der Thrakerin: Eine Urgeschichte der Theorie*. Frankfurt am Main: Suhrkamp.

———. 1987. *The Genesis of the Copernican World*, translated by Robert M. Wallace. Cambridge, MA: MIT Press.

———. 1988. *Matthäuspassion*. Frankfurt am Main: Suhrkamp.

———. 1989. *Höhlenausgänge*. Frankfurt am Main: Suhrkamp.

———. 1996. *Shipwreck with Spectator: Paradigm of a Metaphor for Existence*, translated by Steven Rendall. Cambridge, MA: MIT Press.

———. 1997. "Prospect for a Theory of Nonconceptuality." In *Shipwreck with Spectator: Paradigm of a Metaphor for Existence*, translated by Steven Rendall, 81–102. Cambridge, MA: MIT Press.

———. 2010. *Care Crosses the River*, translated by Paul Fleming. Stanford, CA: Stanford University Press.

———. 2010. *Paradigms for a Metaphorology*, translated by Robert Savage. Ithaca, NY: Cornell University Press.

———. 2014. *Präfiguration: Arbeit am politischen Mythos*, edited by Angus Nicholls and Felix Heidenreich. Berlin: Suhrkamp.

———. 2014. "Und das ist mir von der Liebe zur Kirche geblieben." *Communio: Internationale Katholische Zeitschrift* 43, no. 3: 173–81.

———. 2015. *Rigorismus der Wahrheit: "Moses der Ägypter" und weitere Texte zu Freud und Arendt*, edited by Ahlrich Meyer. Berlin: Suhrkamp.

———. 2017. *Rigorism of Truth: "Moses the Egyptian" and Other Writings on Freud and Arendt*, edited by Ahlrich Meyer, translated by Joe Paul Kroll. Ithaca, NY: Cornell University Press and Cornell University Library.

Blumenberg, Hans, and Jacob Taubes. 2013. *Briefwechsel, 1961–1981, und weitere Materialen*, edited by Herbert Kopp-Oberstebrink und Martin Treml. Frankfurt am Main: Suhrkamp.

Brient, Elizabeth. 2000. "Hans Blumenberg and Hannah Arendt on the 'Unworldly Worldliness' of the Modern Age." *Journal of the History of Ideas* 61, no. 3: 513–30.

Brunner, José. 1982. "Eichmann, Arendt, and Freud in Jerusalem: On the Evils of Narcissism and the Pleasures of Thoughtlessness." *History and Memory* 8, no. 2: 61–88.

Buxton, Richard, ed. 1999. *From Myth to Reason? Studies in the Development of Greek Thought*. New York: Oxford University Press.

Campe, Rüdiger, Paul Fleming, and Kirk Wetters, eds. 2012. "Hans Blumenberg." Special issue. *Telos*, no. 158.

Carchia, Gianni. 1999. "Platonismus der Immanenz: Phänomenologie und Geschichte." In *Die Kunst des Überlebens: Nachdenken über Hans Blumenberg*, edited by Hermann Timm and Franz Josef Wetz, 327–40. Frankfurt am Main: Suhrkamp.

Copeland, Huey, Jennifer Greiman, Ara H. Merjian, Joel Nickels, Jennifer Scappettone, Benjamin S. Jost, Benjamin Graves, Benjamin Lazier, and Catherine Zimmer. 2000. "The End of Nature: Dossier on Hans Blumenberg." Special issue. *Qui Parle* 12, no. 1.

Davis, Creston, John Milbank, and Slavoj Žižek, eds. 2005. *Theology and the Political: The New Debate*. Durham, NC: Duke University Press.

de Vries, Hent, and Lawrence E. Sullivan, eds. 2006. *Political Theologies: Public Religions in a Post-secular World*. New York: Fordham University Press.

Diner, Dan. 2006. *Beyond the Conceivable: Studies in Germany, Nazism, and the Holocaust*. Berkeley: University of California Press.

Forrester, John. 2000. *Truth Games: Lies, Money, and Psychoanalysis*. Cambridge, MA: Harvard University Press.

Freud, Sigmund. 1939. *Moses and Monotheism*, translated by Katherine Jones. New York: Knopf.

Gehlen, Arnold. 1940. *Der Mensch: Seine Natur und seine Stellung in der Welt*. Berlin: Junker und Dünnhaupt.

Ginsburg, Ruth, and Ilana Pardes, eds. 2006. *New Perspectives on Freud's "Moses and Monotheism."* Tübingen: Niemeyer.

Graham, Ruth, ed. 1987. "Symposium: Hans Blumenberg." Special issue. *Annals of Scholarship* 5, no. 1.

Heidenreich, Felix. 2015. "Political Aspects in Hans Blumenberg's Philosophy." *Revista de filosofia aurora*, no. 41: 523–39.

Horkheimer, Max, and Theodor W. Adorno. 2002. *Dialectic of Enlightenment: Philosophical Fragments*, edited by Gunzelin Schmid Noerr, translated by Edmund Jephcott. Stanford, CA: Stanford University Press.

Jay, Martin. 2012. *The Virtues of Mendacity: On Lying in Politics*. Charlottesville: University of Virginia Press.

Levi, Primo. 2014. *If This Is a Man*. Vol. 1 of *The Complete Works of Primo Levi*, edited by Ann Goldstein, translated by Stuart Woolf. New York: Liveright.

Marquard, Odo. 1999. "Entlastung vom Absoluten: In Memoriam." In *Die Kunst des Überlebens: Nachdenken über Hans Blumenberg*, edited by Hermann Timm and Franz Josef Wetz, 17–27. Frankfurt am Main: Suhrkamp.

Masson, Jeffrey Moussaieff. 1992. *The Assault on Truth: Freud's Suppression of the Seduction Theory*. New York: Farrar, Straus and Giroux.

Merker, Barbara. 1999. "Bedürfnis nach Bedeutsamkeit: Zwischen Lebenswelt und Absolutismus der Wirklichkeit." In *Die Kunst des Überlebens: Nachdenken über Hans Blumenberg*, edited by Hermann Timm and Franz Josef Wetz, 68–98. Frankfurt am Main: Suhrkamp.

Morgan, Kathryn A. 2003. *Myth and Philosophy from the Presocratics to Plato*. New York: Cambridge University Press.

Morgan, Michael L., and Peter Eli Gordon, eds. 2007. *The Cambridge Companion to Modern Jewish Philosophy*. Cambridge: Cambridge University Press.

Moyn, Samuel. 2000. "Metaphorically Speaking: Hans Blumenberg, Giambattista Vico, and the Problem of Origins." *Qui Parle* 12, no. 1: 55–76.

Müller, Götz. 1981. "Hans Blumenberg, *Arbeit am Mythos*." *Zeitschrift für deutsche Philologie* 100: 314–18.

Müller, Jan-Werner. 2014. "On Conceptual History." In *Rethinking European Intellectual History*, edited by Darrin M. McMahon and Samuel Moyn, 74–93. New York: Oxford University Press.

Müller, Oliver. 2005. *Sorge um die Vernunft: Hans Blumenbergs phänomenologische Anthropologie*. Paderborn: Mentis.

Nicholls, Angus. 2015. *Myth and the Human Sciences: Hans Blumenberg's Theory of Myth*. New York: Routledge.

———. 2016. "Hans Blumenberg on Political Myth: Recent Publications from the Nachlass." *Iyyun: Jerusalem Philosophical Quarterly* 65: 3–34.

Ohana, David. 2012. *Origins of Israeli Mythology: Neither Canaanites nor Crusaders*, translated by David Maisel. New York: Cambridge University Press.

Parvikko, Tuija. 2008. *Arendt, Eichmann, and the Politics of the Past*. Helsinki: Finnish Political Science Association.

Pippen, Robert B. 1993. "Modern Mythic Meaning: Blumenberg contra Nietzsche." *History of the Human Sciences* 6, no. 4: 37–56.

———. 1999. "Eine Moderne ohne radikale Entzauberung: Zwischen Logos und Mythos." In *Die Kunst des Überlebens: Nachdenken über Hans Blumenberg*, edited by Hermann Timm and Franz Josef Wetz, 99–117. Frankfurt am Main: Suhrkamp.

Recki, Birgit. 1999. "Der praktische Sinn der Metapher: Eine systematische Überlegung mit Blick auf Ernst Cassirer." In *Die Kunst des Überlebens: Nachdenken über Hans Blumenberg*, edited by Hermann Timm and Franz Josef Wetz, 142–63. Frankfurt am Main: Suhrkamp.

Reynolds, Anthony. 2000. "Unfamiliar Methods: Blumenberg and Rorty on Metaphor." *Qui Parle* 21, no. 1: 77–103.

Savage, Robert. 2008. "Laughter from the Lifeworld: Hans Blumenberg's Theory of Conceptuality." *Thesis Eleven*, no. 94: 119–31.

Segal, Robert Alan. 1999. *Theorizing about Myth*. Amherst: University of Massachusetts Press.

Timm, Hermann, and Franz Josef Wetz, eds. 1999. *Die Kunst des Überlebens: Nachdenken über Hans Blumenberg*. Frankfurt am Main: Suhrkamp.

Weber, Samuel. 1987. "The Blindness of the Seeing Eye: Psychoanalysis, Hermeneutics, Entstellung." In *Institution and Interpretation*, 73–84. Minneapolis: University of Minnesota Press.

Whitebook, Joel. 2004. "Omnipotence and Radical Evil: On a Possible Rapprochement between Hannah Arendt and Psychoanalysis." In *Pragmatism, Critique, Judgment: Essays for Richard J. Bernstein*, edited by Seyla Benhabib and Nancy Fraser, 243–60. Cambridge, MA: MIT Press.

Wurgaft, Benjamin Aldes. 2016. *Thinking in Public: Strauss, Levinas, Arendt*. Philadelphia: University of Pennsylvania Press.

Young-Brühl, Elizabeth. 1982. *Hannah Arendt: For Love of the World*. New Haven, CT: Yale University Press.

Zaretsky, Eli. 2015. *Political Freud: A History*. New York: Columbia University Press.

Zill, Rüdiger. 1999. "Wie die Vernunft es macht . . . Die Arbeit der Metapher im Prozeß der Zivilisation." In *Die Kunst des Überlebens: Nachdenken über Hans Blumenberg*, edited by Hermann Timm and Franz Josef Wetz, 164–83. Frankfurt am Main: Suhrkamp.

———. 2002. "'Substrukturen des Denkens': Grenzen und Perspektiven einer Metapherngeschichte nach Hans Blumenberg." In *Begriffsgeschichte, Diskursgeschichte, Metapherngeschichte*, edited by Hans Erich Bödeker, 209–58. Göttingen: Wallstein.

"All Our Theories Are Going to Be Carried Away by History": Alexander Mitscherlich and American Psychoanalysis

Dagmar Herzog

In 1971, at the International Psychoanalytical Association (IPA) congress in Vienna, the eminent West German psychoanalyst Alexander Mitscherlich stood before his peers and demanded that they take sociological and political matters seriously and stop focusing so narrowly and solely on intrapsychic dynamics. "All our theories are going to be carried away by history," Mitscherlich told his colleagues, "unless"—as newspapers from the *Kansas City Times* to the *International Herald Tribune* summarized his argument—"psychoanalysis is applied to social problems."[1] One evident context for Mitscherlich's remark was the war ongoing at that very moment in Vietnam. Indeed, Mitscherlich went on to provoke his fellow analysts with warnings of how irrelevant their models and concepts of human nature would soon be: "I fear that nobody is going to take us very seriously if we continue to suggest that war comes about because fathers hate their sons and want to kill them, that war is filicide. We must, instead, aim at finding a theory that explains group behavior, a theory that traces this behavior to the conflicts in society that actuate the individual drives."[2] Moreover, and pointing to such texts as *Group Psychology and the*

---

1. *New York Times*, "Social Orientation"; *Kansas City Times*, "Analyst Favors"; Whitman, "Revision in Father's Theory"; Mitscherlich, "Psychoanalysis and the Aggression." The published text of the presentation does not include the "all our theories" remark that was carried in the press.

2. *Kansas City Times*, "Analyst Favors."

New German Critique 132, Vol. 44, No. 3, November 2017
DOI 10.1215/0094033X-4162286 © 2017 by New German Critique, Inc.

Analysis of the Ego (1921) and *Civilization and Its Discontents* (1930), Mitscherlich reminded the audience that Sigmund Freud himself had been highly interested in political and cultural phenomena—and thus that concern with extrapsychic conditions and forces would in no way imply a departure from the master's path. Nonetheless, and as the newspapers also reported, "Mitscherlich's suggestion that destructive aggressive behavior is provoked by social factors runs counter to current Freudian orthodoxy—that aggression derives from internal psychic sources that are instinctual."[3] While Mitscherlich's politically engaged comments "evoked a burst of applause from younger participants . . . some of their elders sat in stony silence."[4]

Going into the 1970s, the IPA was dominated by a handful of its British but above all by its American members, many of whom Mitscherlich knew well from numerous travels and research stays in both countries. Why was Mitscherlich's message not welcomed by his senior confreres? Were they not concerned with the war raging at that moment and in their name? What explains the lack of interest not just in political moralizing but also in a way of thinking about psychological dynamics as involving something, anything at all, outside the individual self? The generally chilly or uninterested response at the Vienna meeting is indicative of the fate of Mitscherlich's most famous works, too, in the United States. *Auf dem Weg zur vaterlosen Gesellschaft* (1963) had appeared in English translation already in 1969 as *Society without the Father: A Contribution to Social Psychology*, and *Die Unfähigkeit zu trauern* (1967), partly coauthored with his wife, Margarete Mitscherlich, was translated into English in 1975 as *The Inability to Mourn: Principles of Collective Behavior.*[5] Both took quite some time to find an American audience.

The delayed-reaction reception of Mitscherlich started in the 1980s and gathered force in the 1990s and into the 2000s, including in what would seem the unlikely realms of the turn-of-the-millennium men's movement—in its complex relation to second-wave feminism—and in post–Cold War international diplomacy, especially in sites of interethnic conflict. Those delayed receptions are discussed below, but it is necessary to explicate the delay. That takes us first to postwar West Germany and then to the postwar United States.

---

3. Ibid.

4. *New York Times*, "Social Orientation."

5. On the Mitscherlichs' marriage as a *Denkgemeinschaft* (thinking partnership) involving constant intellectual collaboration, see Freimüller, *Alexander Mitscherlich*, 252; on the process of deciding that *The Inability to Mourn* would be published under both of their names, although six of the eight essays included in the volume (all but chapters 1 and 4) had been singly authored by Alexander—though surely also produced in shared brainstorming and with Margarete's editing—see Hoyer, *Im Getümmel der Welt*, 501–2.

Working both in public and behind the scenes, the re-émigré Frankfurt School philosopher-sociologists Theodor W. Adorno and Max Horkheimer had been striving since at least the early 1950s to get psychoanalysis as a thought system taken seriously in West Germany. Even as they were not consistently impressed with Mitscherlich and privately at times deemed his work merely derivative of their own ideas, they were instrumental in promoting and encouraging Mitscherlich, and Horkheimer had cooperated closely with him to bring prominent émigré analysts back to West Germany to speak in 1956, in a lecture series at the universities of Heidelberg and Frankfurt am Main on the occasion of the hundredth anniversary of Freud's birth.[6] Yet as late as 1965— as Horkheimer lamented in an interview—the West German public remained unenthusiastic about psychoanalysis per se (even though *Auf dem Weg zur vaterlosen Gesellschaft* was selling very well).[7] The reasons were not hard to understand. Contempt for psychoanalysis in the wider public and among medical professionals had, after all, been sown by the Nazis. In the Third Reich, Freud was said to have a "dirty fantasy" and an "Asiatic worldview," and psychoanalysis was deemed both to contain "nothing original"—for to claim otherwise would be "to give too much honor to the unproductivity of the Jewish race"—*and* to be "nothing other than the Jewish nation's rape of Western culture."[8] These attitudes hardly disappeared overnight in the war's aftermath. Yet despite this background, Mitscherlich prevailed spectacularly in convincing West Germans to think about psychoanalysis differently.[9]

Mitscherlich succeeded in his life project of returning psychoanalysis to post-Nazi central Europe—and securing for it far greater cultural prestige than

---

6. See Alexander et al., *Freud in der Gegenwart*; Berger, "'Das Tragen eines Smokings'"; and the glowing reminiscence of Habermas, "Jüdische Philosophen und Soziologen." (In addition to Alexander, other notable visitors were René Spitz, Erik Erikson, Michael Balint, and Herbert Marcuse.) See also the discussion of both sides of Adorno's and Horkheimer's attitudes toward Mitscherlich in Freimüller, *Alexander Mitscherlich*, 210–13. And on Adorno's passionate but ambivalent relationship with psychoanalysis more generally, see Schneider, "Die Wunde Freud."

7. See Shabecoff, "Germans Shunt Psychoanalysis." On the timing, see also Mitscherlich, "Psychoanalyse heute"; and Kauders, *Der Freud-Komplex*, 194–95, 207, 211.

8. Anonymous, "Die Rolle des Juden in der Medizin," 15; Hunger, "Jüdische Psychoanalyse," 314, 317.

9. Paradoxically, an important factor in rising West German public interest in psychoanalysis was the unexpected blockbuster popularity of animal behavior expert Konrad Lorenz's, *Das sogenannte Böse*. On the first page Lorenz had invoked Freud in partial support of his own ideas. Lorenz's success in celebrating aggression as not only a universal and natural but also a positive, life-enhancing force triggered enormous animus from the soon-to-be-ascendant New Left, but additionally caused a wider public to want to know more about what exactly Freud had argued—as it simultaneously motivated Mitscherlich to make theorizing aggression one of the main themes of his life's work. The wide attention received by Lorenz also in the English-speaking world ended up being a major factor in prompting the IPA to make aggression its core theme at the 1971 Vienna meeting. For the details, see Herzog, *Cold War Freud*; cf. Freud, "Comments on Aggression."

it ever had in Freud's own day—by advancing a highly idiosyncratic version of psychoanalysis as a secular moral-political language. (This was to be a major source of the disconnect between Mitscherlich and his American listeners; precisely what worked so well in the West German context was, for overdetermined reasons, anathema in America.) The West German public may not have followed his theoretical work in psychosomatics, his editorship of the flagship journal *Psyche*, or the clinical discussions under his directorship of the Sigmund Freud Institute in Frankfurt am Main, but he was a remarkably effective public intellectual. *Die Unfähigkeit zu trauern* also became a major best seller. His reputation was only amplified by his winning of the Peace Prize of the German Book Trade in 1969. By 1971, when he addressed the Vienna audience, he had without question become *the* public face of psychoanalysis in West Germany. At the same time, Mitscherlich served as "the conscience of the nation," a "gentle repentance-preacher."[10]

Mitscherlich finessed this double role not least by amalgamating creatively elements he had borrowed directly from the dominant American paradigm of ego psychology with frankly left-liberal political commentary on evolving current events with (what in hindsight may seem quite *un*analytic and conceptually clunky) persistent enjoinders to West Germans to develop what he variously referred to as "ego-strength" (*Ichstärke*), "self-control," "capacity for critical thinking," or "the critical thinking-capacity of the ego."[11] The contrast with someone like his French counterpart Jacques Lacan, whose baseline assumption was that there could be no such thing as a stable ego—and who thought the leading American analysts' penchant for ego psychology was ludicrous—could not have been starker. But for West German conditions, Mitscherlich's approach proved ideal. Far from taking offense at his injunctions, many West Germans appreciated Mitscherlich's sensitive mix of empathy and cajoling. Whether out of genuine fellow feeling or shrewd innate instinct in reaction to the hostility he had to endure from medical colleagues in the later 1940s after he had published the exposé of Nazi doctors' crimes—in German *Das Diktat der Menschenverachtung* (1947), in English *Doctors of Infamy* (1949)—Mitscherlich repeatedly communicated that he identified *with* his readers rather than attacking them.[12] Already *Auf dem Weg zur vaterlosen Gesellschaft* had both spoken to cultural conservatives in their preoccupations

---

10. Freimüller, *Alexander Mitscherlich*, 8; Rutschky, "Von Prof. Freud zu Dr. Caligari," 132.

11. Mitscherlich, "Toleranz"; cf. Mitscherlich and Mitscherlich, *Die Unfähigkeit zu trauern*, 171, 318.

12. On the early hostility, see Brandel, "Das Diktat der Menschenverachtung," 19.

with the dangers of "mass society" and the difficulty of developing an independent personality within it *and* attracted young progressives for many of the same reasons. The media received the book as exploring possibilities for "personal freedom." A young reader wrote in to say that the book had given her "courage" in daily life.[13] And *Die Unfähigkeit zu trauern*, too, despite the bombshell argument that it was not the multiple millions of murdered Jews of Europe that Germans had failed to mourn but their own erstwhile passionate love for Adolf Hitler, was compassionate in tone—and continually held out the optimism that both individual healing and a more tolerant world were possible.

Unlike the West German public, however, the postwar US public did not need to be persuaded that psychoanalysis offered useful ways to look at the world or at oneself. The years 1949–69 were the "golden age" of psychoanalysis in the United States. This first half of the Cold War is when psychoanalysis gained the greatest traction in American medicine and mass culture alike. The diffusion was pervasive. Even as, internally, psychoanalysis remained ever defensive about its own institutional legitimacy and was rent by controversies between different theoretical-methodological schools, versions of psychoanalytic thinking came to inflect virtually all other thought systems—a dynamic especially notable across popular advice literature, but also social work and all the social sciences.

The multiform psychoanalysis that evolved in postwar America was the cumulative creation of, on the one hand, (not entirely but predominantly Jewish) émigrés from Germany, Austria, Poland, and Hungary, themselves divided between the neo-Freudians around Franz Alexander, Karen Horney, Erich Fromm, and Erik Erikson and the ego psychologists around Heinz Hartmann, Ernst Kris, and Rudolf Loewenstein in New York and Grete and Edward Bibring and Helene Deutsch in Boston—and about two hundred more fanned out across the nation from Baltimore and Philadelphia to Detroit to Chicago to Los Angeles—with, on the other, native-born gentiles like Karl Menninger, who with his brother William ran a prestigious psychiatric clinic in Topeka, Kansas (though there were also prominent gentile analysts like Clara Thompson and Harry Stack Sullivan more aligned with the neo-Freudians). Additionally, in each cluster—especially in overcrowded New York, though elsewhere as well—there were constant splits, as theoretical and personality differences spawned new analytic associations and coteries.

The spread of popular familiarity with psychoanalysis in America was even more of a collective production. It could be said, from among the émigré

---

13. Freimüller, *Alexander Mitscherlich*, 265–66.

analysts, that it involved the "neos" (especially Horney, Fromm, and Erikson) more than the "egos." Yet within the professional circuits of the American Psychoanalytic Association and among the Americans routinely involved in the IPA, it was clear that the ego psychologists had the higher status (indeed, within US analytic circles, the 1950s and 1960s are often referred to as "the Hartmann era").[14] The circulation greatly depended as well not just on the mass media, from *Ladies Home Journal* to *Newsweek*—which kept the public updated on psychoanalytic ideas through tongue-in-cheek spoofing and sim-plified authoritative explication—but also on the emphatic engagement with psychoanalysis from two unforeseen quarters. One important group promot-ing Freud to its readership included the incipiently neoconservative but in the early postwar decades still self-defined as liberal high-culture New York intel-lectuals Lionel Trilling, Norman Podhoretz, and Irving Kristol.[15] The other—as yet understudied but crucial for the forms taken by postwar American psy-choanalysis—involved the rapprochement between psychoanalysis and the traditional religious communities, especially the mainstream Christian churches (a phenomenon about which Kristol, as it happens, was complaining already as early as 1949).[16]

Certainly this process of rapprochement was evident in Protestantism, encouraged avidly by none other than the "dean of American psychiatry" Karl Menninger. "Busy Dr. Menninger practices Presbyterianism as well as Freud," *Time* had announced to its readers in 1951 under the heading "Psychiatry and Religion"—an essay in which Menninger also talked about his own prayer habits.[17] But it became no less evident in Roman Catholicism. A rabbi named Joshua Liebman had written a book in 1946, *Peace of Mind*, that argued for the benefits of being analyzed to all and sundry. It was a smash hit (on the *New York Times* best-seller list for three years) and a huge impetus for popular American reception of psychoanalysis across the Jewish-gentile divide; Lieb-man arguably became the first postwar American Jewish "celebrity."[18] The Catholic bishop Fulton Sheen, long an enemy of psychoanalysis, published a rival text in 1949, *Peace of Soul*, which angrily insisted on the superiority of the confessional to the couch. Nonetheless, *Peace of Soul*—despite its snarky, verging-on-anti-Semitic hostility to Liebman's proposals that it might be good

14. Bergmann, *Hartmann Era*.
15. ffytche, "Freud and the Neocons."
16. Kristol, "God and the Psychoanalysts."
17. *Time*, "Psychiatry and Religion."
18. Heinze, *Jews and the American Soul*, 213–14.

to unload unnecessary guilt feelings and encourage more general niceness among human beings—unquestionably contributed to the "psychologization" also of Catholicism.[19] For Roman Catholics, and to Sheen's chagrin, this trend would be fostered further by Pope Pius's time-lagging and ambivalent, but eventually granted, partial blessing to psychoanalysis in 1953.[20] And no less significant in helping believing Christians take an interest in psychoanalysis rather than just reflexively warding it off were the books produced by neo-Freudian analysts Fromm (*Psychoanalysis and Religion*, 1950) and Erikson (*Young Man Luther*, 1958). In due time pastoral counseling and religious studies programs as well as theological seminaries regularly incorporated engagement with psychoanalysis into their curricular offerings.

Add to these various currents the positive repute that psychoanalysis had accrued by helping World War II veterans manage reentry into civilian life—as well as the large subsequent influx of government funding into mental health projects from the 1940s on, in a context in which at least half of the leading psychiatry departments in medical schools nationwide were directed by doctors with analytic training—and the overall success in the postwar United States of Freudianism (however profoundly reinvented its content) is perfectly understandable. What also becomes more understandable is the much-speculated-about turn away from culturally critical politics.

Most scholars who have considered the depoliticization of American psychoanalysis—from Russell Jacoby in 1983 to Eli Zaretsky in 2004—have referenced the active silencing and expulsion of more radically inclined analysts from the official fold as well as the blunting impact of medicalization on psychoanalysis' critical political potential (in the United States only MDs were allowed to practice as analysts).[21] Louis Menand in 2011 invoked the Cold War climate of generalized anxiety as both a psychoanalysis-amenable and a conformity-encouraging force, while Elizabeth Ann Danto in 2012 documented the very tangible and extensive redbaiting and intimidating surveillance of analysts—with the foreign-accented émigrés perceived as "queer birds" and especially suspect.[22] Emily Kuriloff in 2009 and Lewis Aron and Karen Starr in 2013 emphasized that postwar psychoanalysis itself needs to be understood as a "Holocaust survivor"—traumatized and manically intent on fitting in to the host society that had, after all, given safe haven to hundreds of analysts and

19. See Herzog, *Cold War Freud*.
20. Pius XII, "On Psychotherapy and Religion."
21. Jacoby, *Repression of Psychoanalysis*; Zaretsky, *Secrets of the Soul*.
22. Menand, "Freud, Anxiety, and the Cold War"; Danto, "'Have You No Shame?'"

their family members.[23] The enticements to offer either pablum or didactic counsel were multiple and evidently intense.

What is indisputable is that—despite some significant countervailing efforts to use psychoanalytic ideas for culturally subversive and emancipatory purposes (Herbert Marcuse's *Eros and Civilization* of 1955 and Norman O. Brown's *Life against Death* of 1959 come to mind), the overwhelming trend in the first two postwar decades was to affirm normative-conservative values (including especially sexual conservatism). For the ego psychologists, the external world mattered in the sense that the emphasis was placed on an individual's ability to adapt to reality. But the main task of psychoanalysis was to help a patient manage intrapsychic conflict. This meant working on modulating and neutralizing libidinal and aggressive drives, and above all developing and expanding autonomous ego functions (such as distinguishing between reality and fantasy, controlling impulses and affects rather than acting out, and integrating synthetically contradictory feelings). Meanwhile, although widely read and influential neo-Freudians like Horney and Fromm differed from the ego psychologists in their express interest in extrapsychic, social pressures (both, in fact, downplayed the idea of instinctual drives, dismissed the Oedipus complex as a figment of Freud's imagination, and pushed the idea that social anxiety and the search for safety in an overwhelming and disempowering world were stronger motivational forces than sexual desire could ever be), they too—as an apoplectic Adorno, who found both of them offensively platitudinous, was the first to point out—encouraged individual accommodation *to* social conditions more than they called for social change. For Adorno, any "desexualization of psychoanalysis" by definition removed its critical political edge as well.[24] (In general, Adorno viewed with scathing disgust how American psychoanalysis "adjusted" people to an unjust society. As he put it already in 1944 in *Minima Moralia*, written in his California exile, "Contemporary sickness exists precisely in what is normal.")[25] Arguably, however, the ego psychologists around the far more respected Hartmann, in their own lack of interest in the themes of sexual repression or expression and in their emphasis on the autonomous strength and positive adaptation-oriented resources of the individual ego—and despite their later rebuttals of claims that they meant

23. Kuriloff, "Revelations in Psychoanalytic History," 580; Aron and Starr, *Psychotherapy for the People*, 111.

24. Adorno first presented his critique of Horney at the San Francisco Psychoanalytic Society on April 27, 1946; the paper was translated by Rainer Koehne and published in 1952 as Adorno, "Zum Verhältnis von Psychoanalyse und Gesellschaftstheorie."

25. Adorno, *Minima Moralia*.

"adaptation" in a conformist way—were no less contributory to the perception that postwar American psychoanalysis was a normative and normalizing enterprise.

Mitscherlich, meanwhile, although initially eager to learn from American analysts, ended up being uninspired by most of them. A keen and frequent traveler, with—as his letters and his recently published diary excerpts from his first trip to the United States in 1951 make clear—a tone of (what can only be called typically European) disdain for what he found to be the general American populace's provinciality and stupefied mindlessness (with the United States, nota bene, not his own country, giving him lots of thoughts about mass pressures to conformity and the difficulty of developing strong individuality), Mitscherlich certainly acquired self-confidence (both in the sense of a firmer grasp of the range of conceptual and clinical possibilities and in the feeling of intellectual superiority) from his contacts with American analysts in New York, Boston, Cincinnati, Chicago, Topeka, Denver, San Francisco, Washington, and elsewhere. He was unabashedly eclectic in his theoretical interests. In Boston he admired the competence of the ego psychologist (and director of the psychiatry division at Beth Israel) Grete Bibring; in Chicago he became good friends with the neo-Freudian (and to Mitscherlich impressively entrepreneurial) Franz Alexander, with whom he shared a strong interest in psychosomatics, even though their approaches differed. His one encounter with Hartmann in New York was mutually courteous but not particularly warm.

Mitscherlich's private observations about American culture could be nasty (though not necessarily unperceptive) or poignant. In his diary he noted: "Consider the slogan I saw on one of the 15 churches I counted on my way home [he was in Cincinnati]: *Wy* [!] *wait to go to church til you are dead*. The despairing emptiness of this country is unsettlingly palpable for me." To his friend Hanni Bally (the Swiss psychoanalyst Gustav Bally's wife) he wrote: "Please, imagine a simultaneous bigamist here. Unthinkable. Here one goes into bed with 4 or 40 women, one after another—out of frantic desperation, you understand, not out of joy." But he could also be funny. Of the sultry strip-teases he (repeatedly) saw in Chicago, he told his diary: "Such an artless, crude power of the obscene such as I have never before encountered. . . . So completely beyond morality and so vital that qualms are misplaced. . . . Too bad that one cannot send German professors of philosophy, also those who teach in Basel, here on a school field trip. Maybe then they would make a better existentialism."[26]

26. Hoyer, *Im Getümmel der Welt*, 291–92, 294.

Mitscherlich was to learn far more about psychoanalysis, and far more happily so, from a year of immersion in the British scenes in 1957–58, when his wife, Margarete, pursued her training analysis with Michael Balint and he undertook one with Paula Heimann, whom he revered. Mitscherlich did, however, repeatedly return to the United States, and in the later 1960s developed close and productive friendships with the highly influential defector from ego psychology and developer of self psychology Heinz Kohut in Chicago and with the nonanalyst but analytically interested Robert Jay Lifton, a psychiatrist and antiwar and anti–atomic weapons activist. One can only speculate that it was the emotional distance each of these men himself felt from the run-of-the-mill US psychoanalytic landscape that contributed to the good rapport. Kohut graciously delivered the laudation for Mitscherlich when he won the Peace Prize in 1969 and in 1976 saw to it that Mitscherlich was granted honorary membership in the American Psychoanalytic Association. Lifton provided the preface to the American edition of *The Inability to Mourn* in 1975. There is no doubt that shared antiwar attitudes made for a strong bond as well. Mitscherlich was a periodic visitor in Lifton's house in Wellfleet, Massachusetts, where left- and left-liberal-leaning psychiatrists and social scientists gathered regularly to discuss psychology, history, and politics.

The whole situation was ripe with ironies. Mitscherlich was, in his first travels in the United States, inevitably more of a supplicant, an apprentice, in relation to his American peers. Germany had, in any case, just been defeated militarily and ideologically, and the horrors of the Third Reich had been exposed to the world's moral outrage. And although Mitscherlich as the documentarian of Nazi medical crimes had been a key player in that exposure, and in general had anti-Nazi bona fides (his somewhat more complicated relationship to rightwing nationalist trends in the Weimar era came out only after his death in 1982, but he definitively never had Nazi sympathies), there was no reason to assume that Americans, whether recent émigrés with fresh memories of Third Reich ordeals or proud native-born winners of World War II, would think they had anything to learn from a gentile German.[27] At the same time, to compound the reception problems, Mitscherlich's tendency to understand psychoanalysis as a valuable toolbox for left-liberal political moralizing did not sit well with émigrés who had preemptively fled into "science" and avoidance of political involvement (whether born of fearful experiences under Nazism, the unmistakable evidence of harsh suppression of psychoanalysis in the Eastern bloc countries, or the McCarthyist climate in the United States). Nor was it compatible with the attitude of analysts whose self-banalization was

27. Dehli, *Leben als Konflikt.*

long since under way even before the Cold War began. Yet a further set of paradoxes concerned theoretical approaches. It was incumbent on Mitscherlich, as a gentile German, to take his cues from the forms of psychoanalysis endorsed by Freud's daughter Anna and her closest associates in the United States, which were Hartmann and Co. (and hence, for example, also to keep his distance from Anna's main British rival, Melanie Klein).[28] This was one main reason for Mitscherlich's otherwise potentially peculiar uncritical adoption of ego psychological tenets. But at the same time, as noted, Mitscherlich persistently conjoined those ego psychological concepts with a culturally critical stance and with attention to social and political dynamics. That made excellent sense in a post-Nazi context. But it gave him little logical audience in the United States.

What West Germans appreciated in Mitscherlich, in sum, did not seem to have immediate use in the United States. It would be some time before English-language reception started in earnest. In the case of both of Mitscherlich's major books, the reception would not be quite what anyone might have expected.

In part, this had to do with the core takeaway ideas, the title concepts, as it were—in the one case too vague and in the other too specific—put forward by Mitscherlich (not to be separated from the problem that, while Mitscherlich was a master of the short essay form, his books tended to be convoluted and associative more than argumentative). *Society without the Father* was concerned less with the absence of literal fathers (though two of the thirteen chapters did touch on the point that while in centuries past children could see their father working and learn directly from him, industrialization had forced him out of sight and intimate relationship) than with the loss of the "father image," that is, an orienting connection to traditional authorities.[29] As anyone raised in the postwar United States with constant injunctions to avoid being "other-directed" and instead become properly "inner-directed" can attest, Mitscherlich was echoing

28. It would take another fifteen years for an energetic Klein reception to emerge in Germany. See Herzog, *Cold War Freud*.

29. Harry Slochower, the editor of *American Imago*, reviewing the German original in 1966, articulately summarized Mitscherlich's views under the headline "Replacing Oedipus by Cain": "Man today attempts to gain individual autonomy while he must subordinate himself to the superorganization of a choking bureaucracy. This situation produces tensions in the relation between the individual and society providing the basis for neurotic modes, manifested in apathy and/or anxiety, aggression and destructiveness. . . . The oedipal father is replaced by competition with siblings—the Joneses. The single father is split into a vast army of neighbors who are envied. . . . An endless chain of Cain-Abel has replaced Oedipus-Laius." And further: "The parentless child grows up into a leaderless adult, directed by anonymous functionaries and engaging in anonymous functions. Here are the phylogenetic roots of narcissism and aggression."

points made by the sociologist David Riesman in *The Lonely Crowd* (1950).[30] In fact, Riesman was one of many US scholars on whom Mitscherlich had explicitly drawn. There was, we can surmise, no need to reimport Riesman home.

No one did more to promote both the notion of a "fatherless society" and the name of Alexander Mitscherlich among Americans than the poet, antiwar activist, and mythology, fairy tale, and Jungian archetype scholar Robert Bly. Already in the opening pages of his blockbuster best seller *Iron John* (1990), Bly referred to Mitscherlich as an important influence on his thinking.[31] Bly was even more free-associative and freewheeling in his writing than Mitscherlich. But he indisputably inspired tens of thousands of men, in the United States and around the world, to seek stronger intergenerational familial relationships and to reclaim emotion in general, in reaction against but also in imitation of many aspects of second-wave feminism. Bly's book was on the *New York Times* best-seller list for sixty-two weeks. And Mitscherlich's name came with him. When Harper Perennial published the first American paperback edition of *Society without the Father* in 1993 (more than two decades after Tavistock in England and Harcourt Brace Jovanovich had published the English translation in hardcover in 1969), Bly wrote the foreword. In it, Bly supplemented his lucid summary of Mitscherlich's key historical-cum-philosophical arguments with remarks that slammed George H. W. Bush for the First Gulf War and lambasted the US press for its self-inflicted ineptitude and cowardice vis-à-vis the powerful.[32] This was heady, militant material.

What was transmitted to a popular readership since then, however, turned out to be quite different. A first wave of renewed (albeit truncated) interest followed quickly in the mid-1990s, as several authors either joined in sounding the alarms about the purported disaster zone that was the American family or the pitiful wreck that was the American man, or sought to cash in on helping men get in healthier touch with their feelings.[33] In the most recent develop-

---

30. Riesman, *Lonely Crowd.*
31. Bly, *Iron John*, xi.
32. Bly, foreword.
33. Kimbrell, *Masculine Mystique*; Blankenhorn, *Fatherless America*. Kimbrell's book was marketed as offering insight into "the alarming increase in male unemployment and homelessness, punitive custody laws that deprive men of their children, and high-pressure competitive jobs that leave men vulnerable to stress-related diseases and substance abuse" (books.google.com/books/about/The_Masculine_Mystique.html?id=fUzaAAAAMAAJ). Blankenhorn was the founder of the Institute for American Values, which helped shape the family policy agenda of President Bill Clinton's administration and was also an inspiration for the founding of the National Fatherhood Initiative (an organization promoting "responsible fatherhood"), and served as its board chairman. As the *Los Angeles Times* reported, Blankenhorn ascribed "Crime. Juvenile delinquency. Teen pregnancy. Welfare. The economy. Homelessness. Substance abuse. Divorce. Moral degeneracy. Domestic violence"

ment—2013 to the present—Mitscherlich serves as a named authority in the context of the "fathers' rights movement," which both in the United States and in the United Kingdom is mobilizing against what it perceives as a problematic cultural tendency, in cases of divorce, to prefer to give custody of children to the mother and, more generally, is offering workshops for thousands of men to strengthen involved parenting.[34] The British branch of the organization runs under the slogan "The Campaign against a Fatherless Society."[35]

Meanwhile, *The Inability to Mourn* had been above all addressed to post-Nazi German conditions. Lifton in his 1975 preface ambitiously tried to elaborate a comparison with "post-Vietnam and post-Nixon America" and to explain the intensity of discovering evil in what one had once loved—in the US case, "faith in American national virtue" turned into brutal killing and meaningless death. He invoked the Mitscherlichs' insights into "the defense against collective responsibility and guilt—guilt whether of action or of toleration."[36] But here, arguably, the same dynamics of denial Lifton was naming also blocked any immediate uptake or sense that the lessons could be applied domestically.

Given the specificity of the Mitscherlichs' diagnosis, it is logical that it was within US-based German literary, film, and historical studies that their thesis was most visibly taken up and its applicability explored. The list of important authors is long and includes, among others (from 1980 on), Andreas Huyssen, Anton Kaes, Eric Santner, Thomas Elsaesser, Dan Bar-On, Susan Linville, Martin Jay, Jeffrey Olick, Samuel Moyn, Dirk Moses, and John Borneman. In time, the concept was applied to other national contexts, from South Africa to Australia to Israel/Palestine.[37] The most prominent book-length

to "the single cause of fatherlessness." See Mehren, "Father Crusader." See also Diamond, *Irritable Male Syndrome. Psychology Today*, too, in 2011, cited the triumvirate of Mitscherlich, Bly, and Blankenhorn, in an article opening with the assertion that "America is rapidly becoming a fatherless society." See Williams, "Decline of Fatherhood." In 2013, in the wake of Democrats' contentions that the Republican Party was engaging in a "war on women" (especially by attacking women's access to contraception), an evangelical Lutheran college professor and editor of a journal called *The Family in America*, working with the conservative organization Concerned Women for America, both cited Kimbrell and offered an extensive exposition of Mitscherlich's views in his rebuttal to the Democrats, as he called as well for "a revival of domesticity" in America. See MacPherson, "'War on Women.'"

34. In 2013 an author writing for the website of the organization Fathers4Justice ("a publication for parents on the wrong side of the standard possession order"), took the occasion of the mass shooting of children by Adam Lanza at Sandy Hook Elementary School in Sandy Hook, Connecticut, to argue that the source of the rising "mindless violence afflicting our world today" was "Fatherlessness." See Marsh, "Remember the Fatherless and Absent."

35. Fathers4Justice, www.fathers-4-justice.org (accessed February 18, 2016).

36. Lifton, preface, vii–viii.

37. E.g., see Falk, *Fratricide in the Holy Land.*

experiment in adapting the concept to another context was without a doubt Paul Gilroy's *Postcolonial Melancholia* (2006). Gilroy found the concept useful for exploring Britain's incapacity to mourn its lost empire.

Before the Mitscherlichs' book had appeared, psychoanalytic writers had recurrently used the phrase "the inability to mourn" in a general sense, whether referring, as Grete Bibring did in 1952 while summarizing a paper by Anna Freud, to the "well-known symptom," in some neurotic patients, of an inability to mourn "the loss of formerly loved persons" or, as John Bowlby did in 1961, to Sigmund Freud's case of the Wolfman (whose inability to mourn the death of his sister Bowlby thought to be associated with an inability to be in a position of "weakness and supplication"), or, as Elizabeth Kleinberger did in a 1965 essay on depression in childhood, especially in cases of adoption and foster care, to toddlers whose incapacity directly to express sadness over the loss of a loved caregiver was often a sign of delayed development or "retardation."[38] After the book was published in English, the term continued to be used in ways unconnected to the Mitscherlichs—simply in relation to an individual patient.

Among US-based psychoanalysts, the most creative and extensive use of the Mitscherlichs' idea that an inability to mourn can be applied to large groups has been made by the Cyprus-born Turkish Muslim and now University of Virginia–based (emeritus) psychoanalyst Vamık Volkan—and he has been responsible for diffusing their idea more broadly among his colleagues and back to historians. In numerous books and countless articles and talks, he has blended ideas from the object relations work on borderline and narcissistically disturbed patients of Melanie Klein, Donald Winnicott, and Otto Kernberg with ideas about group identity drawn from Erikson—and with the Mitscherlichs' central concept. Starting already in 1978 with an examination of the seemingly irresolvable conflicts between Turks and Greeks in his native Cyprus, Volkan adapted the Mitscherlichs' notion to the Cypriot case, referencing the "elation and hyperactivity" that prevented "a more appropriate process of mourning" in the wake of numerous war losses."[39] Volkan soon became a pioneering organizer of Track II diplomacy, serving Presidents Jimmy Carter and Ronald Reagan, heading both postconflict and violence-prevention negotiation teams, and continuing that work into the post–Cold War era. He has functioned as a neutral facilitator with Soviets and US Americans; Egyp-

---

38. Bibring, "Report on the Seventeenth International Psycho-analytical Congress"; Bowlby, "Pathological Mourning and Childhood Mourning"; Kleinberger, "Depression in Infancy and Childhood."

39. Volkan, "Symptom Formation and Character Changes."

tians, Israelis, and Palestinians; Serbs and Croats; Russians and Estonians; Iraqis and Kuwaitis. Throughout, in addition to providing inside tips for negotiators dealing with panicky and bellicose opponents, Volkan has found fresh things to say about such matters as "injured narcissism" and the transgenerational transmission of trauma, about "chosen glories" and "chosen traumas," "societal regression" and "unconscious fantasies." And over and over he has invoked *The Inability to Mourn*.[40]

Strikingly, Volkan has also expressly promoted Alexander Mitscherlich's 1971 call to his fellow analysts in Vienna to consider international politics and interdisciplinary collaboration.[41] Moreover, Volkan was alert to which factors may have come together to cause the impasse of mutual incomprehension that day in 1971 when Mitscherlich had addressed his fellow analysts, so many of them Jewish émigrés who had fled the Third Reich. In a 2011 essay, when Volkan once again invoked the Mitscherlichs as important advocates for the idea that analysts should concern themselves with extrapsychic reality, Volkan surmised that the insistence among so many postwar US analysts that only "classical analyses"—that is, those that avoided any attention to extrapsychic matters—were legitimate might be connected to their inability, at the time, to acknowledge the impact of Holocaust trauma.[42] This is a compassionate interpretation. Other analysts mulling the postwar obsession with excluding extrapsychic factors have in recent years come up with related conjectures; not all of them are equally forgiving. Several focus on the cost of this obsession—to the profession, and to its patients above all.[43]

---

40. In 1983, for example, chairing the first Egyptian-Israeli conversation at which also Palestinians would be present (in Caux, Switzerland), Volkan noted how, at a prior meeting in the wake of the assassination of Egyptian president Anwar Sadat in 1981, while Israelis had expressed "open sorrow," it was the Egyptians who had evinced "an inability to begin mourning." In 1995, in a coauthored essay on "the psychodynamics of ethnic terrorism"—an essay that ranged from the conflicts in Northern Ireland to Basques and Kurds—the Mitscherlichs were cited on the point that "a defeated or victimized group may be too humiliated or too angry to mourn." And in 2006, at the ten-year anniversary of South Africa's Truth and Reconciliation Commission, Volkan was invited to give the keynote celebrating the work of Archbishop Desmond Tutu. This was another occasion at which he cited the Mitscherlichs, noting post-Nazi Germans' tendency to express only "isolated regret, and then only for their own losses," for to mourn "would mean their taking responsibility for war crimes"—even as the talk also went on to discuss the suffering of such groups as African Americans and Armenians. See Volkan, "Arab-Israeli Dialogue"; Volkan and Harris, "Psychodynamics of Ethnic Terrorism"; Volkan, "Memory, Narrative, and Forgiveness."

41. Volkan, "Psychological Concepts."

42. Volkan, foreword.

43. See, e.g., the remarks of Otto Kernberg in Bergmann, *Hartmann Era*, 145–46; cf. Lewes, "Homosexuality, Homophobia, and Gay-Friendly Psychoanalysis."

There was one final irony at play in 1971 as Mitscherlich addressed his colleagues in Vienna and many of the senior Americans sat in stony silence. For the strong fabric of postwar American psychoanalysis was beginning to unravel. The adamant apoliticism that had been so crucial to the success of psychoanalysis in the first two postwar decades in the United States was about to be a major contributing factor to its decline there. Mitscherlich's barb—"all our theories are going to be carried away by history"—could sting his American colleagues, and garner notice in the press, because US American psychoanalysis was in fact, at the turn from the 1960s to the 1970s, in a serious predicament, even though many US analysts had not realized it. The "golden age" of American psychoanalysis that had run from roughly 1949 to 1969 was about to be brought to an end by the combined impact of the feminist and gay rights movements, with their numerous, highly valid complaints about the misogyny and homophobia endemic in postwar analysis; the rise of shorter-term and more behaviorally oriented therapies, not to mention New Age and "human potential" therapies as well as psychopharmacology, but above all the explosion of pop self-help, much of which—as in Wayne Dyer's best-selling *Your Erroneous Zones* (1976)—would expressly style itself in opposition to the expense and purported futility of years on the couch; and the antiauthoritarian climate in general. Psychoanalysis in the United States, specifically its dominant postwar form of ego psychology, would from then on find itself permanently on the defensive. Notably, only one year before Mitscherlich addressed his colleagues about the Vietnam War, gay rights activists were storming the American Psychiatric Association meeting and challenging one of the most overtly homophobic analysts with taunts that he was a "motherfucker."[44] And only six months before the Vienna meeting, the *New York Times Magazine* had run an essay titled "The FemLib Case against Sigmund Freud." As one caption announced: "According to women's liberation leaders (and some male critics today), many of the fundamental ideas of psychoanalysis constitute an ingenious doctrine of male supremacy, traceable to its founder's own underlying misogyny."[45] US analysts had done well in making their "science" acceptable to mainstream, Main Street America. Now America was changing.

But psychoanalysis globally was not in decline. On the contrary, the geographic and generational loci of creativity and influence were shifting. Psychoanalysis was about to enjoy a second "golden age," this time in Western and Central Europe, and (although complicated both by brutal repressions and by self-interested complicities under several dictatorial regimes) also in Latin

44. Bayer, *Homosexuality and American Psychiatry*, 103–5.
45. Gilman, "FemLib Case against Sigmund Freud."

America. This second golden age was nurtured and sustained not least by the New Left generation of 1968 and by those of their elders, Mitscherlich among them, who were in sync with New Left concerns. One could argue that left politics and psychoanalysis engaged in something of a mutual rescue operation. Not only did psychoanalytic insights enrich radical social critiques. A strong case can, in fact needs to, be made that the infusion of moral-political earnestness saved psychoanalysis as an enterprise as well and gave it a longer and richer life in Western and Central Europe as well as in Latin America than it would have had if it had stayed solely within a medical-therapeutic remit.

Why do some theories travel well while others do not? I have argued here, for psychoanalysis, that it is not publishing houses that are determinative (though journals somewhat more so); it is the specificities of cultural climates—and timing. Yet even within a culture it can often be mysterious why some books or theories grab the public while others miss their aim. For it is always also a question of which idea in a book is considered helpful or provocative, and then what valence or spin that idea is given, and which subgroup finds it useful for which objective. Without question, there was not one Freud circulating in the Cold War, and not even only a dozen, but hundreds.

The history of psychoanalysis in general has been one of delayed-reaction receptions, unexpected repurposings, and the ever-evolving coproduction of the meanings of texts and concepts. By the last of those, I mean that often a chronologically later use to which an idea is put shapes what we think the original author's point was in the first place. Ideas accrue significance in the weirdest of sequences. What a particular reading facilitates—emotionally, politically, intellectually—is sometimes as important as what was said in the initial statement. The jury is still out on what we might yet learn from Alexander Mitscherlich.

References

Adorno, Theodor W. 1952. "Zum Verhältnis von Psychoanalyse und Gesellschaftstheorie." *Psyche* 6, no. 1: 1–18.

———. 2005 (1951). *Minima Moralia: Reflections from Damaged Life*, translated by Dennis Redmond. members.efn.org/~dredmond/MM1.html (accessed February 18, 2016).

Alexander, Franz, et al. 1957. *Freud in der Gegenwart: Ein Vortragszyklus der Universitäten Frankfurt und Heidelberg zum hundertsten Geburtstag.* Frankfurt am Main: Europäische Verlagsanstalt.

Anonymous. 1933. "Die Rolle des Juden in der Medizin." *Deutsche Volksgesundheit aus Blut und Boden*, August–September.

Aron, Lewis, and Karen Starr. 2013. *A Psychotherapy for the People: Toward a Progressive Psychoanalysis.* London: Routledge.

Bayer, Ronald. 1987. *Homosexuality and American Psychiatry: The Politics of Diagnosis.* Princeton, NJ: Princeton University Press.

Berger, Falk. 1996. "'Das Tragen eines Smokings wäre ein *Fauxpas*': Die Veranstaltung zum 100. Geburtstag Sigmund Freuds im Jahre 1956." In *Psychoanalyse in Frankfurt am Main: Zerstörte Anfänge, Wiederannäherung, Entwicklungen*, edited by Tomas Plänkers, Michael Laier, Hans-Heinrich Otto, Hans-Joachim Rothe, and Helmut Siefert, 335–48. Tübingen: Diskord.

Bergmann, Martin S., ed. 2000. *The Hartmann Era*. New York: Other Press.

Bibring, Grete L. 1952. "Report on the Seventeenth International Psycho-analytical Congress." *Bulletin of the International Psycho-analytical Association* 33: 249–72.

Blankenhorn, David. 1995. *Fatherless America: Confronting Our Most Urgent Social Problem*. New York: Basic.

Bly, Robert. 1990. *Iron John: A Book about Men*. Reading, MA: Addison-Wesley.

———. 1993. Foreword to Alexander Mitscherlich, *Society without the Father: A Contribution to Social Psychology*, xiii–xxi. New York: HarperPerennial.

Bowlby, John. 1963. "Pathological Mourning and Childhood Mourning." *Journal of the American Psychoanalytic Association* 11: 500–541.

Brandel, Julius. 1949. "Das Diktat der Menschenverachtung." *Aufbau* 15, no. 7: 19.

Brown, Norman O. 1959. *Life against Death: The Psychoanalytical Meaning of History*. Middletown, CT: Wesleyan University Press.

Danto, Elizabeth Ann. 2012. "'Have You No Shame?'—American Redbaiting of Europe's Psychoanalysts." In *Psychoanalysis and Politics: Histories of Psychoanalysis under Conditions of Restricted Political Freedom*, edited by Joy Damousi and Mariano Ben Plotkin, 213–31. New York: Oxford University Press.

Dehli, Martin. 2007. *Leben als Konflikt: Zur Biographie Alexander Mitscherlichs*. Göttingen: Wallstein.

Diamond, Jed. 2004. *The Irritable Male Syndrome: Managing the Four Key Causes of Depression and Aggression*. Emmaus, PA: Rodale.

Dyer, Wayne. 1976. *Your Erroneous Zones*. New York: Funk and Wagnalls.

Erikson, Erik. 1958. *Young Man Luther: A Study in Psychoanalysis and History*. New York: Norton.

Falk, Avner. 2004. *Fratricide in the Holy Land: A Psychoanalytic View of the Arab-Israeli Conflict*. Madison: University of Wisconsin Press.

fffytche, Matt. 2013. "Freud and the Neocons: The Narrative of a Political Encounter from 1949–2000." *Psychoanalysis and History* 15, no. 1: 5–44.

Freimüller, Tobias. 2007. *Alexander Mitscherlich: Gesellschaftsdiagnosen und Psychoanalyse nach Hitler*. Göttingen: Wallstein.

Freud, Anna. 1972. "Comments on Aggression." *International Journal of Psycho-analysis* 53: 163–71.

Fromm, Erich. 1950. *Psychoanalysis and Religion*. New Haven, CT: Yale University Press.

Gilman, Richard. 1971. "The FemLib Case against Sigmund Freud." *New York Times Magazine*, January 31.

Gilroy, Paul. 2006. *Postcolonial Melancholia*. New York: Columbia University Press.

Habermas, Jürgen. 2013. "Jüdische Philosophen und Soziologen als Rückkehrer in der frühen Bundesrepublik." In *Im Sog der Technokratie: Kleine politische Schriften XII*, 13–26. Frankfurt am Main: Suhrkamp.

Heinze, Andrew. 2004. *Jews and the American Soul: Human Nature in the Twentieth Century*. Princeton, NJ: Princeton University Press.

Herzog, Dagmar. 2017. *Cold War Freud: Psychoanalysis in an Age of Catastrophes*. Cambridge: Cambridge University Press.

Hoyer, Timo. 2008. *Im Getümmel der Welt: Alexander Mitscherlich*. Göttingen: Vandenhoeck und Ruprecht.

Hunger, Heinz. 1943. "Jüdische Psychoanalyse und deutsche Seelsorge." In vol. 2 of *Germanentum, Judentum und Christentum*, edited by Walter Grundmann, 307–53. Leipzig: Wigand.

Jacoby, Russell. 1983. *The Repression of Psychoanalysis: Otto Fenichel and the Political Freudians*. New York: Basic.

Kansas City Times. 1971. "Analyst Favors Expanding Base of Freud's Theories." July 28.

Kauders, Anthony D. 2014. *Der Freud-Komplex: Eine Geschichte der Psychoanalyse in Deutschland*. Berlin: Berlin Verlag.

Kimbrell, Andrew. 1995. *The Masculine Mystique: The Politics of Masculinity*. New York: Ballantine.

Kleinberger, Elizabeth. 1965. "Depression in Infancy and Childhood." *Contemporary Psychoanalysis* 2, no. 1: 36–40.

Kristol, Irving. 1949. "God and the Psychoanalysts: Can Freud and Religion Be Reconciled?" *Commentary*, November 1.

Kuriloff, Emily. 2009. "Revelations in Psychoanalytic History." Review of George Makari, *Revolution in Mind: The Creation of Psychoanalysis*. *Contemporary Psychoanalysis* 45, no. 4: 577–80.

Lewes, Kenneth. 2005. "Homosexuality, Homophobia, and Gay-Friendly Psychoanalysis." *Fort Da* 11, no. 1: 13–34.

Lifton, Robert Jay. 1975. Preface to Alexander Mitscherlich and Margarete Mitscherlich, *The Inability to Mourn: Principles of Collective Behavior*, vii–xiii. New York: Grove/Random House.

Lorenz, Konrad. 1963. *Das sogenannte Böse: Zur Naturgeschichte der Aggression*. Vienna: Borotha-Schoeler.

MacPherson, Ryan C. "The 'War on Women'—Myth or Reality?" www.ryancmacpherson.com/presentations/13-invited-speaking/132-the-war-on-women-myth-or-reality.html (accessed February 18, 2016).

Marcuse, Herbert. 1955. *Eros and Civilization*. Boston: Beacon.

Marsh, Warwick. 2013. "Remember the Fatherless and Absent." Fathers4Justice website, July 1. www.f4joz.com/news/newspage.php?yr=13&id=6 (accessed January 25, 2016).

Mehren, Elizabeth. 1995. "Father Crusader: Who Is David Blankenhorn? And Why Is He So Insistent That Missing Fathers Are Responsible for Most of Society's Ills—and That Only a Return to the Traditional Dad Will Do?" *Los Angeles Times*, March 8.

Menand, Louis. 2012. "Freud, Anxiety, and the Cold War." In *After Freud Left: A Century of Psychoanalysis in America*, edited by John Burnham, 189–208. Chicago: University of Chicago Press.

Mitscherlich, Alexander. 1963. *Auf dem Weg zur vaterlosen Gesellschaft: Ideen zur Sozialpsychologie*. Munich: Piper.

———. 1964. "Psychoanalyse heute." In vol. 8 of *Gesammelte Schriften*, 171–93. Frankfurt am Main: Suhrkamp.

———. 1969. *Society without the Father: A Contribution to Social Psychology*. New York: Harcourt Brace and World.

———. 1971. "Psychoanalysis and the Aggression of Large Groups." *International Journal of Psycho-analysis* 52: 161–67.

———. 1974. "Toleranz—Überprüfung eines Begriffs." In *Toleranz—Überprüfung eines Begriffs*, 10–17. Frankfurt am Main: Suhrkamp.

Mitscherlich, Alexander, and Margarete Mitscherlich. 1967. *Die Unfähigkeit zu trauern*. Munich: Piper.

———. 1975. *The Inability to Mourn: Principles of Collective Behavior*. New York: Grove.

New York Times. 1971. "Social Orientation Urged on Freudians." July 28.

Pius XII. 1953. "On Psychotherapy and Religion: An Address of His Holiness Pope Pius XII to the Fifth International Congress on Psychotherapy and Clinical Psychology Given on April 13, 1953." www.papalencyclicals.net/Pius12/P12PSYRE.HTM (accessed February 18, 2016).

Riesman, David. 1950. *The Lonely Crowd: A Study of the Changing American Character*. New Haven, CT: Yale University Press.

Rutschky, Michael. 2006. "Von Prof. Freud zu Dr. Caligari." *Cicero*, January, 132.

Schneider, Christian. 2011. "Die Wunde Freud." In *Adorno-Handbuch*, edited by Richard Klein, Johann Kreuzer, and Stefan Müller-Doohm, 283–94. Stuttgart: Metzler.

Shabecoff, Philip. 1965. "Germans Shunt Psychoanalysis to a Minor Role, Scholar Says: Professor Deplores Neglect of Practice in Region Where It Took Root." *New York Times*, February 22.

Slochower, Harry. 1966. "Replacing Oedipus by Cain." *American Imago* 23, no. 1: 84–86.

Time. 1951. "Psychiatry and Religion." April 16, 65–66.

Volkan, Vamık D. 1987. "Psychological Concepts Useful in the Building of Political Foundations between Nations: Track II Diplomacy." *Journal of the American Psychoanalytic Association* 35: 903–35.

———. 2011. Foreword to Tomas Böhm and Suzanne Kaplan, *Revenge: On the Dynamics of a Frightening Urge and Its Taming*, xi–xvi. London: Karnac.

———. n.d. "Arab-Israeli Dialogue: The Mountain House Meeting." www.vamikvolkan.com/Arab-Israel-Dialogue%3A-The-Mountain-House-Meeting,-Caux,-Switzerland-%281983%29.php (accessed February 18, 2016).

———. n.d. "Memory, Narrative, and Forgiveness: Reflecting on Ten Years of South Africa's Truth and Reconciliation Commission." www.vamikvolkan.com/The-University-of-Cape-Town,-Keynote-Address-Celebrating-Archbishop-Desmond-Tutu%27s-Life-of-Peaceful-Justice-And-The-10th-Anniversary-of-The-Truth-And-Reconciliation-Commission%27s-Activities-%28Cape-Town%29.php (accessed February 18, 2016).

———. n.d. "Symptom Formation and Character Changes Due to Upheavals of War: Examples from Cyprus." www.vamikvolkan.com/Symptom-Formation-and-Character-Changes-Due-to-Upheavals-of-War%3A-Examples-from-Cyprus.php (accessed February 18, 2016).

Volkan, Vamik D., and Max Harris. 1995. "The Psychodynamics of Ethnic Terrorism." *International Journal on Group Rights* 3, no. 2: 149.

Whitman, Alden. 1971. "Revision in Father's Theory Is Proposed by Anna Freud." *International Herald Tribune*, July 31–August 1.

Williams, Ray B. 2011. "The Decline of Fatherhood and the Male Identity Crisis." *Psychology Today*, June 19.

Zaretsky, Eli. 2004. *Secrets of the Soul: A Social and Cultural History of Psychoanalysis*. New York: Knopf.

Koselleck in America

Stefan-Ludwig Hoffmann

In the fall of 1988 Reinhart Koselleck was invited by Michael Geyer and John Boyer to be Lurcy Visiting Professor in the History Department at the University of Chicago. Earlier that year, Koselleck had retired from his position at the University of Bielefeld (what he used to call his "Zwangsvergreisung" [forced senilism] at age sixty-five), and his appointment at Chicago was to be renewable. François Furet, with whom Koselleck had coauthored a book in the late sixties and remained friends with, had already been at Chicago on and off since 1980, more permanently since 1985 when he accepted a five-year one-quarter appointment (with History, Social Thought and the College), which began in 1986. After 1990 Furet shifted completely to the Committee on Social Thought, an arrangement that, according to Geyer, Koselleck would probably have also wanted for himself.[1]

The late 1980s and early 1990s seemed like the perfect moment for a more sustained reception of Koselleck's work in the Anglophone world. In 1986 Koselleck had been already a visiting professor at the New School for Social Research in New York. After a delay of thirty years, his first book, *Critique and Crisis*, was finally published in English translation (1988), as was his important collection of essays *Futures Past* (1985), both with MIT Press. *Futures Past* received prominent reviews by Hayden White and David Carr and established Koselleck's American reputation as "one of Germany's most distinguished philosophers of history."[2] The Columbia political scientist

1. Michael Geyer, pers. comm., February 28, 2014.
2. White, review, 1175; Carr, review.

New German Critique 132, Vol. 44, No. 3, November 2017
DOI 10.1215/0094033X-4162298   © 2017 by New German Critique, Inc.

Melvin Richter tirelessly promoted Koselleck's *Begriffsgeschichte* on this side of the Atlantic since the mid-1980s and organized a symposium on the *Geschichtliche Grundbegriffe* (*Basic Concepts in History*) at the German Historical Institute in Washington, DC, in December 1992, which brought Koselleck into conversation with John Pocock. Moreover, it appeared as if many of Koselleck's theoretical concerns—language, time, secrecy, civil society, public and private, dreams, death, monuments and memory—became mainstream in the 1980s, especially with the linguistic and subsequently the cultural turn in the humanities.

At Chicago Koselleck taught six courses in three fall quarters between 1988 and 1990: on war and its representations, eighteenth- and nineteenth-century German intellectual history, historiography, Nietzsche and Dilthey, the 1848 Revolution in France and Germany (with Furet), and, interestingly, one seminar titled "Carl Schmitt and the Breakdown of the Weimar Republic" with the political scientist Stephen Holmes in the fall of 1990. This last one was apparently one of the few seminars of Koselleck's at Chicago out of which a dissertation emerged (subsequently John McCormick's first book, a critical account of Schmitt's critique of liberalism).[3] Overall, Koselleck's impact at Chicago was much more limited than Furet's. In contrast, Alf Lüdtke (who also taught for two years at Chicago) and other German historians of everyday life, especially Detlev Peukert, inspired a whole cohort of a younger generation of US social and cultural historians in the late twentieth century, not just at Chicago. After three fall quarters Koselleck's appointment was not renewed. He did accept invitations to teach again at the New School for the fall of 1991 and to be Max Kade Visiting Professor at Columbia for the fall of 1992, but this was the last time that Koselleck taught on this side of the Atlantic.[4]

3. Deutsches Literaturarchiv (DLA) Marbach, A, Koselleck, Konvolut: "Unterlagen zum Seminar 'Carl Schmitt and the Breakdown of the Weimar Republic.'" Required readings were Schmitt's "Concept of the Political," "Political Theology," "Crisis of Parliamentary Democracy," "Political Romanticism," "The Necessity of Politics," and "Leviathan." John McCormick, pers. comm., February 15, 2015; Michael Geyer, pers. comm., February 28, 2014. Two other University of Chicago dissertations and subsequent books influenced by Koselleck are Levinger, *Enlightened Nationalism*; and Crane, *Collecting and Historical Consciousness*.

4. DLA Marbach, A: Koselleck, Konvolut: Dokumente und Korrespondenzen zu Aufenthalten in New York: Andreas Huyssen to Reinhart Koselleck, July 4, 1992. At Columbia, Koselleck taught two courses: "Theory of History" (through the History Department) and "Utopia in Literature and Social Thought" as a comparative literature–German course. Koselleck's first visiting professorship abroad, however, was already in September to October 1978 at Tokyo University. He was also twice invited by Furet to be a *directeur associé* at the EHESS Paris (in March 1979 and March 1982) and later received honorary awards from the EHESS and the Collège de France. DLA Marbach, A: Koselleck, Konvolut Lebensläufe und Schriftenverzeichnisse 1993–2002.

Whatever the particular circumstances of the decision not to renew Koselleck's appointment at Chicago were, what I argue here about German theory transfer is the following: although there were repeated transatlantic encounters with Koselleck's work and even with him as a teacher, particularly in the late 1980s and early 1990s, the story of Koselleck's reception in the Anglophone world is one of *misconceptions*: about the politics of *Critique and Crisis*, about the efficacies of *Begriffsgeschichte*, and, finally, about some of its theoretical implications for Koselleck's epistemology of history, his *Historik*.

Koselleck, Habermas, and Schmitt

One of the most important engines for transatlantic theory transfer since the 1980s was MIT Press's series Studies in Contemporary German Social Thought, edited by Thomas McCarthy. *Critique and Crisis* appeared in the series in 1988, almost thirty years after the first German edition; a similarly belated English translation of Jürgen Habermas's *Strukturwandel der Öffentlichkeit* followed in 1989.[5] For comparison, *Strukturwandel* did appear in France in 1978, and *Kritik und Krise* was available in French a year later. Only after the publication of Furet's 1978 reinterpretation of the French Revolution in the shadow of the Gulag and the translation did French scholars discover *Critique and Crisis*.

By locating the origins of twentieth-century totalitarianism in the French Revolution and of revolutionary ideology in enlightened sociability, Furet in a radical departure from his earlier work revived the (Catholic) conservative critique of 1789–94 at a time when the currents of French intellectual life shifted (belatedly) from Marx and Mao to antitotalitarianism. It is fair to assume that it was Koselleck who had pointed Furet to this conservative tradition, particularly to the obscure writings of Augustin Cochin, which had been important for *Critique and Crisis* and became one of the main inspirations for *Interpreting the French Revolution*.[6]

Of course, *Critique and Crisis* was also an important reference point for Habermas's take on some of the same questions. As Anthony La Vopa

5. Koselleck, *Critique and Crisis*. The original dissertation of 1954 had the more precise subtitle "Eine Untersuchung der politischen Funktion des dualistischen Weltbildes im 18. Jahrhundert" ("An Investigation into the Political Function of the Dualistic World View in the Eighteenth Century"). Habermas, *Structural Transformation of the Public Sphere*.

6. Prochasson, *François Furet*, 230; Moyn, "On the Intellectual Origins of François Furet's Masterpiece," esp. n29; Christofferson, "Anti-totalitarian History of the French Revolution." It is unlikely that Furet had read *Kritik und Krise* before its translation into French (apparently, he did not read German), but Koselleck had been a guest of Furet's at EHESS in Paris, and Furet visited Koselleck in Bielefeld while he was writing *Penser la Révolution française*. DLA Marbach, A. Koselleck: François Furet to Reinhart Koselleck, February 3, 1978. See also Koselleck, "Laudatio auf François Furet."

asserted in a 1992 review essay, *Critique and Crisis* and *Transformation of the Public Sphere* both "reflect the political preoccupations of the 1950s, though from opposite ends of the ideological spectrum."[7] Both books are taking Kantian philosophy as their starting points—and both are influenced by Schmitt. While Koselleck aimed for a conceptual genealogy of the political function of Immanuel Kant's critiques (the original working title of his 1954 Heidelberg dissertation had been *Dialektik der Aufklärung*), Habermas wrote an affirmative account of Kant's idea of publicity, which, he argued, had only been corrupted in the nineteenth century by the rise of capitalism and mass culture.[8] However, it was *Transformation of the Public Sphere* that became one of the most influential books by any German theorist in Anglophone academe in the 1990s (only a small part of the reception is documented in a volume edited by Craig Calhoun in the same MIT series in 1992).[9] In contrast, *Critique and Crisis* hardly attracted much scholarly debate, not even in eighteenth-century studies. The question, of course, is why?

Part of why *Kritik und Krise* had become an instant classic in 1960s West Germany was Koselleck's suggestive writing style, which used the different semantic layers of German concepts for making historical arguments. *Kritik und Krise* was itself an early exercise in *Begriffsgeschichte*, something that got lost in the literal translation in the MIT edition (for which, quite unusually, no translator claimed responsibility).[10] The Cambridge historian T. C. W. Blanning articulated what was probably a common reservation for Anglophone historians when he complained in his 1989 review about "the gargan-

7. La Vopa, "Conceiving a Public," 81. See also the chapters on Koselleck and Habermas in Norberg, *Sociability and Its Enemies*.

8. Koselleck, "Dankesrede," 34. Apparently, Koselleck was also not aware of Walter Benjamin and Bertolt Brecht's plan for a journal with the title *Krise und Kritik* in 1930–31. See Wizisla, *Benjamin und Brecht*.

9. Calhoun, *Habermas and the Public Sphere*.

10. One reason for the delay in publishing an English translation of *Critique and Crisis* had been the bankruptcy of Urizen Books in New York, which originally had acquired the English rights in 1976 from Karl Alber Verlag in Freiburg, where the first edition of *Kritik und Krise* had appeared in 1959 (Alber had sold only the German rights to Suhrkamp in 1973). Urizen commissioned a translation (funded by Inter Nationes) and a preface by Victor Gourevitch, but first the translator David Swann died and later the publishing house went bankrupt. Hence the rights were transferred to Crossroad Publ. In 1983 Marion Berghahn expressed an interest to publish *Kritik und Krise* in English with Berg Publishers, as did Cambridge University Press and Columbia University Press. Eventually, Berg acquired the rights from Crossroad to use the translation. The book appeared in 1987 in the United Kingdom with Berg and in the United States with MIT Press in Thomas McCarthy's series. DLA Marbach, A: Koselleck, Konvolut: Unterlagen und Korrespondenz zum Buch "Kritik und Krise" im Alber-Verlag 1958–1995; Briefwechsel Reinhart Koselleck—Urizen Books 1976–1982.

tuan German footnotes" in *Critique and Crisis*, although precisely these footnotes contained many succinct conceptual histories. Moreover, according to Blanning, Koselleck's prose was hard to understand, as it "soars into a metaphysical stratosphere and has no discernible relation to what was happening on the ground."[11] The Cambridge historian compared *Critique and Crisis* unfavorably to Hans-Ulrich Wehler's *German Empire*, which was surely no less Germanic in prose, excessive footnotes, and polemical style. Wehler, of course, was also Koselleck's colleague and intimate enemy at Bielefeld, with close ties to Anglophone academe. Never shy to pick a "lively situation of contestation," Wehler had claimed ten years earlier in Habermas's *Stichworte zur "Geistigen Situation der Zeit"* that Koselleck's conceptual history was a "historicist dead end" at best.[12]

The distance between Koselleck and Wehler (or Habermas) has also to do with different wartime experiences. Koselleck served as a Wehrmacht soldier during World War II (beginning in 1941, when he turned eighteen, on both the eastern and western fronts) and was deported as a prisoner of war first in May 1945 to dismantle the factories at Auschwitz and later to a Soviet Gulag camp in Central Asia (until the fall of 1946).[13] Both of his brothers died during the war, and his mother's schizophrenic sister was gassed by the Nazi euthanasia program in 1940. More than anything else, the wartime experiences shaped his sense of the contingency and absurdity of history. In contrast, Wehler and Habermas were too young to be drafted into the Wehrmacht. Instead, they experienced the end of the war at home in Gummersbach as former members of the Jungvolk, liberated by the US Army.

As a son of a Weimar republican German professor who was initially dismissed from office by the Nazi regime, Koselleck regarded himself intellectually neither as a former Nazi nor as a product of American reeducation (so important for Wehler and Habermas and the "45ers" generation of postwar West German intellectuals) and hence had no difficulties to converse with whomever he found inspiring in postwar Heidelberg.[14] In his 1989 acceptance speech for the Prize of the Historisches Kolleg, for example, Koselleck explicitly stated that his education at Heidelberg would have been unthinkable without the questions raised by Martin Heidegger and Schmitt even though he did

11. Blanning, review.

12. Wehler, "Geschichtswissenschaft heute," 725n23. See also Wehler, *Eine lebhafte Kampfsituation*; and Nolte, *Hans-Ulrich Wehler*, esp. 63–65, 69–72.

13. On the importance of these biographical experiences for Koselleck's work, see Dunkhase, *Kosellecks Gespenst*.

14. Moses, *German Intellectuals and the Nazi Past*.

not necessarily agree with their answers.[15] However, *Critique and Crisis*'s indebtedness to Schmitt, especially to his 1938 *Leviathan in the State Theory of Thomas Hobbes*, proved decisive for its reception, not only in West Germany. Habermas himself had insinuated in his 1960 review that whoever wants to know today what Schmitt is thinking should read *Kritik und Krise*.[16] In the same year, the Harvard émigré political scientist Carl J. Friedrich reviewed *Kritik und Krise* for the *American Political Science Review*. Friedrich was professor of government at Harvard and had advised the US Office of Military Government in Germany on denazification and the drafting of the West German Basic Law. Before coming to Harvard in 1926, Friedrich was a student of Alfred Weber at Heidelberg. As Udi Greenberg shows in *The Weimar Century*, Friedrich essentially transferred his ideas about the origins of democracy from the Weimar context to the early Cold War.[17] As a Calvinist, he argued that democracy was invented in Protestant German-speaking Central Europe in the sixteenth and seventeenth centuries, especially in the Calvinist covenants. The French Revolution with its secularism and incitement of the "masses" was for Friedrich the very opposite of the providential Anglo-Saxon and Germanic democratic traditions, an argument that had a clear-cut political aim (to make democracy and the transatlantic alliance with the United States seem more natural to German traditions and elites) in Weimar and, similarly, in the early Cold War.[18] In 1956 Friedrich had accepted an addi-

---

15. Koselleck, "Wie neu ist die Neuzeit?," 38.

16. Habermas, "Verrufener Fortschritt—verkanntes Jahrhundert." Of course, Habermas's incriminating review also served as a smokescreen for his own indebtedness to Koselleck's analysis of the emergence of a counterpublic within the Old Regime. In a review of Dirk van Laak's important study *Gespräche in der Sicherheit des Schweigens: Carl Schmitt in der politischen Geistesgeschichte der frühen Bundesrepublik* (1993), Habermas conceded thirty years later that "some of the most productive and smartest scholars of the postwar years converted to 'Schmittianism' without buying into his political prejudices." Habermas, "Das Bedürfnis nach deutschen Kontinuitäten." For most present-day critiques of *Kritik und Krise*, however, the influence of Schmitt is sufficient proof for dismissing Koselleck's arguments as conspiratorial and hyperbolic. See, e.g., Fillafer, "Enlightenment on Trial"; similarly, on a methodological level, Pankakoski, "Conflict, Context, Concreteness." While Schmitt's intellectual influence on Koselleck has never been in question, the issue is whether this taints the latter's theoretical writings as well, as Pankakoski argues. If Koselleck claims with Schmitt that all basic concepts emerge historically out of social and political contestations, he articulates the only shared methodological premise of *Begriffsgeschichte*, Pocock and Skinner's contextual approach or Foucault's genealogy (or, in fact, of most historians of political languages). More balanced are Mehring, "Begriffssoziologie, Begriffsgeschichte, Begriffspolitik"; and Mehring, "Begriffsgeschichte mit Carl Schmitt."

17. Greenberg, *Weimar Century*.

18. In 1952 Koselleck had applied to take part in one of Harvard's summer schools in Salzburg, a program organized by Friedrich. One of Friedrich's graduate students at Harvard, the young German-Jewish émigré Henry Kissinger (born like Koselleck in 1923), signed the letter of rejection. DLA Marbach, A. Koselleck: Henry Kissinger to Reinhart Koselleck, May 14, 1952.

tional appointment at Heidelberg, where he taught political education every second semester for ten years until his retirement. That same year Koselleck came back from Bristol where he had been a Deutscher Akademischer Austauschdienst lecturer to accept a position at Heidelberg's Historische Seminar. In other words, Friedrich not only had intimate knowledge of the postwar Heidelberg microcosm but was essentially Koselleck's senior colleague.

Given Friedrich's staunch anticommunism and critical views of the Enlightenment and French Revolution one might have expected sympathy for *Kritik und Krise*'s antitotalitarian bent. Instead, Friedrich focused entirely on the influence of Schmitt on *Critique and Crisis*. Schmitt, Friedrich wrote,

> is singled out for acknowledgment and [his] works are copiously cited. The "decisionism" of this author leads Dr. Koselleck to think of absolutism primarily in terms of "sovereign decisions"—only one of the aspects of this complex system of government. The discussion abounds in certain words fashionable in these circles, such as "sprengen" [bust], "Raum" [space] and its various derivates, "verorten" [locating] and so on.

Friedrich also stressed that Bernard Faÿ's studies on Freemasonry are mentioned in *Kritik und Krise*, another "suspect authority," as he points out. Faÿ had been a professor at the Collège de France, friend and apparently protector of Gertrude Stein and Alice Toklas in Paris under Nazi occupation. But he was also a Vichy collaborator, anti-Semite, and author of the deeply conspiratorial *La Franc-maçonnerie et la révolution intellectuelle du XVIIIe siècle* (1935). Some other reservations against *Kritik und Krise* might have had something to do with Friedrich's deep familiarity with Heidelberg and especially his close ties to his former mentor Alfred Weber, who was also one of Koselleck's teachers after the war. In any case, Friedrich set the tone for the later reception of *Kritik und Krise* by asserting the following: "Inspired by antiliberal and antibürgerlich [antibourgeois] sentiments, it is a brilliant exposition of a theme that seems rather dubious, where it deviates from familiar paths."[19]

Surprisingly, there seems to be not a single review of *Kritik und Krise* in an Anglophone historical journal before the German paperback edition with Suhrkamp, which was reviewed by the Czech social and cultural historian Bedrich Loewenstein in the *Journal of Modern History* three years after its publication in 1973. "Koselleck formulates questions brilliantly," Loewenstein writes;

> he has command over a very rich array of sources which he employs to the point of pedantry, he has a philosophical mind—and yet his analysis is an

19. Friedrich, review.

example of a highly one-sided interpretation. . . . If critical doubts are appropriate, it is certainly not because Koselleck analyzes the present as reflected in the past rather than the past—in my judgment this is to his credit. But his overemphasis on parallels with the twentieth century (the development of moralizing, pseudological philosophy of history leading to rigid political fronts and ideological terror) is not fair to the Enlightenment.

Loewenstein does not make the incriminating connection to Schmitt. Still, the putative politics of *Kritik und Krise* is addressed quite explicitly: "To equate continuous democratic-critical reflection with permanent revolution is demagogy: a causal relationship between criticism and terror has yet to be proved."[20]

Koselleck himself conceded in 2004 the "slightly mannered severity" of his argumentation in *Critique and Crisis*, and he never made a secret of the influence that Schmitt's conceptual rigor (not his politics) had on his writings. In fact, Koselleck developed his own intellectual program of a new epistemology of history in the early correspondence with Schmitt.[21] Yet just as important for his work was Hannah Arendt's *Origins of Totalitarianism*, which appeared in an extended German version in 1955 and guided Koselleck's argumentation for the published version of the dissertation.[22] However, these and other influences were occluded by Koselleck's affiliation with Schmitt. As Koselleck wrote in 2004, two years before he died, with indirect reference to Habermas's 1960 review:

> Thus whoever expressed thanks to Carl Schmitt was labeled a mouthpiece of Carl Schmitt. Whoever cited conspiracy theories of the eighteenth century became himself a conspiracy theorist. Whoever criticized a politically or morally inspired dualism became himself a dualist. The opposite, however, is the case: the mutual dependency of politics and morality was in fact the normative implication of my argumentation. My critique of utopia was based on the disclosure of the polemical juxtapositions of the two entities lurking behind mauvaise foi [bad faith] or hypocrisy: the utopian designs for the future, the implementation of which would make princes disappear as tyrants. And for this reason there would no longer be any tyranny, wars as

20. Loewenstein, review.
21. See esp. DLA Marbach, A. Koselleck: Reinhart Koselleck to Carl Schmitt, January 21, 1953. This letter is the beginning of an extensive correspondence, which lasted until 1983 (two years before Schmitt's death). Landesarchiv Nordrhein-Westfalen, Abteilung Rheinland. Sammlung/Nachlass Carl Schmitt (Bestand RW 0260, 0265). See also Olsen, *History in the Plural*, 58–63; and Olsen, "Carl Schmitt, Reinhart Koselleck, and the Foundations of History and Politics."
22. Hoffmann, "Koselleck, Arendt, and the Anthropology of Historical Experiences."

well would be permanently ended, and ultimately peace-loving citizens would make the state disappear . . . : All of these—as we now know, dangerous and bloody—illusions arose directly from the inadequacy of thinking or executing morality without politics or politics without morality.[23]

It was Koselleck's intention to unveil the agonistic utopian philosophies of history, which he saw as dominating the Cold War confrontation of the 1950s, communism and liberal democracy. Like Jacob Talmon in *Origins of Totalitarian Democracy*, written at the same time in Jerusalem (published 1952, part 1, and 1960, part 2) and reviewed enthusiastically by Koselleck, Koselleck searched for the genealogies of twentieth-century utopian ideologies in the Enlightenment.[24] It was the ideological potential for global self-annihilation in the nuclear age that concerned Koselleck politically, not some Schmittian justification for Third Reich expansionism or postwar German self-pity. Why didn't Koselleck include National Socialism more explicitly in his genealogy of twentieth-century utopian ideologies? In a letter written to Saul Friedländer in 1989, Koselleck gives an explanation surprisingly close to Friedländer's own reflections on the singularity of the Holocaust and the moral, political, and religious boundaries of historical understanding.[25] In any case, in the 1950s Koselleck was like Talmon or Arendt politically a Cold War liberal, "an enlightener of the Enlightenment," as Ivan Nagel put it in his obituary (2006), borrowing a phrase that Koselleck had used to describe himself.[26]

Kant and Schmitt were the two German theorists most widely invoked in the 1990s to make sense of the post–Cold War world. Yet *Critique and Crisis* was too Schmittian for enthusiasts of civil society like Jean Cohen and Andrew Arato or the historian Margaret Jacob (in her book on eighteenth-century Freemasonry *Living the Enlightenment*), who all distanced themselves

23. Koselleck, "Dankesrede," 55–56.

24. Koselleck, "Ursprung der Moderne."

25. "I consider that the history [of the 'Final Solution'] is confronted by demands that are moral, as well as political and religious, and which altogether do not suffice to convey what happened. The moral judgment is unavoidable, but it does not gain in strength through repetition. The political and social interpretation is also necessary, but it is too limited to explain what happened. The escape into a religious interpretation requires forms of observance which do not belong either to the historical, the moral or the political domain. In my thoughts on this issue up to the present day, I did not manage to get beyond this aporetic situation. In any case, these considerations point to a uniqueness which, in order to be determined, creates both the necessity of making comparisons as well as the need to leave these comparisons behind." Quoted by Olsen, *History in the Plural*, 273, from Friedländer, *Memory, History, and the Extermination of the Jews of Europe*, 57.

26. Nagel, "Der Kritiker der Krise"; DLA Marbach, A: Koselleck, Reinhart Koselleck to Stephen Holmes, May 30, 1989. See also Dunkhase, *Kosellecks Gespenst*.

from Koselleck.[27] Conversely, *Critique and Crisis* was perhaps not Schmittian enough for Chantal Mouffe or Ernesto Laclau and other leftist-Schmittian critics of the post–Cold War revival of the idealized normative liberalism connected to Kantian notions of public opinion, civil society, and cosmopolitan democracy.

Beyond Begriffsgeschichte

It was not only the affiliation with Schmitt or the *völkisch* past of Koselleck's coeditors at the *Geschichtliche Grundbegriffe*, Otto Brunner and Werner Conze, that made the reception of *Begriffsgeschichte* difficult in the Anglophone world. Koselleck's reputation in German intellectual life, but especially among German historians in the 1960s and 1970s, was not only built on *Kritik und Krise*. In many ways he became a historian (and received an appointment in history, a *Lehrstuhl*) as a result of his Heidelberg *Habilitation* "Preußen zwischen Reform und Revolution" ("Prussia between Reform and Revolution," 1967), which has not yet been translated into English, as well as for his ambitious lexicon project *Geschichtliche Grundbegriffe* (1972–92).[28] Some of the essays in *Vergangene Zukunft* (1979) were also part and parcel of Koselleck's studies in the history of particular *Sattelzeit* concepts like crisis, critique, revolution, history, and modern time (*Neuzeit*), which had also informed his empirical work in *Kritik und Krise* and *Preußen zwischen Reform und Revolution*. Becoming the main editor of the *Geschichtliche Grundbegriffe* and participating in the Poetik und Hermeneutik group propelled Koselleck into the center of German intellectual life in the 1960s and 1970s. Hans Ulrich Gumbrecht, who had himself contributed to the lexicon but is now convinced that there is no place for *Begriffsgeschichte* in the "broad present," claimed recently that the lexicon gave Koselleck the unique opportunity to impose his very personal conceptions of what constituted the modern time regime (the *Neuzeit*) on an entire generation of authors for this multivolume lexicon project.[29]

But the lexicon also made Koselleck's theoretical reflections seem like explorations of *Begriffsgeschichte* as a method. *Begriffsgeschichte* became

27. Jacob, *Living the Enlightenment*, esp. 14 on Koselleck and Furet; Cohen and Arato, *Civil Society and Political Theory*, esp. chap. 5: "The Historicist Critique"; Scheuerman, "Unsolved Paradoxes," 221–42, esp. 234–40 on Koselleck and Schmitt, with reference to the "devastating effectiveness" of Habermas's critique of Koselleck's argumentation forty years ago.

28. According to Keith Tribe, Columbia University Press had planned a translation of the *Preußen* book but dropped these plans because of the poor sales of *Futures Past*, for which Columbia had acquired the rights from MIT. Keith Tribe, pers. comm., June 22, 2015.

29. Gumbrecht, *Dimensionen und Grenzen der Begriffsgeschichte*, 22.

almost synonymous with Koselleck's name and the *Geschichtliche Grundbegriffe*, hence a straitjacket not only for his own writings but perhaps also for his reputation abroad.[30] In an interview with the Italian historian Edoardo Tortarolo in 1989, Koselleck himself articulated the intellectual constraints imposed on him by what he called his "Strafarbeit" (penal labor) on the *Geschichtliche Grundbegriffe*. "Because I am really not interested in this method anymore. If you invested a quarter of century into something it's just no fun anymore to work with this method, it has become boring for me."[31]

Preußen zwischen Reform und Revolution remained Koselleck's most heavily archive-based work, a brilliant combination of social, legal and conceptual history, which attracted much critical appraisal on this side of the Atlantic. Mack Walker, who two years later published his deeply influential study *German Home Towns*, which traced some of Koselleck's themes with different conclusions, wrote in his 1969 review: "One may judge it one of the half-dozen most important historical studies to appear in Germany since 1945 while retaining some skepticism of his argument."[32] But Walker and the other reviewers do not mention at all the main theoretical concern underpinning Koselleck's account of the reform efforts of the Prussian bureaucracy after 1789: his attempt to explain the failure of the reforms and the 1848 revolution as a result of the clash of the different velocities of historical time in law, administration, and social movements. In his 1975 preface to the second edition, Koselleck prominently addresses "Mack Walker's exciting question whether my account introduces constellations, which were perhaps more salient before 1789 or after 1948 than in the time period of my study."[33] Yet, even if *Preußen zwischen Reform und Revolution* paved the way for more nuanced histories of eighteenth- and nineteenth-century Prussia, exemplified more recently by Christopher Clark's *Iron Kingdom* (2006), the unique combination of social, legal, and conceptual history did not find much resonance among Anglophone historians.

Koselleck thought of *Begriffsgeschichte* not as a new form of intellectual history or yet another subdiscipline of history but merely as a methodological and empirical starting point (therefore the lexicon format) for historical explorations of any kind. This is precisely how his otherwise quite diverse group of

30. Olsen, *History in the Plural*, 196. Similarly, Jordheim, "Thinking in Convergences."

31. DLA Marbach, A: Koselleck, Edoardo Tortarolo, interview with Reinhart Koselleck, manuscript 17 pp., here p. 12.

32. Walker, review; Walker, *German Home Towns*. See also Sperber's extensive review essay "State and Civil Society in Prussia."

33. Koselleck, preface.

students at Bielefeld (Jörg Fisch, Gerhard Dohrn–van Rossum, Lucian Hölscher, Willibald Steinmetz, Monika Wienfort, and Michael Jeismann, among others) employed *Begriffsgeschichte* for their own research on the histories of international law, timekeeping, religious and socialist utopias, English parliamentary politics, Prussian patrimonial courts as well German and French nationalism. In other words, not only were Anglophone historians skeptical of Koselleck's politics and his theoretical interests (his "soaring into metaphysical stratospheres"), but they also failed to see how conceptual or intellectual history and social and political history belonged together for Koselleck. The reservations against *Begriffsgeschichte* in James J. Sheehan's review of the first volumes of the *Geschichtliche Grundbegriffe*, for example, echo Wehler's skepticism. As a social and cultural historian with similar methodological sensibilities, Sheehan also articulates precisely and unwittingly Koselleck's views:

> Despite its many virtues, the Lexikon does not convince me that Begriffsgeschichte will establish itself as an independent branch of historical inquiry with its own subject matter and methods. It will, I think, usually be drawn into the orbit of other methods. On the one hand, if Begriffsgeschichte is to have the chronological sweep, which Koselleck regards as the method's definitive characteristic, it will be pushed toward selectivity and abstraction and will strongly resemble the history of ideas. On the other hand, if it is to provide a concrete analysis of a concept's usage and historical context, it will also become part of an intensive and wide-ranging analysis, which will be difficult to distinguish from social, political, or economic history.[34]

In retrospect, one can only admire Richter's relentless yet slightly misguided advocacy for *Begriffsgeschichte* as a historical method on this side of the Atlantic since the mid-1980s (without lasting success) by pointing out its similarities, particularly to early modernists John Pocock and Quentin Skinner's analysis of political languages. Richter had met Koselleck in 1978 in Bielefeld and proposed at this very first meeting a conference with Pocock and Skinner, both of whom agreed to participate; Koselleck, however, seemed reluctant and did not pursue the possibility of a conference, despite Richter's yearly reminders.[35]

Of course, there were probably more differences than similarities between the two approaches, and the main differences are less methodological (which

34. Sheehan, "Begriffsgeschichte," 319.
35. DLA Marbach, A. Koselleck: Melvin Richter to Reinhart Koselleck, July 8, 1978, October 9, 1978, December 31, 1980, December 24, 1981.

was at the heart of the debate) than theoretical, something Koselleck might have been aware of. (Conversely, Skinner was also skeptical and had remarked in 1987 famously that it is impossible to write a history of concepts; all that can be done is to write a history of their uses.)[36] In December 1992 Richter finally was able to put together a symposium on the *Geschichtliche Grundbegriffe* at the German Historical Institute in Washington, DC; the event marked the completion of the lexicon that same year. The symposium brought Koselleck and Pocock into direct dialogue for the first time.

Language, ironically enough, turned out to be one of the main barriers for this conversation. Pocock (like Skinner) did not have any firsthand knowledge of Koselleck's writings (he was familiar with them only through Richter's summaries).[37] Still, his comments were more cautiously critical than Skinner's earlier assertion that a diachronic history of individual concepts in toto is flawed. On the other hand, as Koselleck later explained to Richter, he had difficulties answering Pocock on the spot because he had been unable to understand Pocock's English accent with its unique blend of Cambridge with New Zealand. But even years later, when Koselleck did find the time to write a more formal response to Pocock, his tone was uncharacteristically brusque ("As my previous comments indicate, I dealt with the issues he raises already long ago").[38] Thus the Anglophone history of political languages and German *Begriffsgeschichte* existed in parallel after the symposium, Richter's advocacy to combine the two notwithstanding. *Begriffsgeschichte* went global in the last twenty years and is today particularly strong in Scandinavia, eastern Europe, and the Spanish-speaking world, with the curious exception of Anglophone academe.[39] Koselleck's theoretical underpinnings of *Begriffsgeschichte*, including his idea that conceptual history is informed by the contemporary, has more in

36. DLA Marbach, A. Koselleck: Melvin Richter to Reinhart Koselleck, November 19, 1987. See also Richter, *History of Social and Political Concepts*. Similarly, Palonen, *Die Entzauberung der Begriffe*; and Müller, "On Conceptual History."

37. Koselleck's library (now at the DLA Marbach), contains three of Pocock's books: *The Machiavellian Moment*, sent in 1979 by Princeton to Koselleck at Richter's recommendation; *Virtue, Commerce, and History*, given to Koselleck by Pocock; and *Politics, Language, and Time*, given to Koselleck by Richter in 1986 (originally inscribed by Pocock to *Richter*). Koselleck usually annotated books heavily while reading; from the annotations it appears as if he read only the introduction to *Virtue, Commerce, and History*, and the chapter "Languages and Their Implications" in *Politics, Language, and Time*. Apparently, there is no book by Skinner in Koselleck's library.

38. Koselleck, "Response to Comments on the *Geschichtliche Grundbegriffe*," 65.

39. The History of Political and Social Concepts Group was established in 1998 primarily at the initiative of Richter and Kari Palonen. It holds annual conferences and has its own journal. See also the short contributions on Koselleck's reception in France, Spain, Italy, Poland, Turkey, and Russia in Müller, *Forum Interdisziplinäre Begriffsgeschichte*.

common with Michel Foucault's genealogies than with Pocock's and Skinner's much more antiquarian interests.[40] In fact, Foucault used the *Geschichtliche Grundbegriffe* for his lectures on governmentality at the Collège de France in the late 1970s and early 1980s. He first heard about Koselleck in 1977—two years before the publication of the French translation of *Critique and Crisis*— from Walter Seitter at a meeting with Pasquale Pasquino and the Merve Verlag publishers Heidi Paris and Peter Gente in Paris.[41]

This makes the nonreception of *Begriffsgeschichte* in the excruciating debates about the linguistic turn in the late twentieth century even more striking. Martin Jay's programmatic 1982 essay, "Should Intellectual History Take a Linguistic Turn?," which in some ways tried to contain the impact of French poststructuralist imports on the practice of history, does not mention Koselleck or *Begriffsgeschichte* at all.[42] Instead, it introduces Anglophone readers to the Habermas-Gadamer debate. If there was one historian in the 1970s and 1980s who had thought long and hard about language and history and, in response to Hans-Georg Gadamer, about why history is not a subdiscipline of hermeneutics, it was Koselleck. Yet, in the avalanche of manifestos in the 1980s and 1990s debating whether "all the world is a text," Koselleck (unlike Habermas, Clifford Geertz, Jacques Derrida, Gilles Deleuze, Jacques Lacan, and, of course, Foucault) is not mentioned at all by Dominick LaCapra, John Toews, or Joan Scott, to name just a few authors of landmark interventions.[43] This is all the more striking because the debate revolved around questions (the evidence of experience, the extralinguistic preconditions of linguistic change, etc.) that were at the center not only of Koselleck's writings on *Begriffsgeschichte* but, more generally, of his theory of possible histories, his *Historik*, to which I turn now in conclusion.

On Possible Histories
Again, we need to keep in mind that many of Koselleck's theoretical writings were not translated into English, and that *Futures Past* (1985, 2nd ed. 2004)

---

40. Edwards, "Ideological Interpellation of Individuals as Combatants."

41. Tape recordings of the meeting, in possession of the Merve Verlag. I am grateful to Philipp Felsch for making this tape available to me. See Felsch, *Der lange Sommer der Theorie*. See also Foucault, "Birth of Biopolitics," 315n26, on Riedel, "Gesellschaft, bürgerliche."

42. Jay, "Should Intellectual History Take a Linguistic Turn?" Koselleck is mentioned briefly in Jay, *Songs of Experience*, 20.

43. Judith Surkis's splendid article "When Was the Linguistic Turn?" invokes Koselleck's writings on time and acceleration as a way of introduction but does not notice the curious absence of Koselleck from debates on the linguistic turn.

and *The Practice of Conceptual History* (2002) did not contain some of his most important essays on the *Historik* (published mainly in *Zeitschichten*, 2000). Still, this is only part of the answer and does not explain the puzzlement and skepticism that some of his translated works provoked in the Anglophone world—in marked contrast to France, by the way, where Koselleck has been recognized as the most inspiring German theorist of history of the late twentieth century, first by Paul Ricoeur in *Temps et récit* (1983–85), especially volume three, *Le temps raconté*, and more recently by François Hartog in his explorations of contemporary experiences of time, what he calls "presentism."[44]

Instead of borrowing theoretical concepts from other disciplines, Koselleck believed that historians should develop their own epistemology, with being in time (following Heidegger) as its defining episteme.[45] As I have argued elsewhere, Koselleck's studies in conceptual history were for him only a kind of propaedeutic for a fundamental theory of history, the first systematic outline of an epistemology of history since Johann Gustav Droysen's *Historik*.[46] No doubt there is something German about the idea that a discipline needs theoretical *Grundlagen* (principles). While Habermas and Niklas Luhmann, who had similar ambitions for their own disciplines, were able to produce large systematic works, Koselleck preferred for various reasons the pointed essay as the vehicle to develop his theoretical claims.

A good example is his inaugural public lecture as Lurcy Visiting Professor at Chicago, "Language and History," to a somewhat puzzled and unreceptive audience, which the *Journal of Modern History* published in December 1989. Largely ignored, the lecture is probably the most cogent summary of Koselleck's *Historik* in English.

In his lecture Koselleck insisted on the fundamental difference between language and history. At a moment when theoretically infatuated Anglophone historians debated whether "all the world is a text," the *Begriffshistoriker* Koselleck delivered an untimely reminder of the *prelinguistic* conditions of all possible histories. For Koselleck, these conditions included the tensions between "earlier" and "later," "inner" and "outer," "above" and "below"—abstract sets

44. Hartog, *Regimes of Historicity*. The most comprehensive introduction to Koselleck's work in French is Escudier, "Le temps de l'histoire."

45. Like Heidegger, Koselleck believed that understanding historical temporality is the defining theoretical domain of history as a discipline. See esp. Heidegger, "Der Zeitbegriff in der Geschichtswissenschaft," 433.

46. Hoffmann, "Koselleck, Arendt, and the Anthropology of Historical Experiences"; Hoffmann, "Was die Zukunft birgt," as well as the review essays Zammito, "Koselleck's Philosophy of Time(s) and the Practice of History"; and Scuccimarra, "Semantics of Time and Historical Experience."

of universal contraries, which condition all particular histories. His second set of arguments concerned the temporal differences between language and events. History is always more than language can grasp, but concepts contain more or less than what is carried out in the actual course of events. "It is language above all that decides about the potentialities of history in actu," as Koselleck asserts. Language "bundles, as a storehouse of past experiences, conditions of possible events."[47] We cannot know how a particular event—whether a revolution, civil war, defeat, or social and economic crisis—might unfold, but we do know from historical experience, captured by language, some of the possibilities.

For Koselleck, history is above all an *Erfahrungswissenschaft* (experiential science), and experiences also determine the language of the historian. Here Koselleck applies his abstract, systematic categories of the prelinguistic conditions of all possible histories to the historiography itself. The historian's perspective is conditioned by temporality, the question of whether historians are contemporaries of the events they report on or whether they are born later. Next it is important whether they are "higher" or "lower," for example—whether they belong to the winners or the losers. Finally, it is decisive whether they are "inner" or "outer," that is, if they are part of the polity they are describing or are looking on from the outside. From here Koselleck moves on to discern three dominant modes of historiographical writing, structured by temporality, which capture past experiences linguistically: writing down (*Aufschreiben*) at the moment when events occur; copying (*Abschreiben*), transmitting the meaning once attached to particular events; and finally revising (*Umschreiben*) under the pressure of new experiences that compels the historian to come up with new explanations for familiar events.[48]

Recently, there has been an uptick of interest in Koselleck's theoretical writings, as is evident in new work on or with Koselleck since his untimely death in 2006, especially with the publication of Niklas Olsen's excellent intellectual biography.[49] Whenever scholars across the humanities deal with issues of temporality, with present pasts or past futures, Koselleck's writings are being invoked.[50] With Hartog one might argue that in our current crisis of

47. Koselleck, "Linguistic Change and the History of Events," 656. The German original was published as "Sprachwandel und Ereignisgeschichte."

48. See also Koselleck, "Transformations of Experience and Methodological Change."

49. Olsen, *History in the Plural*; Joas and Vogt, *Begriffene Geschichte*; Dutt and Laube, *Zwischen Sprache und Geschichte*; Locher and Markantonatos, *Reinhart Koselleck und die politische Ikonologie*; Jordheim, "Special Forum"; Dunkhase, *Kosellecks Gespenst*; Imbriano, *Le due modernità*.

50. See, e.g., Huyssen, *Present Pasts*; Scott, *Conscripts of Modernity*; Davis, *Periodization and Sovereignty*; Gumbrecht, *Broad Present*; Roitman, *Anti-crisis*; Traverso, *Left-Wing Melancholia*.

time, the collapse of the past and the future into a present that has become "omnipresent," Koselleck's theory of multiple temporalities and possible histories gains critical urgency. Yet it remains to be seen if this will change some of the widespread misconceptions about (or mistranslations of) Koselleck's work. Up until very recently in the Anglophone reception of his writings, Koselleck was perceived *either* as a conservative historian and anti-utopian critic of the French Revolution à la Furet *or*, more narrowly, as a *Begriffshistoriker*, that is, a historian of concepts à la Pocock and Skinner, *or* as a metahistorian à la Hayden White (or as a "philosopher of history," something Koselleck had always abhorred). Of course, Koselleck repeatedly insisted that all these different interests belong together. Yet only the three volumes of essays, *Zeitschichten*, *Begriffsgeschichte*, and *Vom Sinn und Unsinn der Geschichte*, published in the years immediately before and after his death in 2006 (and only now being translated into English), make apparent how these different interests are laced together in his theory of possible histories, his *Historik*.[51] To put it differently, Koselleck was not entirely ignored in the Anglophone world, but he was also not recognized for what he was, a social and conceptual historian in search of the theoretical foundations of History—a "théoricien de l'histoire," as Hartog writes in his obituary, whose seemingly untimely abstract categories open up historical questions critical for understanding our (or, in fact, any) time.[52]

References

Blanning, T. C. W. 1989. Review of Reinhart Koselleck, *Critique and Crisis: Enlightenment and the Pathogenesis of Modern Society*. *German History* 7, no. 2: 265–66.

Calhoun, Craig, ed. 1992. *Habermas and the Public Sphere*. Cambridge, MA: MIT Press.

Carr, David. 1987. Review of *Futures Past*. *History and Theory* 26, no. 2: 197–204.

Christofferson, Michael Scott. 1999. "An Anti-totalitarian History of the French Revolution: François Furet's *Penser la Révolution* in the Intellectual Politics of the Late 1970s." *French Historical Studies* 22, no. 4: 557–611.

Cohen, Jean, and Andrew Arato. 1992. *Civil Society and Political Theory*. Cambridge, MA: MIT Press.

Crane, Susan. 2000. *Collecting and Historical Consciousness in Early Nineteenth-Century Germany*. Ithaca, NY: Cornell University Press.

Davis, Kathleen. 2008. *Periodization and Sovereignty: How Ideas of Feudalism and Secularization Govern the Politics of Time*. Philadelphia: University of Pennsylvania Press.

Dunkhase, Jan Eike. 2015. *Kosellecks Gespenst: Das Absurde in der Geschichte*. Marbach: Deutsche Schillergesellschaft.

51. See Koselleck, *Sediments of Time*.
52. Hartog, "Reinhart Koselleck, théoricien de l'histoire."

Dutt, Carsten, and Reinhard Laube, eds. 2013. *Zwischen Sprache und Geschichte*. Göttingen: Wallstein.

Edwards, Jason. 2007. "The Ideological Interpellation of Individuals as Combatants: An Encounter between Reinhart Koselleck and Michel Foucault." *Journal of Political Ideologies* 12, no. 1: 49–66.

Escudier, Alexandre. 2009. "Le temps de l'histoire: 'Temporalisation' et modernité politique; Penser avec Koselleck." *Annales: Histoire, sciences sociales* 64, no. 6: 1269–301.

Felsch, Philipp. 2015. *Der lange Sommer der Theorie: Geschichte einer Revolte, 1960–1990*. Munich: Beck.

Fillafer, Franz Leander. 2007. "The Enlightenment on Trial: Reinhart Koselleck's Interpretation of *Aufklärung*." In *The Many Faces of Clio: Cross-Cultural Approaches to Historiography; Essays in Honor of Georg G. Iggers*, edited by Q. Edward Wang and Franz L. Fillafer, 322–45. Oxford: Berghahn.

Foucault, Michel. 2008. *The Birth of Biopolitics: Lectures at the Collège de France, 1978–1979*, edited by Michel Senellart. Basingstoke: Palgrave/Macmillan.

Friedländer, Saul. 1993. *Memory, History, and the Extermination of the Jews of Europe*. Bloomington: Indiana University Press.

Friedrich, Carl. 1960. Review of Reinhart Koselleck, *Critique and Crisis. American Political Science Review* 54, no. 3: 746–48.

Greenberg, Udi. 2014. *The Weimar Century: German Émigrés and the Ideological Foundations of the Cold War*. Princeton, NJ: Princeton University Press.

Gumbrecht, Hans Ulrich. 2006. *Dimensionen und Grenzen der Begriffsgeschichte*. Munich: Fink.

———. 2014. *Broad Present: Time and Contemporary Culture*. New York: Columbia University Press.

Habermas, Jürgen. 1960. "Verrufener Fortschritt—verkanntes Jahrhundert: Zur Kritik an der Geschichtsphilosophie." *Merkur*, no. 147: 468–77.

———. 1989. *The Structural Transformation of the Public Sphere: An Inquiry into a Category of Bourgeois Society*, translated by Thomas Burger. Cambridge, MA: MIT Press.

———. 1993. "Das Bedürfnis nach deutschen Kontinuitäten." *Die Zeit*, December 3.

Hartog, François. 2006. "Reinhart Koselleck, théoricien de l'histoire, il était tenu par la profession pour un historien à part entière." *Le Monde*, February 10.

———. 2015. *Regimes of Historicity: Presentism and Experiences of Time*. New York: Columbia University Press.

Heidegger, Martin. 1978. "Der Zeitbegriff in der Geschichtswissenschaft (1916)." In *Frühe Schriften*. Vol. 1 of *Gesamtausgabe*, 413–33. Frankfurt am Main: Klostermann.

Hoffmann, Stefan-Ludwig. 2009. "Was die Zukunft birgt: Über Reinhart Kosellecks Historik." *Merkur*, no. 721: 546–50.

———. 2010. "Koselleck, Arendt, and the Anthropology of Historical Experiences." *History and Theory* 49, no. 2: 212–36.

Huyssen, Andreas. 2003. *Present Pasts: Urban Palimpsests and the Politics of Memory*. Stanford, CA: Stanford University Press.

Imbriano, Gennaro. 2016. *Le due modernità: Critica, crisi e utopia in Reinhart Koselleck.* Rome: Derive Approdi.

Jacob, Margaret. 1991. *Living the Enlightenment: Freemasonry and Politics in Eighteenth-Century Europe.* New York: Oxford University Press.

Jay, Martin. 1982. "Should Intellectual History Take a Linguistic Turn?" In *Modern European Intellectual History: Reappraisals and New Perspectives*, edited by Dominick LaCapra and Steven L. Kaplan, 86–110. Ithaca, NY: Cornell University Press.

———. 2005. *Songs of Experience: Modern American and European Variations on a Universal Theme.* Berkeley: University of California Press.

Joas, Hans, and Peter Vogt, eds. 2011. *Begriffene Geschichte: Beiträge zum Werk Reinhart Kosellecks.* Berlin: Suhrkamp.

Jordheim, Helge. 2007. "Thinking in Convergences: Koselleck on Language, History, and Time." *Ideas in History* 2, no. 3: 65–90.

———, ed. 2014. "Special Forum: Multiple Temporalities." *History and Theory* 53, no. 4.

Koselleck, Reinhart. 1963. "Der Ursprung der Moderne." *Neue politische Literatur* 8, nos. 11–12: 863–66.

———. 1975. Preface to the second edition. In *Preußen zwischen Reform und Revolution: Allgemeines Landrecht, Verwaltung und Soziale Bewegung von 1791 bis 1848.* Stuttgart: Klett-Cotta.

———. 1988. *Critique and Crisis: Enlightenment and the Pathogenesis of Modern Society.* Cambridge, MA: MIT Press.

———. 1989. "Linguistic Change and the History of Events." *Journal of Modern History* 61, no. 4: 649–66.

———. 1989. "Sprachwandel und Ereignisgeschichte." *Merkur*, no. 486: 657–73.

———. 1990. "Wie neu ist die Neuzeit?" In *Historisches Kolleg 1980–1990: Vorträge anläßlich des zehnjährigen Bestehens und zum Gedenken an Alfred Herrhausen am 22. November 1990*, 37–52. Munich: Historisches Kolleg.

———. 1996. "A Response to Comments on the *Geschichtliche Grundbegriffe.*" In *The Meanings of Historical Terms and Concepts*, edited by Hartmut Lehmann and Melvin Richter, 59–70. Washington, DC: German Historical Institute.

———. 1997. "Laudatio auf François Furet." *Sinn und Form* 49, no. 2: 297–300.

———. 2002. *The Practice of Conceptual History: Timing History, Spacing Concepts*, translated by Todd Samuel Presner et al. Stanford, CA: Stanford University Press.

———. 2002. "Transformations of Experience and Methodological Change: A Historical-Anthropological Essay." In *The Practice of Conceptual History: Timing History, Spacing Concepts*, translated by Todd Samuel Presner et al., 45–83. Stanford, CA: Stanford University Press.

———. 2004. "Dankesrede." In *Reinhart Koselleck (1923–2006): Reden zum 50. Jahrestag seiner Promotion in Heidelberg*, 33–60. Heidelberg: Universitätsverlag Winter.

———. Forthcoming. *Sediments of Time: On Possible Histories*, translated and edited by Sean Franzel and Stefan-Ludwig Hoffmann. Stanford, CA: Stanford University Press.

La Vopa, Anthony. 1992. "Conceiving a Public: Ideas and Society in Eighteenth Century Europe." *Journal of Modern History* 64, no. 1: 79–116.

Levinger, Matthew. 2000. *Enlightened Nationalism: The Transformation of Prussian Political Culture, 1806–1848*. Oxford: Oxford University Press.

Locher, Hubert, and Adriana Markantonatos, eds. 2013. *Reinhart Koselleck und die politische Ikonologie*. Berlin: Deutscher Kunstverlag.

Loewenstein, Bedrich. 1976. Review of Reinhart Koselleck, *Kritik und Krise*. *Journal of Modern History* 48, no. 1: 122–24.

Mehring, Reinhard. 2006. "Begriffssoziologie, Begriffsgeschichte, Begriffspolitik: Zur Form der Ideengeschichtsschreibung nach Carl Schmitt und Reinhart Koselleck." In *Politische Ideengeschichtsschreibung im 20. Jahrhundert: Konzepte und Kritik*, edited by Harald Bluhm and Jürgen Gebhardt, 31–50. Baden-Baden: Nomos.

———. 2011. "Begriffsgeschichte mit Carl Schmitt." In *Begriffene Geschichte: Beiträge zum Werk Reinhart Kosellecks*, edited by Hans Joas and Peter Vogt, 138–67. Berlin: Suhrkamp.

Moses, Dirk. 2009. *German Intellectuals and the Nazi Past*. New York: Cambridge University Press.

Moyn, Samuel. 2008. "On the Intellectual Origins of François Furet's Masterpiece." *Tocqueville Review/Revue Tocqueville* 29, no. 2: 1–20.

Müller, Ernst, ed. 2015. *Forum Interdisziplinäre Begriffsgeschichte* 4, no. 1.

Müller, Jan-Werner. 2014. "On Conceptual History." In *Rethinking Modern European Intellectual History*, edited by Darrin M. McMahon and Samuel Moyn, 74–93. Oxford: Oxford University Press.

Nagel, Ivan. 2006. "Der Kritiker der Krise: Über den Historiker Reinhart Koselleck." *Neue Zürcher Zeitung*, January 8–9.

Nolte, Paul. 2015. *Hans-Ulrich Wehler: Historiker und Zeitgenosse*. Munich: Beck.

Norberg, Jakob. 2014. *Sociability and Its Enemies: German Political Theory after 1945*. Evanston, IL: Northwestern University Press.

Olsen, Niklas. 2012. "Carl Schmitt, Reinhart Koselleck, and the Foundations of History and Politics." *History of European Ideas* 37, no. 2: 197–202.

———. 2012. *History in the Plural: An Introduction to the Work of Reinhart Koselleck*. New York: Berghahn.

Palonen, Kari. 2004. *Die Entzauberung der Begriffe: Das Umschreiben der politischen Begriffe bei Quentin Skinner und Reinhart Koselleck*. Münster: LIT.

Pankakoski, Timo. 2010. "Conflict, Context, Concreteness: Koselleck and Schmitt on Concepts." *Political Theory* 38, no. 6: 749–79.

Pocock, J. G. A. 1971. *Politics, Language, and Time: Essays on Political Thought and History*. New York: Atheneum.

———. 1975. *The Machiavellian Moment: Florentine Republican Thought and the Atlantic Republican Tradition*. Princeton, NJ: Princeton University Press.

———. 1985. *Virtue, Commerce, and History: Essays on Political Thought and History, Chiefly in the Eighteenth Century*. Cambridge: Cambridge University Press.

Prochasson, Christophe. 2013. *François Furet: Les chemins de la mélancolie*. Paris: Stock.

Richter, Melvin. 1997. *The History of Social and Political Concepts: A Critical Introduction*. Oxford: Oxford University Press.

Riedel, Manfred. 1975. "Gesellschaft, bürgerliche." In *Geschichtliche Grundbegriffe*, vol. 2, edited by Otto Brunner, Werner Conze, and Reinhart Koselleck, 719–800. Stuttgart: Klett-Cotta.

Roitman, Janet. 2014. *Anti-crisis*. Durham, NC: Duke University Press.

Scheuerman, William. 2002. "Unsolved Paradoxes: Conservative Political Thought in Adenauer's Germany." In *Confronting Mass Democracy and Industrial Technology: Political and Social Theory from Nietzsche to Habermas*, edited by John P. McCormick, 221–42. Durham, NC: Duke University Press.

Scott, David. 2004. *Conscripts of Modernity: The Tragedy of Colonial Enlightenment*. Durham, NC: Duke University Press.

Scuccimarra, Luca. 2008. "Semantics of Time and Historical Experience: Remarks on Koselleck's *Historik*." *Contributions to the History of Concepts* 4, no. 2: 160–75.

Sheehan, James. 1978. "Begriffsgeschichte: Theory and Practice." *Journal of Modern History* 50, no. 2: 312–19.

Sperber, Jonathan. 1985. "State and Civil Society in Prussia: Thoughts on a New Edition of Reinhart Koselleck's *Preussen zwischen. Reform und Revolution*." *Journal of Modern History* 57, no. 2: 278–96.

Surkis, Judith. 2012. "When Was the Linguistic Turn? A Genealogy." *American Historical Review* 117, no. 3: 700–722.

Traverso, Enzo. 2016. *Left-Wing Melancholia: Marxism, History, and Memory*. New York: Columbia University Press.

Van Laak, Dirk. 1993. *Gespräche in der Sicherheit des Schweigens: Carl Schmitt in der politischen Geistesgeschichte der frühen Bundesrepublik*. Berlin: de Gruyter.

Walker, Mack. 1969–70. Review of Reinhart Koselleck, *Preußen zwischen Reform und Revolution*. *Journal of Social History* 3, no. 2: 183–87.

———. 1971. *German Home Towns: Community, State, and General Estate, 1648–1871*. Ithaca, NY: Cornell University Press.

Wehler, Hans-Ulrich. 1979. "Geschichtswissenschaft heute." In vol. 2 of *Stichworte zur "Geistigen Situation der Zeit*," edited by Jürgen Habermas, 709–53. Frankfurt am Main: Suhrkamp.

———. 2006. *Eine lebhafte Kampfsituation: Ein Gespräch mit Cornelius Torp und Manfred Hettling*. Munich: Beck.

White, Hayden. 1987. Review of *Futures Past*. *American Historical Review* 92, no. 5: 1175–76.

Wizisla, Erdmut. 2004. *Benjamin und Brecht: Die Geschichte einer Freundschaft; Mit einer Chronik und den Gesprächsprotokollen des Zeitschriftenprojekts "Krise und Kritik."* Frankfurt am Main: Suhrkamp.

Zammito, Jon. 2004. "Koselleck's Philosophy of Time(s) and the Practice of History." *History and Theory* 43, no. 1: 124–35.

Niklas Luhmann

William Rasch

In his *Spektator Brief* (spectator letter) of June 26, 1919, immediately after the terms of the Versailles Treaty became public, Ernst Troeltsch wrote with great resignation, "The Anglo-Saxon world domination has been decided on." Then, in English in the original, *"The world is rapidly becoming english."*[1] Whatever one wants to think about Anglo-Saxon (Anglo-American) hegemony, the world *has* become English, or rather: the world now speaks, writes, and reads English as the global lingua franca. Anglo-Saxony's political, military, and economic hegemony may be on the wane, but its linguistic reach grows ever stronger. No longer is it common to learn French, German, or some other language in order to study in Europe and bring back the latest intellectual news; it is even rarer to learn, say, Chinese or Spanish for anything other than winning a competitive edge in doing business. Rather, and to the extent that we Anglophones still wish to learn anything coming from beyond our shores, we wait for translations. Accordingly, the first hurdle to any transatlantic (or, for that matter, transchannel) transmission of ideas is the politics of translation. The second hurdle, intimately linked to the first, is finding fertile ground for the reception of translated work. Columbia University Press, for instance, brought out translations of two works by Arnold Gehlen, including his magnum opus, *Man* (*Der Mensch*), to no discernible effect.[2] And finally, the translated body of work needs a cadre of proselytizers to spread the good news of the new

1. Troeltsch, *Die Fehlgeburt*, 61.
2. See Gehlen, *Man in the Age of Technology*; and Gehlen, *Man*.

New German Critique 132, Vol. 44, No. 3, November 2017
DOI 10.1215/0094033X-4162310   © 2017 by New German Critique, Inc.

wisdom. In discussing the relative failure of igniting interest in the work of Niklas Luhmann, I touch on, but also go beyond, these three general factors. Despite the work of a dedicated few who have internalized and work with some facets of Luhmann's theoretical architecture on this side of the Atlantic, a measure of defeat that remains somewhat puzzling yet also quite readily explicable must be acknowledged.

Grand Theory

One important factor is the history of a discipline. Luhmann called himself a sociologist, working within the paradigm pioneered by Talcott Parsons, with whom Luhmann studied during a Fulbright year at Harvard. What Parsons represented is often called "Grand Theory," an ironic title thrust on him by his chief critic, C. Wright Mills. Stanley Aronowitz defined grand theory as the effort made by figures like Parsons, Paul Lazarsfeld, and Robert Merton to move the discipline "toward criteria they believed prevailed in the natural sciences—that statements about the social world could be verifiable or, in Karl Popper's terms, 'falsifiable'; that the truth is written in the language of mathematics and expressed in quantitative terms; and that speculation be rigorously excluded from scientific discourse."[3] As the epitome of a grand theorist, Parsons was the prime target of attack. It was Mills who offered the classic critique, indicting Parsons on two counts.[4]

First, Mills faults him for his needlessly abstruse language. In *The Sociological Imagination* Mills portrays "Grand Theory," as practiced by Parsons, as illusory, one of social science's grandest distortions. He charts four responses to Parsons's puzzling obscurity: (1) those who understand it and find it good, (2) those who do not understand it because it is written in a clumsy and ponderous style, (3) those who do not understand it and find it exciting anyway, and (4) those who understand Parsons and find him a charlatan.[5] Mills counts himself among this final group. Citing interminably long passages from Parsons's *Social System*, Mills "translates" them into obvious claims that have been made, and made better, by numerous less-celebrated practitioners of the social sciences, enunciated in easy-to-understand English. For example, Mills reduces a page-length disquisition on social order in which values provide normative orientations to two simple sentences: "People often share standards and expect one another to stick to them. Insofar as they do, their society may be

---

3. Aronowitz, *Thinking It Big*, 86.

4. See the brief discussion in Aronowitz, *Thinking It Big*, 218–20.

5. Mills, *Sociological Imagination*, 26.

orderly."[6] Mills thereby condemns Parsons for his pretentious abstractions, his focus on distinctions that do not elucidate social phenomena, and his inability to move from conceptual thinking to empirical observation; in short, he accuses Parsons of an "organized abdication of the effort to describe and explain human conduct and society plainly."[7] When, therefore, Luhmann appeared on the American scene with a translation of essays written in the 1970s on social differentiation, systems theory, and the future relevance of systems theory,[8] he could be easily dismissed as the ghostly shadow of the recently departed Parsons, and Mills's old accusations could be aimed at a new target. The only thing worse than Parsons, on this view, is Parsons rehashed by a German in language even more obscure than the original.

Second, what many, following Mills, also found egregiously problematic in Parsons was the question of power and social order. At fault here is not merely Parsons's abstractions but his reliance, developed during the 1950s, on cybernetics, especially the concept of homeostasis. Parsons's system theory study of society, so the attack goes, rejects change in favor of stability, conservatively locating social homogeneity in the seemingly unchanging role of the family as providing the single most important ground for decision and action. After all, as has been repeatedly noted, the term *cybernetics* is derived from the Greek word for steering, piloting, guiding, in other words, control and justification of the status quo. As the world moved into the 1960s with its political agitations and demands for domestic and international change (civil rights, anticolonial liberation movements, peace movements, and eventually women's liberation and ecology), and with the waves of European intellectual influences crashing on US shores, Parsons began to feel outdated, apologetic, irrelevant. Perhaps fittingly (if one can ever find death fitting), Parsons died during a triumphant tour of Germany to celebrate the fiftieth anniversary of his degree from Heidelberg, a tour in which Luhmann, Jürgen Habermas, and others participated. Nevertheless, Parsons had, in a sense, died in the United States long before that.

Intellectual Context

When Luhmann began to be translated into English in the 1980s, the intellectual climate had changed. On this side of the Atlantic, grand theory was replaced first by critical theory and then by poststructuralism. Luhmann eventually did clear

6. Ibid., 27.
7. Ibid., 33.
8. Luhmann, *Differentiation of Society*; Luhmann, *Trust and Power.*

the hurdle of association with Parsons and 1950s grand theory, but waiting for him as his next obstacle was Habermas. In Germany, second-wave Frankfurt School thought, of which Habermas is the leader, could be said to have two major rivals. Within philosophy, the so-called Münster or Ritter School represented a counterweight to Marxian-inflected critical theory. Though he was condemned by Habermas as neoconservative (a term he also used to describe much, if not all, of French poststructuralist thought), conventional opinion tends to view Joachim Ritter and company as liberal, championing the West German *Rechtsstaat* (rule-of-law state), a position to which Habermas himself gradually inclined. The other, often more visible rival was Luhmann and systems theory. Early in Luhmann's university career, students organized a debate between the two social theorists, which resulted in a classic *Auseinandersetzung*, starting with two essays by Luhmann, two by Habermas, one of near-monograph length, followed by Luhmann's response.[9] The debate launched a continuous engagement, each with the other, until Luhmann's death in 1998.

To date, Habermas has refused to grant the rights to translate the volume, claiming lack of contemporary relevance. Nevertheless, the impact of that encounter has left indelible traces in his works that *have* been translated; thus for much of the two decades following their dispute, Habermas exerted a controlling influence on the Anglophone perception of Luhmann's thought. In its simplest version, Habermas's rebuttal pits his normative, critical theory against what he sees as Luhmann's affirmative, technocratic functionalism. In *Legitimation Crisis*, for instance, Habermas characterizes Luhmann's emphasis on a system's need to reduce environmental complexity as an "expansion of power" that "transform[s] *questions of validity* into *questions of behavior*" ("ought" into "is," in other, neo-Kantian, words), and sees in Luhmann's "comprehensive conceptual strategy" (i.e., his grand theory) a form of "conceptual imperialism."[10] There may have been a protest-too-much aspect of this initial condemnation, for Habermas increasingly incorporated aspects of both Parsons's and Luhmann's system-theory approach in his monumental *Theory of Communicative Action*. Perhaps to compensate for his concessions and to keep a critical edge, Habermas continued to emphasize a normative refuge, the lifeworld, from which "social pathologies" can be observed and corrected. With respect to these "pathologies," Luhmann's "functional perspective" is said to be "insensitive." Luhmann's performed cool detachment, his belief in

9. Habermas and Luhmann, *Theorie der Gesellschaft oder Sozialtechnologie.*
10. Habermas, *Legitimation Crisis*, 5–6.

the inefficiency of oversimplified, morally normative critique, has continuously elicited handwringing. Accordingly, Habermas sees in Luhmann a complacent observer of Weberian rationalization and thus concludes: "For Adorno, this 'administered world' was a vision of extreme horror; for Luhmann it has become a trivial presupposition."[11] Ultimately, the "normative content of modernity" that Habermas wishes to rescue is gutted by Luhmann's "subject-centered reason" that devolves into mere "systems rationality," into mere instrumentality without the wherewithal to engage in critiques of "metaphysics" and "power." Yet, acknowledging that his ongoing debate with Luhmann remains unresolved, perhaps even irresolvable, Habermas ends his Paris lectures on the philosophical discourse of modernity with this observation: "It may be that 'linguistically generated intersubjectivity' [Habermas] and 'self-referentially closed system' [Luhmann] are now the catchwords for a controversy that will take the place of the discredited mind-body problematic."[12]

Those who read these volumes in the 1970s and 1980s had a singularly negative introduction to Luhmann. One had in these snapshots all one needed to know about this epitome of the status quo. Luhmann could be safely ignored. Ironically, Habermas's reservations about Luhmann's purported technocratic functionalism were echoed by one of Habermas's most resolute enemies, Jean-François Lyotard. In *The Postmodern Condition*, Lyotard, very much echoing the older Frankfurt School of Max Horkheimer and Theodor W. Adorno, also uses the distinction between traditional and critical theory to condemn Luhmann as a technocrat, also sees in Luhmann's reduction of complexity an affirmation of power, and thus objects to legitimacy based on the success of mere procedure to be a form of bureaucratic terror.[13] From both sides of the modernity-postmodernity divide, then, we had identical dismissals of this pesky shadow of the complacent past.

With the name Lyotard we now encounter the third barrier to an Anglophone understanding of Luhmann's system theory, namely, the loosely knit web of late twentieth-century French thought brought together under the name of poststructuralism. Think for a moment of terms commonly associated with Luhmann: *system, communication, information, observation, differentiation, binary distinction.* Then think of some of the terms most thoroughly excoriated by Jacques Derrida, Michel Foucault, Gilles Deleuze, and a host of others

11. Habermas, *Theory of Communicative Action*, 1:377, 312.
12. Habermas, *Philosophical Discourse of Modernity*, 385.
13. Lyotard, *Postmodern Condition*, 12, 60–61, 63–64.

generally associated with poststructuralism. You will come up with a strikingly similar list. When "system" does not evoke the "iron cage" of reified modernity, it calls up, for many, even worse specters, like G. W. F. Hegel (or post-Marxist caricatures of Hegel). What are "communication" and "information" if not the nightmare versions of human interaction associated with a specifically "scientistic" view of the world represented by Noam Chomsky's linguistics, computer science, genetic engineering, empirical social science, mass marketing, and advertising, in short, the various rationalized bureaucracies of the soul routinely chastised by the philosophical avant-garde?[14] What is "observation" if not "ocularcentric" and thus "logocentric." And need one be strictly a feminist scholar to worry about the effects of binary distinctions, known now simply as "binaries"? With such terminological baggage, how could one even begin to take Luhmann seriously? Such questions fairly represent the zeitgeist in North American humanities disciplines of the final third of the twentieth century, a spirit nourished on a critique of metaphysics that saw everywhere, but especially in cybernetics and systems theory, Adorno's "administered society" populated by Friedrich Nietzsche's "last man" and Martin Heidegger's *das Man.* It was also a spirit schooled on the linguistic turn, the view that meaning was a product of language's self-referential capacities, not its ability to point to an extralinguistic reality. The linguistic turn nurtured the cognitive taste for "readings," that is, research by way of precise, rhetorical, and aesthetic examinations of landmark texts (verbal and visual) and popular culture. Readings (*Lektüre*), Luhmann fiercely claimed, was not theory. In this atmosphere, Luhmann's views fell on deaf ears. Those on the left could separate themselves from Karl Marx and leave Frankfurt because in Paris they now had Foucault. Literary scholars and those social scientists engaged in qualitative research could find in the Heideggerian tradition (from Hans-Georg Gadamer to Derrida) reading strategies that could be applied to Goethe, Jean-Luc Godard, or the semiotics of kinship structures. In the poetry of Friedrich Hölderlin, Stéphane Mallarmé, or Paul Celan, and the theory of Walter Benjamin, one sought at best the roots of communicability (or its impossibility), certainly not communication or, God forbid, information. And in the analyses of modernity—now called postmodernity—one found hybrid formations that transgressed, even made a mockery of boundaries. Clear distinctions, oppressively *binary* ones in particular, were signs of masculine metaphysics. Where after all this could there be room for an engagement with Luhmann?

The answer: almost everywhere.

14. Deleuze and Guattari, *What Is Philosophy?*, 9–12.

Poststructuralist Openings

Commonalities were found. With the Luhmann of the late 1980s, Lyotard could initiate a kind of rapprochement. He remained critical, to be sure, but his critique is now tinged with self-effacing irony—"All politics is only (I say 'only' because I have a revolutionary past and hence a certain nostalgia) a program of administrative decision making, of managing the system"—and not without reexamination and newfound appreciation: "What Niklas Luhmann calls 'reduction of complexity' is not the suppression of complexity at all, it is what might be called feasibility, the capacity to make use of a complex memory."[15] He even pens an affectionate tribute to "N.L.," commenting on Luhmann's "Baudelairian elegance" and their "common front against the waves of ecologist eloquence" at a conference in Siegen.[16] But their common front was not merely Baudelairian or based on weary skepticism. There is a fundamental difference between what Habermas called the "project of modernity" and what Lyotard is famous for enunciating as postmodernity. That difference centers on—difference. What Luhmann and Lyotard shared was a belief that modernity (Luhmann)/postmodernity (Lyotard) was characterized by incommensurability, not just a historical disarticulation of the body of the past, not just a paradigm shift, epistemic break, or move from feudal to bourgeois capitalist production (though all of this too), but a structural incommensurability centered firmly in the now. The difference both Lyotard and Luhmann have with Habermas is clearly signaled in the title of one of the latter's essays, in which Habermas critiques the critique of reason: "The Unity of Reason in the Diversity of Its Voices."[17] Odo Marquard, another interesting German thinker who failed to make the Atlantic crossing, nicely brings the Habermasian position to a point, namely, plurality is not a value in itself but merely the starting point of a process meant to produce ultimate conformity, "consensus."[18] Lyotard sees "terror" in this aim, Luhmann merely "old European" conservatism. "Nie wieder Vernunft!" Luhmann cries, ironically parodying the post–World War I pacifist slogan *nie wieder Krieg* (war). Reason—never again.[19]

15. Lyotard, *Political Writings*, 99, 98.
16. Ibid., 81.
17. Habermas, *Postmetaphysical Thinking*, 115–48.
18. Marquard, "Menschliche Endlichkeit und Kompensation I," 32–33.
19. Lyotard's response to Habermas is most famously included in the Kantian-titled "Answering the Question: What Is Postmodernism?" (Lyotard, *Postmodern Condition*, 71–82; retranslated in Lyotard, *Postmodern Explained*, 1–16). The word *terror* is found in the final paragraph, which has both Hegel and Habermas as its target. I use the 1993 translation. "Finally, it should be made clear that it is not up to us to *provide reality*, but to invent allusions to what is conceivable but not presentable. And this task should not lead us to expect the slightest reconciliation between 'language games.'

Luhmann's castigation of the nostalgia for substantial, ultimately metaphysical reason (no matter how procedurally arrived at) was matched by Lyotard's own violent negation: metanarratives—never again!

In "Speaking and Silence" Luhmann gives a concise overview of what unites and separates him from Lyotard. What Lyotard calls a phrase, Luhmann calls an operation. Each operation is an event linked in a recursive network with other events of the same type. Linkage can occur only selectively, producing possibilities that are ignored ("victims" in Lyotard's terminology) but thereby establishing orders, "regimes," that create regularities, definitive "cuts" in the world. Speaking, in other words, also produces silence; inclusion excludes. All this is taken in stride by Luhmann, but underlying Lyotard's precise description, Luhmann detects a nostalgia, a sadness.

> Yet despite this insight into the operative inevitability of difference, for Lyotard the temptation remains strong to think the unity of difference as well—no longer in the sense of "spirit" but in the problematization of normativity, in the question of justice . . . and further in a rather hopeless appeal to politics, or finally in the historical self-characterization as "postmodern." Thus a defiant sadness rests on the renunciation of unity—that old rhetorical unity of *orgé/lý pe* (*ira/tristitia*) which at least in its mood holds on to what one knows to be lost.[20]

Luhmann is more optimistic and uses the cybernetic device of the "blind spot" to imagine a concatenation of observers observing the blind spot of other observers, each with a blind spot of its own that can be seen only by yet others. Unity can never be recouped, not even nostalgically. Still, something of Lyotard seemed to stick with Luhmann, just as Lyotard may have been stimulated by Luhmann to reflect on his own nostalgia for his revolutionary past. Toward the end of his career, Luhmann reserved a place for a more comprehensive exclusion than he had ever acknowledged before. Systems operate through inclusion and necessary exclusion. There is no system that encom-

---

Kant, in naming them the faculties, knew that they are separated by an abyss and that only a transcendental illusion (Hegel's) can hope to totalize them into a real unity. But he also knew that the price of this illusion is terror. The nineteenth and twentieth centuries have given us our fill of terror. We have paid dearly for our nostalgia for the all and the one, for a reconciliation of the concept and the sensible, for a transparent and communicable experience. Beneath the general demand for relaxation and appeasement, we hear murmurings of the desire to reinstitute terror and fulfill the phantasm of taking possession of reality. The answer is this: war on totality. Let us attest to the unpresentable; let us activate the differends and save the honor of the name" (16). Luhmann's ironic phrase can be found in Luhmann, *Observations on Modernity*, 35.

20. Luhmann, "Speaking and Silence," 28.

passes all, no Habermasian integration of society through rational consensus. Yet Luhmann acknowledges that individuals who are excluded from one or more systems (e.g., education) may become victims of a chain reaction (e.g., no education, no career) that results in a more or less total exclusion from society, a "negative integration," marked by the favelas of Brazil or the inner cities of North America. There is no mourning, no pathos in his description, but perhaps a recognition of "loss" that may in time destroy the fine web of incommensurability that is modernity.[21] Unfortunately, this dialogue between Luhmann and Lyotard, which was made available in English in the 1990s, was cut short by the death of both participants in 1998.

Luhmann, a seemingly voracious reader, kept abreast of other developments in France and elsewhere. He was quite taken by Michel Serres's notion of the parasite and cites it often. With their similar set of interests in information theory, cybernetics, and scientific systems theory, both scholars apprehended the role the parasite plays with reference to objects, or quasi objects as Serres would have it, meaning the role of that network of observers who are constitutively unable to complete their mission.[22] Luhmann also appreciated Derrida's deconstruction, masterfully explaining it in terms of second-order observation.[23] He found little in Foucault to be of use, as the "Preface to the English Edition" in *Love as Passion* demonstrates. Indeed, that short preface is one of the clearest expositions in English of what Luhmann did and did not value in some of the scholarly traditions, especially historical, related to his own activities. However, apart from Lyotard, there was little or no reciprocal interest. Luhmann's language ("system" etc.) was off-putting for the chic theory of the age, his politics was insufficiently "critical" (though, in reality, stood as a massive critique of critique), and his interest in science was perceived to be, well, too "scientistic." In Germany, because of the dominance of historical (over "structural") thinking, the various strands of Marxism, and the resurrection or, some would say, domestication of Heideggerian hermeneutics by Gadamer, placing Luhmann's work in the context of new French thought was only very belatedly undertaken. Therefore, if with no little irony, discussion of Luhmann in terms of the dominant theoretical currents of the last third of the twentieth century coming from France had to take place in English.

---

21. See, e.g., Luhmann, *Soziologische Aufklärung 6*, 237–64.

22. See Cary Wolfe's introduction to Serres, *Parasite*, esp. xxi–xxv, in which he articulates Serres by way of Luhmann and vice versa.

23. Luhmann, *Theories of Distinction*, 94–112.

Translation and Reception

I started this investigation with the observation that the world has become "English," leading to the enhanced importance of translations. I mentioned one of the relatively early collection of essays in English (Luhmann, *Differentiation of Society*) and can add a few subsequent volumes: *Trust and Power, Ecological Communication* (one of his crankiest books), *Essays on Self-Reference*, and *Political Theory in the Welfare State*. These works would have been of interest almost exclusively to practitioners of the social sciences, especially sociology and political theory. They tended to be more conservative in tone and lacked much of the more sophisticated theoretical apparatus (except *Essays on Self-Reference*) that began appearing in German during the 1980s. For the most part, these volumes were not designed to introduce Luhmann to the audience in the humanities eager for devouring new manifestations of "theory." The one volume that may have had a chance on that score, *Essays on Self-Reference*, lacked any introduction, no Gayatri Spivak introducing *Of Grammatology* with a quasi monograph of her own, for instance. On the back of its dust jacket three volumes of sociology, two authored by Jeffrey Alexander, are advertised, indicating the intended audience. No groundswell, it seemed, could emerge from this scattershot beginning.

It was only after Stanford University Press undertook the herculean task of translating seminal works that any sophisticated examination of Luhmann's "postmodern" modernity could be hoped for. *Social Systems*, with its splendid preface by Eva Knodt that very precisely and clearly articulated the relationship of Luhmann's thought to dominant German, French, and American traditions, was published mid-decade, roughly coinciding with a special Luhmann edition of *New German Critique* (1994) and two consecutive issues of *Cultural Critique* dedicated to "the politics of systems and environments" (1995). A string of titles followed over the next two decades: *Love as Passion* (1998, a reprint), *Observations on Modernity* (1998), *Art as a Social System* (2000), *The Reality of the Mass Media* (2000), *Theories of Distinction* (2002), *A Systems Theory of Religion* (2013), and his two-volume magnum opus, *Theory of Society* (2012–13). Stanford University Press was not alone, but without Stanford and its then editor, Helen Tartar, and her successors, this mass of material would never have seen the light of day in such a short time.

During this same period, secondary literature, aimed at the broad spectrum of humanities-based theory-a-holics, began to appear. Examples include Wolfe, *Critical Environments*; Rasch, *Niklas Luhmann's Modernity*; Rasch and Wolfe, editors, *Observing Complexity*; Moeller, *Luhmann Explained*; Wolfe, *What Is Posthumanism?*; Moeller, *The Radical Luhmann*; and articles in prominent journals and essay collections. It was argued that Luhmann's "grand narrative" of modernity placed the contentious debate about postmodernity in a far more comprehensively historical and theoretical context, that, in fact, with "postmodernism" the syntax of modernity caught up with its structure. Similarly, his "constructivist epistemology" was seen to have affinities with poststructuralist critiques of reason, representation, intersubjective dialogue, and foundationalism. Furthermore, his contention that communication (*not* the individual) ought to be regarded as the basic element of society aligned him with emerging "posthumanist" and "cyborg" perspectives on questions of embodied cognition, artificial intelligence, and animal rights, among others; and it was realized that his interpretation of information had nothing to do with a conventional transfer model of messages through a channel—rather, it contributed to ongoing analyses of language and the generation of meaning more narrowly associated with poststructuralism. Cary Wolfe and Bruce Clarke,[24] among others, have carried Luhmann, along with associated "neocybernetic" literature, into the research on "posthumanities," the title of the series Wolfe edits for the University of Minnesota Press. These discussions about the relevance of Luhmann to contemporary debates emerged largely in language and literature departments (German, English, comparative literature), where much of contemporary European theory finds its American home, but even in sociology, anthropology, and science studies, where systems theory could be compared productively with network theory, Luhmann was no longer strictly looked on as a Parsonian persona non grata.

At roughly the same time, Luhmann's work in legal and political theory began to emerge as an independent force to explain the post-1989 and post-2001 world. In the United Kingdom (thanks, in part, to the influence of Günther Teubner, who taught at the London School of Economics), the translation of Luhmann's *Law as a Social System* has been accompanied by King and Thornhill (*Niklas Luhmann's Theory of Politics and Law*); King and Thornhill, editors (*Luhmann on Law and Politics*); Philippopoulos-Mihalopoulos (*Niklas Luhmann*); and Borch (*Niklas Luhmann*), among others. Although part of the Anglophone literature on Luhmann, the reception of British work seems to have more resonance in the Commonwealth and on the European continent than it does in the United States. The volume *Luhmann Observed* (2013), edited by Anders la Cour and Andreas Philippopoulos-Mihalopoulos, reflects a strong interest in Luhmann that exists in pockets of the British Isles and at the Copenhagen Business School. Even in non-German Europe, reception of

---

24. Clarke, *Neocybernetics and Narrative*.

Luhmann takes place more in English translation than in the original German.[25] There is, in other words, an Anglophone Luhmann discrete from these coasts, the flavor (or rather, flavour) of which is markedly different from the American variety.

The Puzzle

And yet! Luhmann is hardly a household name, even in the relatively small house of North American humanities. The importance of his work is recognized, but it has never caught fire. A simple test suffices to explain the difference between the *availability* of a body of work and the *necessity* of wrestling with that corpus. Does the question "Have you read Luhmann?" strike terror in the heart of a graduate student? The clear answer is no. Mention affect (today, tomorrow—who knows), or even Carl Schmitt, and the need to be interested is mobilized. Luhmann? Communication? Complexity? Contingency? Cybernetics? Systems? Only among a select few.

One can conjure reasons why the name Luhmann served no terrorist function in the humanities. His work is obscure, seemingly remote from text-based studies; his concepts reek of science but somehow fail to conjure the same fascination that, say, Bruno Latour's work manages; systems are not as sexy as networks; his politics are conventionally liberal, ergo reactionary in the environment of academic radicalism; his insistence on the persistence of modernity was seen as antiquated in the hothouse days of postmodernism; his aesthetics, unlike Lyotard's, lacks the pathos of the sublime and pays little attention to the avant-garde; the linguistic turn that gave pride of place to text and communication (in Luhmann's sense) has given way to the "new materialisms" and affect; and although his champions include leaders in their respective fields, perhaps none treated Luhmann with the appropriate awe and wonder necessary to project charisma on the master. But even if true, are these musings really obstacles? Is Jacques Lacan or Deleuze easier to read? Do Alain Badiou's mathematics make sense? Is having "a revolutionary past" a necessary visa allowing entry? Is the linguistic turn gone for good? If so, is it really good that it is gone?

One wonders what a failed transatlantic theory transfer means. Certainly Lyotard's theory transferred quite successfully for roughly twenty years, and then it disappeared overnight, as if the death of his body had immolated the paper pages of his soul. What one now sees is an occasional obligatory reference to *The Postmodern Condition*, a citation that betrays no evidence that the

25. See also Thornhill, "Niklas Luhmann."

referrer has actually read the work. It seems that we live in an age when the half-life of intellectual trends can almost be counted in days or months, not years or decades.

Could Luhmann's story be the opposite? Unlike other German intellectual figures of the late twentieth century whose work has never or barely been translated—Marquard, as I said; Gehlen, the efforts of Columbia University Press notwithstanding; Silvia Bovenschen's foundational feminist historical work *Die imaginierte Weiblichkeit*, still important despite the current pivot away from history and the subordination of feminism to gender theory—Luhmann left behind translated work that sits quietly on the shelves to be discovered, and those scholars who have shown interest in it have not given up their interest. And even on the American side of the Atlantic we have access to the Anglophone literature "over there." Max Weber famously defined politics as the "slow, powerful drilling through hard boards."[26] This may also be the definition of the politics of reception. Perhaps the slow, powerful drilling will prove longer lasting than the whipsaw twists and turns in the ever more rapid replacement of the new with the newer.

Were I you, however, I would not hold my breath.

References

Aronowitz, Stanley. 2012. *Thinking It Big: C. Wright Mills and the Making of Political Intellectuals*. New York: Columbia University Press.

Borch, Christian. 2011. *Niklas Luhmann*. New York: Routledge.

Clarke, Bruce. 2014. *Neocybernetics and Narrative*. Minneapolis: University of Minnesota Press.

Deleuze, Gilles, and Félix Guattari. 1994. *What Is Philosophy?*, translated by Hugh Tomlinson and Graham Burchell. New York: Columbia University Press.

Gehlen, Arnold. 1980. *Man in the Age of Technology*, translated by Patricia Lipscomb. New York: Columbia University Press.

———. 1988. *Man*, translated by Clare McMillan and Karl Pillemer. New York: Columbia University Press.

Habermas, Jürgen. 1975. *Legitimation Crisis*, translated by Thomas McCarthy. Boston: Beacon.

———. 1987. *The Philosophical Discourse of Modernity*, translated by Frederick G. Lawrence. Cambridge, MA: MIT Press.

———. 1987. *The Theory of Communicative Action*, translated by Thomas McCarthy. 2 vols. Boston: Beacon.

———. 1994. *Postmetaphysical Thinking: Philosophical Essays*, translated by William Mark Hohengarten. Cambridge, MA: MIT Press.

26. Weber, *Vocation Letters*, 93.

Habermas, Jürgen, and Niklas Luhmann. 1971. *Theorie der Gesellschaft oder Sozialtechnologie—Was leistet die Systemforschung?* Frankfurt am Main: Suhrkamp.

King, Michael, and Chris Thornhill. 2003. *Niklas Luhmann's Theory of Politics and Law.* Houndmills: Palgrave Macmillan.

———, eds. 2006. *Luhmann on Law and Politics: Critical Appraisals and Applications.* Oxford: Hart.

la Cour, Anders, and Andreas Philippopoulos-Mihalopoulos, eds. 2013. *Luhmann Observed: Radical Theoretical Encounters.* New York: Palgrave Macmillan.

Luhmann, Niklas. 1982. *The Differentiation of Society*, translated by Stephen Holmes and Charles Larmore. New York: Columbia University Press.

———. 1982. *Trust and Power.* New York: Wiley.

———. 1989. *Ecological Communication*, translated by John Bednarz Jr. Chicago: University of Chicago Press.

———. 1990. *Essays on Self-Reference.* New York: Columbia University Press.

———. 1990. *Political Theory in the Welfare State*, translated by John Bednarz Jr. Berlin: de Gruyter.

———. 1994. "Speaking and Silence." *New German Critique*, no. 61: 25–37.

———. 1995. *Social Systems*, translated by John Bednarz Jr. with Dirk Baecker. Stanford, CA: Stanford University Press.

———. 1995. *Soziologische Aufklärung 6: Die Soziologie und der Mensch.* Opladen: Westdeutscher Verlag.

———. 1998. *Love as Passion: The Codification of Intimacy*, translated by Jeremy Gaines and Doris L. Jones. Stanford, CA: Stanford University Press.

———. 1998. *Observations on Modernity*, translated by William Whobrey. Stanford, CA: Stanford University Press.

———. 2000. *Art as a Social System*, translated by Eva M. Knodt. Stanford, CA: Stanford University Press.

———. 2000. *The Reality of the Mass Media*, translated by Kathleen Cross. Stanford, CA: Stanford University Press.

———. 2002. *Theories of Distinction: Redescribing the Descriptions of Modernity*, translated by Joseph O'Neil, Elliott Schreiber, Kerstin Behnke, and William Whobrey. Stanford, CA: Stanford University Press.

———. 2004. *Law as a Social System*, edited by Fatima Kastner, Richard Nobles, David Schiff, and Rosamund Ziegert, translated by Klaus A. Ziegert. Oxford: Oxford University Press.

———. 2012–13. *Theory of Society*, translated by Rhodes Barrett. 2 vols. Stanford, CA: Stanford University Press.

———. 2013. *A Systems Theory of Religion*, translated by David A. Brenner with Adrian Hermann. Stanford, CA: Stanford University Press.

Lyotard, Jean-François. 1984. *The Postmodern Condition: A Report on Knowledge*, translated by Geoff Bennington and Brian Massumi. Minneapolis: University of Minnesota Press.

———. 1993. *Political Writings*, translated by Bill Readings and Devin Paul Geiman. Minneapolis: University of Minnesota Press.

————. 1993. *The Postmodern Explained*, edited by Julian Pefanis and Morgan Thomas, translated by Don Barry, Bernadette Maher, Julian Pefanis, Virginia Spate, and Morgan Thomas. Minneapolis: University of Minnesota Press.

Marquard, Odo. 1995. "Menschliche Endlichkeit und Kompensation I." In *Menschliche Endlichkeit und Kompensation*, 19–34. Bamberg: Verlag Fränkischer Tag.

Mills, C. Wright. 1959. *The Sociological Imagination*. New York: Oxford.

Moeller, Hans-Georg. 2006. *Luhmann Explained: From Souls to Systems*. Chicago: Open Court.

————. 2011. *The Radical Luhmann*. New York: Columbia University Press.

Parsons, Talcott. 1951. *The Social System*. Glencoe, IL: Free Press.

Philippopoulos-Mihalopoulos, Andreas. 2010. *Niklas Luhmann: Law, Justice, Society*. Abingdon, VA: Routledge.

Rasch, William. 2000. *Niklas Luhmann's Modernity: The Paradoxes of Differentiation*. Stanford, CA: Stanford University Press.

Rasch, William, and Eva M. Knodt, eds. 1994. "Special Issue on Niklas Luhmann." *New German Critique*, no. 61.

Rasch, William, and Cary Wolfe, eds. 1995. "The Politics of Systems and Environments, Part I." Special issue. *Cultural Critique*, no. 30.

————, eds. 1995. "The Politics of Systems and Environments, Part II." Special issue. *Cultural Critique*, no. 31.

————, eds. 2000. *Observing Complexity: Systems Theory and Postmodernity*. Minneapolis: University of Minnesota Press.

Serres, Michel. 2007. *The Parasite*, translated by Lawrence R. Schehr. Minneapolis: University of Minnesota Press.

Thornhill, Chris, ed. 2012. "Niklas Luhmann." Special issue. *Revue Internationale de Philosophie*, no. 259.

Troeltsch, Ernst. 1994. *Die Fehlgeburt einer Republik: Spektator in Berlin 1918 bis 1922*, edited by Johann Hinrich Claussen. Frankfurt am Main: Eichborn.

Weber, Max. 2004. *The Vocation Letters*, edited by David Owen and Tracy B. Strong, translated by Rodney Livingstone. Indianapolis, IN: Hackett.

Wolfe, Cary. 1998. *Critical Environments: Postmodern Theory and the Pragmatics of the "Outside."* Minneapolis: University of Minnesota Press.

————. 2009. *What Is Posthumanism?* Minneapolis: University of Minnesota Press.

The Kittler Effect

Geoffrey Winthrop-Young

The following remarks trace the North American engagement with "German media theory" over the last twenty-five years. The main focus is on the contested centerpiece of that strange construct, the transatlantic reception of Friedrich Kittler (1943–2011). However, this is not a reception history but a double-layered scrutiny of key points that have shaped the North American engagement with Kittler. I am using the term *engagement* in its broadest sense, from the marital to the martial, from informed admiration and strategic appropriation to irritated rebuttal and flat-out rejection. Its semantic fullness stands in contrast to the hollowness of German media theory, a designation that recalls one of history's more suspect brand names, the so-called Holy Roman Empire. It is frequently said of the latter that it was neither an empire nor Roman and certainly not holy. German media theory, in turn, is neither a theory nor really centered on media, and its Germanness is a contested issue. The term's only trustworthy feature are the quotation marks. Sometimes minor discourse operators determine the state of our theories.

But when and where did this term emerge? To the best of my knowledge, we have Geert Lovink to thank; who in the 1990s he published print and online papers on the media-technological contributions of German scholars like Kittler, Norbert Bolz, Hartmut Winkler, and others. To be sure, Lovink was not

Portions of this article draw on previously published material, especially Winthrop-Young, "Krautrock, Heidegger, Bogeyman." I am grateful to Claudia Breger, Paul Feigelfeld, Philipp Felsch, Erich Hörl, Peter Uwe Hohendahl, Sybille Krämer, and Bernhard Siegert for additional suggestions.

New German Critique 132, Vol. 44, No. 3, November 2017
DOI 10.1215/0094033X-4162322   © 2017 by New German Critique, Inc.

the first to talk about German media theorists within the Anglosphere. The journal *October*—which together with *Grey Room* deserves a lot of credit for initiating the engagement with German media-theoretical production—had already in 1987 published a translation of the introduction of Kittler's *Gramophone Film Typewriter.* Neither was Lovink the first to highlight the obvious French connection. The ways in which German theorists like Kittler elaborated a media-technological grounding of what in those days was called French poststructuralism are already explained in David Wellbery's 1990 introduction to *Discourse Networks.* However, Lovink was the first to move from German media *theorists* to German media *theory*, thus intimating the emergence of an identifiable collective enterprise. Rumors began to spread that there was something noteworthy going on in Germany. To quote the most pithy title of the countless recent German introductions to media theory, Germans in Freiburg, Siegen, and Berlin appeared more informed when it came to doing *Was mit Medien* (best rendered into congenial slacker English as "Like, media and stuff").[1]

Germans soon heard what others were saying about them, and when in October 2004 Lovink asked in the online forum Rohrpost whether there indeed was such a thing as German media theory, he received a slew of responses that revived George Berkeley's doctrine of *esse est percipi.* If such a national body of theory existed at all, Lovink was told, then it was the result of internalizing an external observation. "That means there wasn't one until it was perceived out there, in countries speaking other languages."[2] Or maybe it had less to with Bishop Berkeley than with Louis Althusser: German media theory was interpellated from the outside, and that call to order contributed to its self-awareness.

German media theory, in short, is not a homegrown label. In the prolix idiolect known as a *Luhmanndeutsch* it would rank as *eine rezeptionssteuernde Fremdbeobachtung*—a reception-guiding hetero-observation, a look in from the outside instrumentally involved in constructing the scrutinized object. As many second-order observers have pointed out, this questionable first-order observation resembles the construct known as "French theory." It, too, was an observer product, a brew concocted on the other side of the Atlantic that threw into one pot a motley crew of theorists, many of whom were surprised to find themselves in such close company with each other (and some of whom eagerly jumped into the cauldron to increase their exposure). Of course, there are dif-

---

1. See Heinevetter and Sanchez, *Was mit Medien*, which elevates Kittler to the lofty status of the "MacGyver of media theory" (52).

2. Mercedes Bunz, quoted in Lovink, "Whereabouts of German Media Theory," 84.

ferences, the most obvious being size. The impact of French theory—judging by some accounts, "impact" can here be read with large extraterrestrial objects in mind—took place on a different level of magnitude. Kittler may enjoy his share of attention, but he is not Michel Foucault—and Kittler, a lifelong admirer of Foucault, never claimed to be. Neither was Kittler Theodor W. Adorno, a theorist he came to despise with relish despite noticeable similarities. German media theory is not Critical Theory; it does not enjoy, as did the Frankfurt School in Daimler/Chrysler fashion, a bicephalous institutional base on both sides of the Atlantic.

Yet as hollow as the term may be, there is nothing less productive than the futile exchange of accusations of essentialism versus constructivism.[3] To be sure, German media theory is not the outgrowth of some essentially German way of theorizing. But then again, there is more to it than the trivial fact that it was produced by theorists who happened to be writing in German. Kittler has produced a German theory because the deeper layers of his work, the basis and the bias of his arguments as well as the recurrence of certain references and associations, have to be understood against the background of debates about technology, humanism, and identity formation that over the last two centuries emerged in the German-speaking countries. The media theory is "German" in the sense that it reflects German collective experiences in which media structures, from the eighteenth-century attempts to culturally construct a politically not yet existing nation by means of books and letters to the Nazi propaganda apparatus and beyond, appear first and foremost as instances of collective homogenization.

With this in mind, observers north of the forty-ninth parallel will note similarities between "German" and "Canadian" media theory. In both cases we are dealing with controversial founding figures who usurped media theory from the outside (philosophers and literature scholars in Germany, economists and literature scholars in Canada). In both cases, the origins can be linked to the dynamics of specific academic locales (e.g., Freiburg and Toronto) as well as to the aforementioned collective media experiences. In both cases, theory production was marked by a generous deployment of the key term *media/Medien* that, however vague, was clearly at odds with the ruling association of media with *mass media*. In both cases, a familiarity with hermeneutic literary techniques was a significant part of the challenge to the media-indifferent

3. For different views of the debate, see Breger, "Zur Debatte um den 'Sonderweg Deutsche Medienwissenschaft'"; Lethen, "Wie deutsch ist die deutsche Kultur- und Medienwissenschaft?"; Pias, "What's German about German Media Theory?"; Peters, "Strange Sympathies"; and Winthrop-Young, "Von gelobten und verfluchten Medienländern."

"channel theory" of established communication and information theory.[4] In both cases, the focus on hitherto neglected media-specific materialities stressed both the categorical differences between media *and* the fact that this difference was the prerequisite for any understanding of media. In other words, in both cases the intellectual brand products amounted to theories of contrastive intermediality aimed at disrupting hegemonic narratives of continuity and autonomy. In both cases, this foregrounding of media specificities was widely decried as technodeterminist, an objection that determines little else than the ignorance of those who raise it.

In retrospect it appears that German media theory was a mutable construct with an hourglass shape. It arose from a fairly wide base, passed through an interim period of constriction, and then once again fanned out. The 1999 *New German Critique* special issue "German Media Studies" offered a somewhat indiscriminate collection of different approaches, while the 2007 *Grey Room* special issue "German Media Studies" explicitly focused on the type of *Medienwissenschaft* inspired by Kittler's work.[5] During its first decade, then, the observer construct known as "German media theory" progressed from ecumenic inclusion to selective exclusion. Names that initially appeared side by side with Kittler's—such as Bolz and Winkler, both of whom featured more prominently and positively in the *New German Critique* special issue than Kittler himself[6]—tended to fall by the wayside. German theorists in particular have been critical of this focus on Kittler. Is it fair, is it historically justified, that he should hog the limelight? First, brusque answer: reception is a form of communication; communication, following Claude Shannon, is a form of selection; and selection is unfair. If Kittler's high profile is indeed unjustified, let's skip the lamenting and ask how and why it came about.

It comes as no surprise that a theorist as contested and idiosyncratic as Kittler should have enjoyed an equally slippery and skewered reception. In his case *reception* is an umbrella term that covers refraction, projection, appropriation, truncation, amputation, dissection, and remediation. The difficulties begin with a couple of basic points.

While Kittler did not indulge in the Pynchonesque reticence of a Hans Blumenberg, he was not an overly proactive self-promoter in the Anglosphere. As a result, he came to depend on intermediaries, many of whom have definite

---

4. On this point, see the excellent paper by Schüttpelz, "'Get the Message Through!'"
5. See Horn, "Editor's Introduction."
6. See Geisler, "'From Building Blocks to Radical Construction."

ideas of what his work is about. This is by no means unique to Kittler, but it is of greater importance in his case. We are dealing, as it were, with several abridged or truncated Kittlers rather than with one whole Kittler: the cool techno-archaeologist who appears, for instance, in Jussi Parikka's accounts is worlds and discourse networks apart from the "Mythographer of Paradoxes" Hans Ulrich Gumbrecht makes him out to be.[7] These different refractions also emerge on the national level. At first glance there appears to be an Anglo-American division of Kittlerian labor. In the beginning the Americans did almost everything; now both sides are at work. Two of the first three books translated into English (or, as the Germans say, into American)—*Discourse Networks* (1990) and *Gramophone, Film, Typewriter* (1999)—were issued by US publishers, while the third, the collection *Literature, Media, Information Systems* (1997), was edited and translated by American scholars for a Dutch press. Prior to 2005 virtually all the papers translated into English appeared in North American journals or collections. Then came a noticeable shift. In 2006 the British journal *Theory, Culture and Society* published the world's first Kittler special issue; it was followed in 2011 by a special issue edited by Axel Fliethmann for the Australian journal *Thesis Eleven*. The first conference ever dedicated to Kittler, and the only one during his lifetime, took place at the Tate Gallery in 2008. At the moment of this writing, the only book-length introduction to Kittler in English, *Kittler and the Media* (2011), as well as the only two book collections dedicated to him—*Media after Kittler* (2015) and *Kittler Now* (2015)—were published in the United Kingdom.

Of course, matters are not that simple. Scholarship is not divided by mid-ocean rifts and tectonic plates. Numerous American scholars contributed to the British collections; in turn, *Cultural Politics*, the British journal most active in translating Kittler, is published by Duke University Press. Nonetheless, given the traditionally anemic relationship between Britain and Germany in matters of high theory—as exemplified by the bygone phony war between Birmingham's cultural studies and Frankfurt's Critical Theory—Kittler's cross-channel incursion is no small feat. Yet it is not always clear whether recent British engagements are dealing with a "German" Kittler or one preprocessed by his American reception. Sometimes the circuitous routes of theory recall the triangular arrangements of the old slave trade. Here the real difficulties start.

To grasp what is at stake, it is necessary to briefly step back into Kittler's disciplinary beginnings. The story goes that he started out as a Germanist who then moved into media studies. Good riddance, some accounts written from a

---

7. See Parikka, *What Is Media Archaeology?*; and Gumbrecht, "Mythographer of Paradoxes."

slightly resentful Germanist perspective appear to say; he was always more interested in philosophy and technology than mere literature, and he finally got to migrate into a domain that satisfied his engineering envy. There is some truth to this caricature, but it may be more instructive when turned on its head: Kittler did not abandon *Germanistik* because he was more taken by Shannon than by Friedrich Schiller; he left because *Germanistik did not take literature seriously enough*. It failed to grasp literature's role as a cultural technique of inscription involved in constructing subjectivity on a much deeper level than was dreamed of in Frankfurt and beyond. What ultimately emerges from Kittler's early work on the coevolutionary and mutually constitutive feedback between philosophy, education, and literature in the "Discourse Network 1800" is the image of *Germanistik* as a Münchhausen discipline: producing a bevy of texts about texts, it pulled itself into a swamp of texts by its own beard and then claimed to pull itself out again by its own hair by producing yet more texts. What is necessary, Kittler claimed, was a discourse-analytic "step aside" to join Foucault *au dehors*,[8] on the outside, from which things can be seen that are forever invisible to those who hermeneutically imprison themselves inside.

You do not have to buy the diagnosis, but at the very least it should make you more skeptical of what others are peddling. More to the point, you would have expected Germanists residing in countries in which Foucault, Jacques Lacan, and Jacques Derrida had received a warmer welcome than in Germany to be more interested. As I have described in greater detail elsewhere,[9] this expectation played into Stanford's publication of *Discourse Networks*. In hindsight, Wellbery's excellent introduction performed a complex docking maneuver designed to highlight Kittler's poststructuralist connections to generate greater connectivity in the theory-heavy Francophile climate of the early 1990s.[10] Yet it did so by insinuating that in contrast to the widespread epigonal deconstructionism pervading large swaths of US academe, Kittler's work was truly radical because it spelled out the full implications of the approaches pioneered in France. Kittler was poststructuralism as it really should be. At the same time, Wellbery drew attention to those features of *Discourse Networks* that had been sidelined in Germany but that stood a greater chance of appreciation in the United States: most notably, Kittler's contingent discursive constructions of gender that allowed for an alternative to biological determination

---

8. Kittler, *Dichter Mutter Kind*, 14.

9. For a more detailed analysis of the following, see Winthrop-Young, "Krautrock, Heidegger, Bogeyman." See also Graw, Martin, and Rottmann, "Do Media Determine Our Situation?"

10. Cf. Wellbery, foreword.

without falling prey to a no less inescapable Lacanian determination. At the same time, Robert Holub, though from a more critical viewpoint, provided the first informed survey of how Kittler's work continued and revised poststructuralism.[11] Nonetheless, and even though several prominent representatives of German studies in North America (e.g., Avital Ronell, Lawrence Rickels, and Samuel Weber) continued to engage Kittler, the bulk of the reception took place elsewhere.

Why? The simple answer is that Kittler's voyage took place when the traditional transatlantic theory currents changed direction. His *inter*disciplinary shift from literature to media coincided with an *intra*disciplinary shift in North American German studies. After decades in which the latter appeared to have mimicked *Mutterlandsgermanistik*, the 1980s and 1990s witnessed a noticeable reversal of the umbilical cord. An array of isms and ologies, paradigms and approaches related to feminism, gender studies, gay studies, identity studies, (post)colonial studies, and New Historicism, was communicated east across the Atlantic. Some, no doubt, will disagree with this disparaging view of pre-1980s North American German studies. Others, however, have argued that matters were even worse. In a highly critical essay from the early 1990s Arnd Bohm summoned the spirit of Harold Innis to describe the crippling triple dependency of Canadian *Germanistik* on the disciplinary knowledge monopolies of Germany, Britain, and the United States. One of Bohm's examples of the disciplinary backwardness was the absence of any engagement with Kittler.[12] By contrast, Peter Uwe Hohendahl argued that the postwar similarities between, for instance, North American New Criticism and German *werkimmanente* hermeneutics had less to do with dependence and personnel overlap than with the fact that similar institutional and social conditions obtaining in both Germany and the United States had given rise to similar disciplinary developments.[13] To rephrase Hohendahl's analysis in biological terms, it was not a matter of homology (similarity based on common descent) but of analogy (similarity based on convergent adaptation to similar environments). The relationship between North American Germanists and their German counterparts did not resemble that between dolphins and whales but that between dolphins and sharks. But regardless of who is right, the outcome was inevitable and can be summarized in two points. (1) At the very moment in which Germany once again produced interesting and challenging theorists

---

11. Cf. Holub, *Crossing Borders*, 97–107.
12. Bohm, "Anachronisms of Canadian *Germanistik*," 62.
13. See Hohendahl, "Nationale Ausdifferenzierung der Germanistik."

such as Kittler and Niklas Luhmann, North American Germanists were less inclined to import them. (2) If you look at the list of isms and ologies that made up this second Marshall Plan, you will realize that Kittler does not fit the bill. Not only did he and Luhmann face opposing disciplinary currents, large parts of the usual welcoming committees were missing in action because they had taken offense at the new arrivals.

As a result, the formative and most interesting phase of Kittler's North American reception fell to Americanists like John Johnston, Joseph Tabbi, Bruce Clarke, Mark Seltzer, Mark Hansen, and Michael Wutz—most of whom were twentieth-century experts, many of whom came to specialize in the cross-relationships between literature, media, and culture, and few of whom had access to Kittler's untranslated texts. In hindsight, the first "Kittler collection" may well have been *Reading Matters: Narratives in the New Media Ecology* (1997), edited by Tabbi and Wutz, which featured several contributions clearly inspired by Kittler as well his well-known essay on *Gravity's Rainbow*, "Media and Drugs in Pynchon's Second World War." This collection—to which one could add Johnston's *Information Multiplicity: American Fiction in the Age of Media Saturation* (1998)—signals that Kittler's first large-scale deployment as a theorist in the Anglosphere was part of the trend toward technologically informed and theoretically updated intermedial case studies that gathered steam in the 1990s and centered on texts published between 1850 and 1950. At the risk of oversimplifying matters for the sake of producing a tangible narrative, I would argue that the common denominator of this engagement with Kittler is an antidotal impulse. His reception was part of an underlying shift in the humanities that found its institutional expression in the creation of electronic writing centers, media studies departments, and digital humanities initiatives, most of which coexist uneasily with established media and communications programs. Kittler was deployed the way Marshall McLuhan could and should have been deployed a generation earlier—as a shifter who moves the materialities of communication to the front of the stage and serves as a counterweight to precisely those paradigms that had partly scuttled his acceptance by German studies.

The net result was a conspicuous truncation: the Kittler who first emerged in (decidedly non-Germanist) North American literary studies is the Kittler of *Gramophone, Film, Typewriter*. It says something about Kittler's North American reception that "Media and Drugs in Pynchon's Second World War" has been translated no fewer than three times, while much of his work devoted to earlier epochs—the Lacanian dissertation on Conrad Ferdinand

Meyer, the study of Friedrich Hebbel, the long essays on Goethe's *Wilhelm Meister's Apprenticeship*, Schiller's *Don Carlos*, and E. T. A. Hoffmann's "Sandman"—remains untranslated.

But this is Kittler. We need to take a step back and question some of the basic assumptions underlying the preceding section.

First, metaphors like refraction, truncation, and amputation, or claims that the Atlantic transfer resulted in multiple incomplete Kittlers, imply that back home in Germany there was one whole Kittler to begin with. Conventional reception histories tend to presuppose sufficiently processed entities; a theorist abroad resembles a German car you can drive straight off the lot rather than a box of Swedish furniture you are forced to assemble. Recent discussions in reception theory, taking their cue from more complex notions of *transferts culturels*, have challenged these assumptions. As Zaur Gasimov and Carl Antonious Lemke Duque demonstrated in the instructive case of Oswald Spengler, it is misleading to reduce reception to a unidirectional communication between a defined sender and an equally defined receiver culture. Cultures—pace Kittler—are not designed by Shannon. Neither is what is communicated a clearly defined information package: instead of "so-called culturemes [*Kultureme*], that is, transfer objects with a distinct identitary essence," reception involves "so-called structuremes, that is, transfer objects with a merely identitary potentiality [*mit lediglich identitärer Potenz*]."[14] The emphasis shifts from transmitting a closed proposal to conveying an open debate that, in turn, feeds into further debates at the other end. That is precisely what mediators like Wellbery or Parikka had and have in mind when introducing some of Kittler's more volatile structuremes. It is less a matter of adding a helpful perspective than of shaking things up.

Such receptive fracturing and dissolving of theorists is easier to accomplish when the original habitat already experiences difficulty trying to pin them down. The editors of the 2003 *Festschrift FAKtisch* made the valid point that Kittler's "stupendous versatility" was able to influence so many disciplines because he never remained in one. These fertile interdisciplinary moves, in turn, were linked to the productive way in which he shuttled to and fro between academic research and less academic pursuits involving saxophones, soldering irons, and silicon: "Fortunately, though, he always did both, he welded *and* wrote, he calculated *and* taught, he programmed at night and

14. Gasimov and Lemke Duque, "Oswald Spengler als europäisches Phänomen," 9.

spent his days scribbling code on the blackboard of his office—thus he was never where his poor fellow human beings thought he was when they tried to confine him to one of their pitiful drawers."[15] Kittler is like the Scarlet Pimpernel: they seek him here, they seek him there, those interpreters seek him everywhere—which is why he is found all over the place. The North American truncations are enabled by the breaks and questionable transformations of Kittler's theorizing.

Transnational reception processes frequently involve a focus on fault lines that are of less concern—or that are deliberately blurred—at the site of original production. Immanuel Kant's epistemology is to no small degree a complex shotgun marriage of French rationalism with Anglo-Scottish empiricism; not surprisingly, French and English discussions of Kant tend to pry matters apart and focus on their respective traditions. The most prominent example by far is Charles Darwin. At the heart of Darwinian theory are a conjoined That and How. We have the notion of the transformation of species (ultimately involving a common origin), and we have the variation/selection-mechanism by which this transformation is said to come about. The first century of the international discussion of Darwin can be parsed according to how the reception habitats insisted that you can have the former without the latter. On the one hand, there is the neo-Lamarckian rewrite of Darwin in North America that tends to replace random mutation with the inheritance of acquired features (as Darwin himself was prone to do later in life). On the other hand, there is the orthogenetic approach in Germany with its Goethean reminder that the transformation of species occurs because of the unfolding of inner forces or typological blueprints.

On a more trivial level, something similar happened to both Luhmann and Kittler. The North American reception of Luhmann frequently operates by splitting his theory along horizontal lines. The "upper" epistemic or cybernetic level with its complex discussions of reentries and second-order observations is peeled off and incorporated into current debates, while the "lower" historic and semantic levels receive far less attention. In Kittler's case there is the conspicuous split along the vertical lines alluded to in the preceding section. To put it bluntly, there are at the very least three Kittlers: the discourse analyst of the 1970s, the media theorist of the 1980s and 1990s, and the Hellenistically inclined cultural technician of the early 2000s, and only the second one has really been processed in North America. However, it is insufficient (as I just did) to refer this near-exclusive focus on the "media" Kittler of the 1980s and 1990s

15. Berz, Bitsch, and Siegert, *FAKtisch*, 11.

to the academic dynamics of the receiving habitat and leave it at that. Kittler's theory—with its early, polemical mobilization of Foucauldian ruptures—is itself marked by ruptures. Driven by an affect against continuity, the younger Kittler invoked ruptures; hence his own progress as a theorist was marked by caesuras that allowed, indeed invited, the breaking off of isolated portions. As a result, the North American reception opened up some of the seams and sutures glossed over by Kittler himself. Not surprisingly, the interest has shifted from explaining what Kittler has to say to illuminating how what he said came about and evolved. This is attempted either by historicization or by identifying a mechanism that may explain how the theory jumps from discourse to media and on to cultural techniques through recursive feedback.[16]

Second, the preceding section still pays homage to an obsolete canopy model of reception. It is all summit and slide, peak and percolation: high-ranking academic *A* or school of thought *B* in country *C* is processed by theorist *X* or intellectual coterie *Y* in country *Z*, and the net result of this penthouse encounter oozes downward through graduate and undergraduate seminars, scholarly papers, conferences, and other academic habitats into the usual intellectual catchment areas that in many cases do not extend much beyond campus perimeters. Judging by recent accounts, the reception or construction of North American "French theory" seems to have followed this pattern.[17] Derrida and Lacan come to Johns Hopkins, and Ivy League schools start secreting a peculiar variant of deconstruction that is then picked up and recycled by less ivied institutions. Foucault and Deleuze come to the New York Schizo Conference, and across the nation adventurous academic habitats turn anti-oedipal, rhizomatic, or biopolitical. Jean Baudrillard is invited to haunt the coasts, and sections of Manhattan and the Bay Area go into full simulation mode that is then mimicked in the hinterland. Ultimately, everything coalesces into a scandalous bubbling morass that barrels down the academic pyramid like pyroclastic flows on the slopes of an erupting volcano to clog and bury the American Mind. Such reception models double down on the trickle-down model. However, accounting for the reception or construction of German media theory in this way erases precisely what the theory professes to be about: media.

We need to approach matters differently. In a world of decentralized global terror networks, intelligence experts increasingly rely on "intelligence chatter," a form of signals traffic analysis that monitors the rates, spikes, and

16. E.g., Pias, "Friedrich Kittler und der 'Mißbrauch von Heeresgerät'"; Winthrop-Young, "Discourse, Media, Cultural Techniques."

17. Cf. Cusset, *French Theory*; and Lotringer and Cohen, *French Theory in America*.

lulls of suspect communication channels. In one of the more interesting extensions of both metaphor and procedure, epidemiologists now speak of "viral chatter."[18] Rather than wait for a virus such as HIV to cross the simian-human interspecies boundary, work its way up the infection pyramid, and mutate into a pandemic threat, we need to monitor the front lines of first contact. Ideally, every time a hunter in the African jungle kills a monkey (and killing complete with skinning and gutting is the most intimate encounter and therefore the most effective viral conduit), blood samples should be taken, analyzed, and centrally registered. Monitoring these encounters will allow virologists to keep track of which viruses are circulating through which monkey population at a given time and, if need be, correlate the data with the localized outbreak of human diseases. The same applies to theories. A theory, after all, is a viral form of intelligence (though admittedly not always an intelligent virus). The equivalent of a pandemic, in turn, is the influential book "one has to read." But why wait for the latter to be translated, reviewed, and canonized? There is, of course, nothing wrong with books or academic monographs as long as you keep in mind that they are relatively late-aggregate states in the evolution and transfer of knowledge. Increasingly, however, the guiding conditions for reception processes are located in other media.

One amusing example known to the Kittlerati: between September 2014 and February 2016 a Twitter account run by "Justin Kittler"—the avatar is a composite image of Justin Bieber and Friedrich Kittler—featured over twenty thousand messages that attributed the tabloid life of Bieber to Kittler, from "Friedrich Kittler to cover up his Selena Gomez tattoo" to "Friedrich Kittler planning to adopt another pet monkey." Does this help us understand the intricacies of German subhermeneutics? Or the Lacanian logic of the mediatized unconscious? Probably not. But it somehow makes sense; or at least more so than a Rihanna/Reinhart Koselleck mash-up. The tongue-in-many-cheeks remediation of the media theorist (which also highlights the dynamics of media-enabled intellectual celebrity culture) serves as a reminder that any full account of the Kittler effect needs to pay attention to the *theory chatter* of social media (remember that in the intelligence context *chatter* is not a disparaging term). This, needless to say, is just another indication of the decline of authority suffered by traditional academic gatekeepers. Webpages, blogs, forums, snapchats, e-mail discussions, and so on are among the initial crucibles of the American Kittlers, Luhmanns, or Sloterdijks—not to mention the monocled Adorno who appears as the avatar on Eric Jarosinski's popular *Nein* Twitter account. (Which makes a lot of sense: Are not some of the one-liners

18. Wolfe, *Viral Storm*, 179.

in *Minima Moralia* among philosophy's greatest predigital tweets?) Media—social media—determine the situation of our media theorists, also and especially of those who had little to say about social media.

Third, there is a moment of allopatric appropriation. It recalls the Bible's repeated claim (Matthew 13:57, Mark 6:4, Luke 4:24, and John 4:44) that prophets count for little in their home country. At first glance this does not apply to Kittler, who certainly enjoyed his share of domestic success. However, it is less a matter of home countries ignoring their prophet than of other countries claiming to better understand them because, somehow, what these prophets had to say can only be fully understood abroad.

A few years ago Milan Kundera published a beautiful essay in which he chided the French for not appreciating one of their major authors, even though he happens to bear the name of their nation: Anatole France.[19] Specifically, Kundera cited the lack of domestic appreciation for France's 1912 novel *Les dieux ont soif*. But why did the novel invite such domestic disregard? It appears that France bit off more history than any French novelist can chew. He violated the specifically French variant of the Second Commandment: Thou shalt not make a graven image of *la Grande Révolution*. Since the ideological bandwidth of his well-intended sentimental plot fell short of the revolution's real amplitude, France resembled an overly ambitious music teacher trying to get the local brass band to do justice to Beethoven. But Kundera went a step farther. Not only were French readers compelled to dismiss any attempt to contain the mythic singularity at their core of their history within a novel, Kundera also insinuated that he, a foreigner who had fled communism and its claim to have wrought an even greater revolution, was better equipped to appreciate some of the core achievements of *Les dieux ont soif*. In the figure of the painter and revolutionary juror Évariste Gamelin, France was the first writer to have depicted one of the great banes of the twentieth century: the politically committed artist who, if given power, will send people to the guillotine with the same zeal that he executes his brushstrokes. This was beyond the scope of French readers.

There are numerous other examples. It is difficult to read Carl Schmitt's *Leviathan in the State Theory of Thomas Hobbes* without rubbing up against the insinuation that English political theory—not to mention English political reality—never took the full measure of Hobbes and thus lags behind German discussions of Hobbes.[20] But closer to Kittler (not that Schmitt is that far removed from him), in his engaging look back at the US reception of Deleuze

19. See Kundera, *Encounter*, 41–60.
20. Cf. Dyzenhaus, "Leviathan in the 1930s."

and Baudrillard in the wild early 1980s, Sylvère Lotringer notes that their theories, brushed off as a "Science Fiction" in their home country, received such an enthusiastic welcome in places like New York because they seemed so "uncannily realistic."[21] Parts of Parisian poststructuralism were always already about America; no wonder it flourished more abundantly over there. A lot of the hypertext hype of the 1990s followed the same lines. The new (American) possibilities of electronic writing were described as "an almost embarrassingly literal embodiment" of Derrida and Roland Barthes.[22] Hypertext was nothing less than "a vindication of postmodern literary theory."[23] Much like an oversized airplane that arrives years ahead of schedule over an underdeveloped region and is forced to circle the clouds and wait for the ground crew to build an adequate runway, French theory appeared to be locked in a holding pattern with little chance of a touchdown in reality. But once the new technologies are in place, they will bring about nothing less than the promise/prospect of making theory itself superfluous, since "what is unnatural in print becomes natural in the electronic medium and will soon no longer need saying at all, because it can be shown."[24] Computers redeem the philosophers of Gulliver's Lagado: Why use words if we can wield digital things instead? While Europeans are subject to repetition compulsion, Americans are prone to suffer from redemption compulsion (*Erlösungszwang*): just as the America of the early 1800s would cleanse and redeem dirty European steam-age technology,[25] the America of the late 1990s would redeem convoluted European computer-age theories.

There is a similar gesture in the appropriations of Kittler, whose media theory is decoded—not without some justification—as the theoretical equivalent of American visions of the future, including the *Terminator* and *Matrix* movies.[26] Many obituaries implied that Kittler had described a world in which humans are targeted by merciless computers. This is narcissist nonsense. Kittler was too deeply influenced by Martin Heidegger to peddle the old Pinocchio fallacy that our creations have nothing better to do than covet our humanity. To claim that we are in the crosshairs of machines is a feeble attempt to prop up an endangered anthropocentrism. Kittler's technological gloomsday scenario was more complex, but on a deeper zeitgeist level the Kittler-Hollywood link

---

21. Lotringer, "Better than Life," 195.
22. Landow, *Hypertext*, 34.
23. Bolter, "Literature in the Electronic Writing Space," 24.
24. Bolter, *Writing Space*, 43.
25. See the classic study by Marx, *Machine in the Garden*.
26. For a more detailed discussion of the Kittler-cyberpunk connection, see Winthrop-Young, "Machine Learning."

hits the mark. To return to the beginning of this article, in terms of (dark chrome) content and (hourglass-shaped) appearance, German media theory resembles cyberpunk. Cyberpunk, too, was first described as an accumulation of individual writers (William Gibson, Bruce Sterling, John Shirley, and others); then, in a purist reduction, Gibson's *Neuromancer* trilogy was singled out as the only truly representative achievement; and now we are back to a broader view in which cyberpunk is almost as it appears in the first footnote of Fredric Jameson's canonical essay on postmodernism—"the supreme literary expression if not of postmodernism, then of late capitalism itself."[27] On this level, the construct called German media theory, and its Kittlerian centerpiece in particular, was associated with the inebriating future fatigue that emerged in 1980s. It became part and parcel of a cultural constant cutting across medial, academic, and cultural domains. "If you wish to know an era," William Gibson noted, "study its most lucid nightmares."[28] These days, theorists rise to prominence when their dreams are no less stark than those of the best science fiction writers.[29]

At the end of the first section I gave a brusque rejoinder to the sour-grapes question of why Kittler enjoyed so much attention. It is time for a more diplomatic response that, in conclusion, offers a short outlook on the fate of German media theory *after* Kittler—with the inevitable reminder that *nach*, the German word for "after," also means "according to."[30]

Kittler was a bit like his idol Heidegger. Apart from the fact that they both spent a lot of time in Freiburg and shared an appreciation for the poetry of Friedrich Hölderlin and the achievements of the German Wehrmacht, there is a revealing similarity between the two related to their progeny. Throughout his career Heidegger attracted students who embarked on notable careers of their own that took them far away from the master. By contrast, none of those who remained too close to the nest and came to think and write like Heidegger ever came up with anything Heidegger had not already written or thought better.

27. Jameson, *Postmodernism*, 491.

28. Gibson, *Distrust That Particular Flavor*, 171.

29. To be sure, Kittler himself is partly to blame for this allopatric appropriation. Before he voiced decidedly less flattering assessments of US academe, he was happy to recycle hackneyed notions of America as a haven of technophilia, claiming that *Gramophone, Film, Typewriter* would be better understood by Americans than Germans because it starred Thomas Edison. "Edison . . . is an important figure for American culture, like Goethe for German culture. But between Goethe and myself there is Edison. Germans don't like to hear this, but naturally Americans do" (Griffin and Herrmann, "Technologies of Writing," 735).

30. On this point, see Geoghegan, "After Kittler."

The same applies to Kittler. The most uninteresting portion of the Kittler effect is the ongoing production of epigonal, if not downright cloned, Kittlerian analyses written as if the master were still in Bochum taking apart his first PCs (known to insiders as "totally eighties"). Among the contributors to the *Grey Room* special issue "German Media Studies," however, are scholars such as Bernhard Siegert, Cornelia Vismann, and Markus Krajewski, for whom at one point the engagement with Kittler may have been as decisive as Kittler's with Heidegger or Foucault, but who cannot be labeled Kittlerians (as little as Hans Jonas, Günther Anders, Hannah Arendt, Karl Löwith, or Herbert Marcuse can be labeled Heideggerians). But these are the scholars—to which one must add Wolfgang Ernst—who presently are at the center of the transatlantic engagement with the next iteration of German media theory.

I would suggest that this spectrum—the wide bottom of the hourglass—is best described as unfolding between two names: Siegert and Ernst. In terms of publication profile and theory chatter, they have become the most debated representatives of two approaches that are both tied to and untied from Kittler's work: Siegert stands for the cultural techniques approach and Ernst for the more radical German variant of media archaeology. To rephrase this in facetious terms: if Kittler, the late paterfamilias of a rambunctious theory clan, was also a bit like Hegel (and on occasion he came close to insinuating this), then think of Siegert as the leading left-wing and Ernst as the leading right-wing Kittlerian.

Once again, *Grey Room* deserves a lot of credit, especially with the publication of several essays by Siegert that have attracted considerable interest.[31] This time there is no transatlantic delay in the Anglosphere. *Theory, Culture and Society* published the first Anglophone special issue dedicated to *Kulturtechniken* already in 2013. The same applies to Ernst. Several English translations have appeared almost simultaneously in the United States, Britain, and Holland.[32] There is, however, one revealing difference between the two in terms of their respective receptions. Observers in the Anglosphere were quick to note that the cultural techniques concept represents a refined softening of Kittler's media-theoretical work. It goes beyond *Medienwissenschaften* by carefully teasing apart, among many other things, the reified concept of media at the center of Kittler's work up until the late 1990s. More to the point, by describing cultural techniques as operative chains and distinction-generating mechanisms that give rise to ontological entities that are then said to precede

31. Siegert, "Cacography or Communication"; Siegert, "Doors." See also Siegert, *Cultural Techniques*.

32. Ernst, *Chronopoetics*; Ernst, *Sonic Time Machines*; Ernst, *Digital Memory and the Archive*.

these distinctions (and that include the ontologized entity *media*), the approach includes moments of praxis and agency sidelined by Kittler. It comes as no surprise, therefore, that the interest in the *Kulturtechniken* concept is to no small degree based on the perception that the concept is very similar to, and therefore maybe compatible with, approaches already established in North America: actor-network-theory, the work of Bruno Latour, various shades of OOO (object-oriented ontologies), and parts of US-style posthumanism up to and including critical animal studies. Siegert himself is not too happy with these parallels; there is the danger that too much transatlantic harmony may extract the concept's canine teeth inherited, in no small part, from Kittler.

Matters are different in the case of Ernst. For those who went through Kittler's Foucauldian purgatory, the media archaeology practiced in the Anglosphere is a hybrid affair because it tends to waver between two very different orientations. On the one hand, media archaeology is the excavation, retrieval, and resuscitation of media dead, lost, forgotten, discarded, and silenced. It is in many instances a highly political project that takes issue with conventional media histories by offering alternate micro-archaeologies and technological counterhistories. Yet as rebellious as these critical tales may be, they remain well within established historiographical paradigms. The winners and losers of media history may change; the emplotments do not. From a narratological perspective, such redemptions of preterit media remain pretty conventional. On the other hand, media archaeology professes to be the technological update of Foucault's archaeology of knowledge. Foucault's contested *historical a priori*, which Kittler and others updated into a *technological a priori*, but which is any case an *archival a priori*, signifies successive sets of ongoing initial ruling conditions that are both *within* history insofar as they determine a finite regime of time, and *without* insofar as they, first, defy attempts to weave together successive regimes into a continuous narrative and, second, raise the epistemological quandary of how one is to reflect on the conditions that determine such reflection in the first place. This is precisely where Ernst enters the debate. His work, like Kittler's, comes as a challenge, an antidotal reminder that the machines are maybe even more of a force than even Kittler ever made them out to be. Not only have they become their own archivists, but, by means of digitally enabled axis manipulation, they operate outside historical time.[33] Here the work of German media theory turns into something that Kittler hinted at in one of his cryptic asides and that Ernst made the focus of countless texts. We are no longer dealing with media determining our situation but *with media generating and determining their own*

---

33. For more on this point, see Winthrop-Young, "Siren Recursions."

time. This, finally, links so-called German media theory to current debates about the fracturing of times out of joint.[34] When Kittler pronounced that media cross one another in a time that is no longer history,[35] he may have provided the first impulse for a possible progression from German media theory to German time theory. If under conditions of machine time, it still makes sense to speak of here and now, this is where we are now.

References

Berz, Peter, Annette Bitsch, and Bernhard Siegert, eds. 2003. *FAKtisch: Festschrift für Friedrich Kittler zum 60. Geburtstag*. Munich: Fink.

Bohm, Arnd. 1992. "Anachronisms in Canadian *Germanistik*." In *Challenges of Germanistik: Traditions and Prospects of an Academic Discipline*, edited by Eitel Timm, 48–68. Munich: Iudicium.

Bolter, Jay. 1991. *Writing Space: The Computer, Hypertext, and the History of Writing*. Hillsdale, NJ: Erlbaum.

———. 1992. "Literature in the Electronic Writing Space." In *Literacy Online: The Promise (and Peril) of Reading and Writing with Computers*, edited by Myron C. Tuman, 19–42. Pittsburgh: University of Pittsburgh Press.

Breger, Claudia. 2009. "Zur Debatte um den 'Sonderweg deutsche Medienwissenschaft.'" *Zeitschrift für Medienwissenschaft*, no. 1: 124–27.

Cusset, François. 2008. *French Theory: How Foucault, Derrida, Deleuze, and Co. Transformed the Intellectual Life of the United States*, translated by Jeff Fort. Minneapolis: University of Minnesota Press.

Dyzenhaus, David. 2002. "Leviathan in the 1930s: The Reception of Hobbes in the Third Reich." In *Confronting Mass Democracy and Industrial Technology: Political and Social Theory from Nietzsche to Habermas*, edited by John P. McCormick, 163–91. Durham, NC: Duke University Press.

Ernst, Wolfgang. 2013. *Digital Memory and the Archive*, edited by Jussi Parikka. Minneapolis: University of Minnesota Press.

———. 2016. *Chronopoetics: The Temporal Being and Operativity of Technological Media*, translated by Anthony Enns. London: Rowman and Littlefield.

———. 2016. *Sonic Time Machines: Explicit Sound, Sirenic Voices, and Implicit Sonicity*. Amsterdam: Amsterdam University Press.

Gasimov, Zaur, and Carl Antonius Lemke Duque. 2013. "Oswald Spengler als europäisches Phänomen: Die Kultur- und Geschichtsmorphologie als Auslöser und Denkrahmen eines transnationalen Europa-Diskurses." In *Oswald Spengler als europäisches Phänomen*, edited by Zaur Gasimov and Carl Antonius Lemke Duque, 7–14. Göttingen: Vandenhoeck und Ruprecht.

---

34. E.g., Lorenz and Bevernage, *Breaking Up Time*; Hartog, *Régimes d'historicité*. For a good overview (including links to Koselleck's notion of *Zeitschichten*), see Jordheim, "Introduction: Multiple Times."

35. Kittler, *Gramophone*, 115.

Geisler, Michael. 1999. "From Building Blocks to Radical Construction: West German Media Theory since 1984." *New German Critique*, no. 78: 75–107.

Geoghegan, Bernard Dionysius. 2013. "After Kittler: On the Cultural Techniques of Recent German Media Theory." *Theory, Culture and Society* 30, no. 6: 66–82.

Gibson, William. 2012. *Distrust That Particular Flavor.* New York: Putnam.

Graw, Isabelle, Reinhold Martin, and André Rottmann. 2015. "Do Media Determine Our Situation? Reflections on the Transatlantic Reception of Friedrich Kittler." *Texte zur Kunst*, no. 98: 46–79.

Griffin, Matthew, and Susanne Herrmann. 1996. "Technologies of Writing: Interview with Friedrich A. Kittler." *New Literary History* 27, no. 4: 731–42.

Gumbrecht, Hans Ulrich. 2016. "Mythographer of Paradoxes: How Friedrich Kittler's Legacy Matters." *Critical Inquiry* 42, no. 4: 952–58.

Hartog, François. 2012. *Régimes d'historicité: Présentisme et expériences du temps.* Paris: Points.

Heinevetter, Nele, and Nadine Sanchez. 2008. *Was mit Medien: Theorie in 15 Sachgeschichten.* Munich: Fink.

Hohendahl, Peter Uwe. 2000. "Nationale Ausdifferenzierungen der Germanistik: Das Beispiel der USA." In *Literaturwissenschaft und Wissenschaftsforschung*, edited by Jörg Schönert, 357–81. Stuttgart: Metzler.

Holub, Robert. 1992. *Crossing Borders: Reception Theory, Poststructuralism, Deconstruction.* Madison: University of Wisconsin Press.

Horn, Eva. 2007. "Editor's Introduction: 'There Are No Media.'" *Grey Room*, no. 29: 6–13.

Jameson, Fredric. 1991. *Postmodernism; or, The Cultural Logic of Late Capitalism.* London: Verso.

Jordheim, Helge. 2014. "Introduction: Multiple Times and the Work of Synchronization." *History and Theory* 53, no. 4: 498–518.

Kittler, Friedrich. 1991. *Dichter Mutter Kind.* Munich: Fink.

———. 1999. *Gramophone, Film, Typewriter*, translated by Geoffrey Winthrop-Young and Michael Wutz. Stanford, CA: Stanford University Press.

Kundera, Milan. 2010. *Encounter*, translated by Linda Asher. New York: HarperCollins.

Landow, George. 1992. *Hypertext: The Convergence of Contemporary Critical Theory and Technology.* Baltimore, MD: Johns Hopkins University Press.

Lethen, Helmut. 2010. "Wie deutsch ist die deutsche Kultur- und Medienwissenschaft?" In *Kulturwissenschaften in Europa—eine grenzüberschreitende Disziplin?*, edited by Andrea Allerkamp and Gérard Raulet, 128–36. Münster: Westfälisches Dampfboot.

Lorenz, Chris, and Berber Bevernage, eds. 2013. *Breaking Up Time: Negotiating the Borders between Present, Past, and Future.* Göttingen: Vandenhoeck und Ruprecht.

Lotringer, Sylvère. 2003. "Better than Life—My 80s." *Artforum*, April, 194–97, 252–53.

Lotringer, Sylvère, and Sande Cohen. 2001. *French Theory in America.* New York: Routledge.

Lovink, Geert. 2008. "Whereabouts of German Media Theory." In *Zero Comment: Blogging and Critical Internet Culture*, 83–98. New York: Routledge.

Marx, Leo. 2000. *The Machine in the Garden: Technology and the Pastoral Ideal in America.* New York: Oxford University Press.

Parikka, Jussi. 2012. *What Is Media Archaeology?* Cambridge: Polity.

Peters, John. 2008. "Strange Sympathies: Horizons of German and American Media Theory." In *American Studies as Media Studies*, edited by Frank Kelleter and Daniel Stein, 3–23. Heidelberg: Winter.

Pias, Claus. 2015. "Friedrich Kittler und der 'Mißbrauch von Heeresgerät': Zur Situation eines Denkbildes 1964–1984–2014." *Merkur*, no. 791: 31–43.

———. 2015. "What's German about German Media Theory?" In *Media Transatlantic: Developments in Media and Communication Studies between North American and German-Speaking Europe*, edited by Norm Friesen, 15–27. Hamburg: Springer.

Schüttpelz, Erhard. 2010. "'Get the Message Through': From the Channel of Communication to the Message of the Medium (1945–1960)." In *Media, Culture, and Mediality: New Insights into the Current State of Research*, edited by Ludwig Jäger, Erika Linz, and Irmela Schneider, 109–38. Bielefeld: Transcript.

Siegert, Bernhard. 2007. "Cacography or Communication? Cultural Techniques in German Media Studies." *Grey Room*, no. 29: 27–47.

———. 2012. "Doors: On the Materiality of the Symbolic." *Grey Room*, no. 47: 6–23.

———. 2015. *Cultural Techniques: Grids, Filters, Doors, and Other Articulations of the Real*, translated by Geoffrey Winthrop-Young. New York: Fordham University Press.

Wellbery, David. 1990. Foreword to Friedrich Kittler, *Discourse Networks 1800/1900*, translated by Michael Metteer and Chris Cullens, vii–xxxiii. Stanford, CA: Stanford University Press.

Winthrop-Young, Geoffrey. 2008. "Von gelobten und verfluchten Medienländern: Kanadischer Gesprächsvorschlag zu einem deutschen Theoriephänomen." *Zeitschrift für Kulturwissenschaften*, no. 2: 113–27.

———. 2011. "Krautrock, Heidegger, Bogeyman: Kittler in the Anglosphere." *Thesis Eleven* 107, no. 1: 6–20.

———. 2012. "Machine Learning: Friedrich Kittler (1943–2011)." *Artforum*, September, 473–79.

———. 2015. "Discourse, Media, Cultural Techniques: The Complexity of Kittler." *Modern Language Notes* 130, no. 3: 447–65.

———. 2015. "Siren Recursions." In *Kittler Now: Current Perspectives in Kittler Studies*, edited by Stephen Sale and Laura Salisbury, 71–94. Cambridge: Polity.

Wolfe, Nathan. 2011. *The Viral Storm: The Dawn of a New Pandemic Age*. New York: Holt.

"Half a Heart and Double Zeal": Critical Theory's Afterlife in the United States

Robert Zwarg

In an essay called "Tradition," added to the third edition of *Dissonanzen* in 1963, Theodor W. Adorno begins with referencing a famous metaphor for philosophy's relationship to history: the owl of Minerva. Originally from Greek mythology, the ancient symbol for wisdom and knowledge in his *Elements of the Philosophy of Right*, where he declared that "the owl of Minerva begins its flight only with the onset of dusk."[1] Only when the day is drawing to a close— or, in Hegel's words, "when actuality has gone through its formative process and attained its completed state"[2]—can philosophy comprehend "its own time . . . in thoughts."[3] Philosophy, in other words, always comes too late and is endowed with a fundamental, constitutive secondarity. Adorno's reiteration of Hegel's dictum in the still untranslated essay, however, renders it more specific, as if informed by the wreckage that had piled up by the mid-twentieth century and with more attention to the consequences of said secondarity for the subject of thought:

An earlier version of this article was presented at the conference "Transatlantic Theory Transfer: Missed Encounters?" in New York City, May 27–28, 2015. I want to warmly thank the organizers for the invitation and their comments on my paper as for their support during the work on my dissertation, which has been published under the title *Die Kritische Theorie in Amerika: Das Nachleben einer Tradition*. I also thank Martin Jay for the use of his private collection for the dissertation and this article and Paul Reitter for his thoughts on the paper.

    1. Hegel, *Elements of the Philosophy of Right*, 23.
    2. Ibid.
    3. Ibid., 21.

New German Critique 132, Vol. 44, No. 3, November 2017
DOI 10.1215/0094033X-4162335   © 2017 by New German Critique, Inc.

> Hegel's word that the owl of Minerva begins its flight only with the onset of dusk affirms itself in the history of spirit, insofar as thought tends to focus on concepts which, as they say, have become problematic; when they're no longer adequate to what they designate and when they seem to be doomed to vanish. The contemplation, which then seizes upon these concepts, seeks, with half a heart and double zeal, to salvage them.[4]

While uncannily true for a whole array of political issues of our time, this is also likely to be the most poignant formulation for the extraordinary efforts— the "double zeal"—to appropriate, understand, and continue critical theory in the United States of America that began in the wake of the crisis of the New Left at the end of the 1960s, most notably in journals like *Telos* (founded in 1968 in Buffalo, New York) and, of course, *New German Critique* (founded in 1973 in Madison, Wisconsin). And even though these efforts were by no means, in a literal sense, undertaken halfheartedly, this formulation does aptly catch the doubts that have accompanied the reception of critical theory almost from the outset. Ever present was the question of whether Adorno et al.'s words speak to the decades after 1968 or whether they work in America at all. Regarding the latter, the subconscious insecurities over the historical adequateness of critical theory's texts lead into the discourse on the differences between the Old and the New Worlds—a juxtaposition most commonly associated with Hegel as well, who in *Lectures on the Philosophy of World History* had dubbed America "a land of the future,"[5] outside world history. The travels of critical theory across the ocean, to a country once scorned as the least philosophical of all,[6] are thus not only to be measured in miles, so to speak; the cultural-geographic distance is much longer. On the shores of the other side, the words of critical theory absorb more and another history than the one already ingrained in them, for, as Adorno said, words and history are not separate things but "history breaks into words, establishing their truth-character."[7] Studying the American reception of critical theory, if only in this specific fragment of a field, which by the 1980s had become vast and complex, is as much about the Frankfurt tradition and its legacy as about the United States.

First Encounters; or, The Owl of Minerva in Waterloo

Unlike the cases of other German luminaries of theory, like Niklas Luhmann, it is obvious, evidenced by libraries filling up with an ever-growing

---

4. Adorno, *Dissonanzen*, 127. My translation.
5. Hegel, *Lectures on the Philosophy of World History*, 193.
6. Tocqueville, *Democracy in America*, 698.
7. Adorno, "Theses on the Language of the Philosopher," 35n (translation modified).

research literature, that there has been an encounter between the United States and the so-called Frankfurt School (a denomination not coined by the critical theorists themselves but reluctantly adopted once it became widely used in the postwar Federal Republic of Germany). Critical theory and its cultural and historical context are, in fact, firmly established in the university, in reading, writing, and teaching, so much so that in 2001 a Columbia University professor, Mark Anderson—certainly angering his German studies colleagues—complained about the displacement of the traditional canon of Goethe and Friedrich Schiller in favor of the works by Theodor W. Adorno, Walter Benjamin, and Paul Celan, who, as he alleged, persisted in the curriculum only because of politically correct solidarity with the Jewish victims of the Holocaust.[8] Thus, on a factual level, the encounter between America and the Frankfurt tradition was not at all missed. A heuristic look, however, at the etymology of the word *encounter* discloses a more complex semantic field. Not only does the French noun *encontre* mean "meeting"; it also means "fight" and "opportunity." Farther down this road we arrive at the original Latin root *incontra*, meaning "in front of" or, even more literally, "in-against." One could thus posit that the depth and complexity of the American reception of critical theory comes into light only when understood literally as an "in-against," that is, something that happened *in* a special context and was directed *against* certain social, political, and academic conditions as well as *against* certain elements of critical theory itself. The afterlife of critical theory in America, in other words, is to be understood as an intellectual transformation, fraught with frictions, understandings, and misunderstandings.

The early period of the reception of critical theory in the United States, the 1960s and 1970s, is indicative of the larger context in which the Frankfurt tradition was appropriated and contains many topoi and arguments that persist until the beginning of the 1990s. After all, the American reception of critical theory is part and parcel of the "long Sixties"—the cultural and intellectual ramifications of which are still debated today. One important event from this early period, after the reception picked up speed in scattered places like Berkeley, Buffalo, New York City, and Madison, takes us out of the United States to Canada, far away from the centers of student activism on the East and West Coasts or Chicago. In 1970 *Telos* held its first of many conferences in a city that got its name from the most iconic of defeats: Waterloo (Ontario).[9] The

8. Anderson, "German Intellectuals, Jewish Victims."

9. See Anonymous, "First *Telos* International Conference," as well as the thorough and indispensable article by Genosko, Gandesha, and Marcellus, "Waterloo."

"First *Telos* International Conference" originally had no title, nor was it supposed to be more than a discussion forum for the editors and authors of the still very young journal, which was started in 1968 in Buffalo and edited from the third issue until his death in 2004 by the energetic yet controversial Paul Piccone, born in 1940 in L'Aquila, Italy. His family had emigrated to the United States when he was thirteen years old, to Rochester, New York.[10] The conference could take pride in its internationalism; among the panelists was the later editor of *New Left Review*, Robin Blackburn; the late secretary of Leon Trotsky, Raya Dunayevskaya (who allegedly arrived in a limousine with a chauffeur); the structural Marxist Lucio Colletti; and Albrecht Wellmer. It should be stressed that neither critical theory nor Western Marxism was the explicit object of the conference, mostly because its contours were not known yet. Rather, the discovery of the Frankfurt theorists was part of an excursion, a large-scale unearthing of a hitherto unknown tradition. The conference proceedings were published by *Telos* as *Towards a New Marxism*.[11] On the cover was an alphabetical sequence of names that indicates how rough the contours of what is now known as Western Marxism were at the time: the names included Adorno, Ernst Bloch, and Georg Lukács but also Immanuel Kant and Edmund Husserl, as well as forgotten authors like Tran Duc Thao or a Stalinist like Andrei Zhdanov. This was a visible attempt to construct genealogies and to make sense of an unfamiliar history—an "unknown dimension," according to a later volume edited by Dick Howard and Karl E. Klare.[12]

More interesting than the actual presentations (e.g., on Lukács, Bloch, Vladimir Lenin, and the Second International) are the overall character of the conference and its evaluation by the organizers. Only about a hundred people attended, a mixture of young activists ("politicos"), people in the midst of their dissertations, interested students, and so on. This heterogeneity as well as the diverging interests of the participants seemed to result in rocky proceedings. The conference was interrupted many times, plans were changed, talks pushed back or canceled, mostly because of escalating discussions about strategy and tactics, and the persistent confrontation of the two key concepts at the time: theory and practice. "As it turned out," an anonymous report (judging by its tone, authored by Piccone) in *Telos* said,

> the conference was attacked for being abstract, obscure and incomprehensible. The organizers' only defense from these charges is that people for whom

10. For a biographical sketch, see Jacoby, "Outside Academe," 59.
11. See Grahl and Piccone, *Towards a New Marxism*.
12. Howard and Klare, *Unknown Dimension*.

names such as Lukács, De Leon, or Korsch connote the local brand of hot dogs or Spanish *conquistadores* should not have bothered to come or, if they chose to come, they should have listened rather than immediately demanding, how can I use things such as Lukács's theory of reification to obliterate the bourgeoisie.[13]

Contrary to this evaluation, however, the report concluded: "Most people left with a general feeling that a conference dealing with theoretical problems might be a good idea! After creeping down the runway for four days, the owl of Minerva finally got airborne!"[14]

This is yet another echo of Hegel's famous remark and its Adornian reprise, one, however, that bears the mark of the political crisis that the New Left found itself in at the time, exemplifying what one could call, to borrow Russell Jacoby's phrase, a "dialectic of defeat":[15] the transformation of practical failure into theoretical success, rendering a political impasse into an opportunity for a much-needed pause and reflection. The epitome of this crisis is, of course, the 1969 convention of the Students for a Democratic Society in Chicago, which resulted in a split that gave birth to numerous competing factions, the most notorious being the Weathermen. A volume, published in 1970 and edited by Paul Breines, bears the telling title *Critical Interruptions*, evoking the gesture of breaking through the chatter of New Left common sense. Even though Herbert Marcuse was and is still proclaimed the "guru" of the New Left, Breines's volume was arguably the first thorough engagement with Marcuse from a New Left perspective. Breines's depiction of the crisis could not have been more dramatic:

> At present the New Left appears to have utterly and decisively freaked out—and it may have. . . . Actions and theories are now upheld or denounced in the name of Marxism-Leninism, proletarian internationalism, revolutionary discipline, the working class, the Black Panther Party, Chairman Mao, the National Liberation Front of Vietnam, the dictatorship of the proletariat, the seizure of state power, armed struggle, and, here and there, Stalin, Georgi Dimitrov, and the Peoples' Republic of Albania. At least momentarily, genuine *auto-critique* or critical self-reflection is scarce.[16]

This crisis resounded not only in Waterloo but also in Madison, where at the beginning of the 1970s plans were made to start a journal—the early

13. Anonymous, "First *Telos* International Conference," 296.
14. Ibid., 317.
15. Jacoby, *Dialectic of Defeat*.
16. Breines, "From Guru to Spectre," 9.

history of which has been recalled in these very pages—that eventually came out in 1973: *New German Critique*.[17] Familiar with the *Telos* milieu—not the least because Piccone not only wrote in the journal but also typeset and printed *New German Critique* until the 1990s, even though he had predicted not more than one issue[18]—the journal then embarked on its own journey to make sense of what had happened to the New Left, whose ever more militant and violent reverberations could be felt at the very spot of *New German Critique*'s founding, when an army research center on the campus of UW Madison was bombed in 1970, killing one graduate student. Not as vocal or programmatic as its older sister *Telos*, *New German Critique* was nevertheless shaped by the same political and cultural context. While *Telos* directed its anti-institutional rage against established philosophy and academic discourse *tout court*, *New German Critique* emerged as an immanent critique of German studies, which resulted first in the successful establishment of the study of the German Democratic Republic as a legitimate field and second in the introduction of the canon of German-Jewish thought into the discipline. For years to come, both *Telos* and *New German Critique* looked for answers on the other side of the pond, in the intellectual history of not just the Frankfurt tradition but Western Marxism and the Weimar Republic as well; the energy that went into writing, commenting, and not the least, translating previously unavailable texts can hardly be overstated. It was only in the 1980s that the trajectories of both journals began to diverge sharply, mostly through debates (in either of the journals) on the German peace movement, German attempts to cope with the past, and the emerging civil democracies in eastern Europe. At the outset, however, both journals' intensive engagement with critical theory, their efforts to familiarize themselves with an unknown dimension—efforts of "double zeal," so to speak—exemplify a crucial difference between the German and the American reception of the Frankfurt tradition. While in Germany the "short summer of theory" (Detlev Claussen) happened at the political climax of the student movement, its most optimistic phase, before turning against the former intellectual forefathers (epitomized in the occupation of the Institute for Social Research in January 1969), the American reception was the product of a crisis. In a way, the American reception was actually closer to the dynamic that Adorno describes in the quote at the beginning of this article. While in Germany, critical theory at the end of the 1960s was slowly ground down between a conservative political landscape and inner-school, academic quarrels, with some exceptions

17. Huyssen and Rabinbach, "*New German Critique*."
18. Ibid., 12.

resulting in philology being the hiding place of the Frankfurt tradition, what happened in the United States were indeed efforts to salvage various concepts that had become problematic.

There is, however, another dimension applicable to Adorno's curious formulation of the "double zeal." It speaks to the hypothesis—most recently argued by Philipp Felsch[19]—that "Theorie" as a genre distinguishes itself from other modes of thinking through an affective or emotional surplus, an unnamed, often subconscious desire attached to the books of Adorno or Benjamin, one that goes beyond the arguments of these writings. In other words, theory as it emerges in the late 1960s, lauding the ascendance of Hegel's owl of Minerva, is itself a specific practice, embedded in an extratextual force field of political aspirations, almost existential matters, and a certain dissatisfaction with the academic and political discussion. This undercurrent in the American reception of critical theory does not often manifest itself overtly. It does, however, emerge in commemorations of teachers—recall, for instance, Ron Aronson's letter to Marcuse, "Dear Herbert"[20]—or in passing biographical remarks about the very places that critical theory emerged from. In fact, the concrete dimension of what would otherwise remain a bloodless process of importing ideas becomes visible when we take into account that not just ideas crossed the ocean but people as well. In fact, spending time in Europe became something of a standard among the American readers of critical theory, facilitated by an increasing internationalization of the academy. Thus it is no coincidence that Shierry Nicholson, who had studied with Samuel Weber in Frankfurt and cotranslated the first English edition of Adorno's *Prisms*, in her contribution to the volume *Critical Interruptions*, on the question of practice, highlights traveling as the way to recapture the possibility of experience that was lost in the one-dimensional society: "Adventure means excursion into something unknown and exciting; it also means arriving somewhere. One of the characteristics of life today is that the possibility of adventure, of the out-of-the-ordinary, seems to have been foreclosed by the increasing homogeneity of the world and the increasing programming of possible experience."[21] This explains why, on the one hand, Marcuse's importance for the 1960s is so widely acknowledged, when, on the other hand, as Thomas Wheatland's *Frankfurt School in Exile* shows, Marcuse was read intensively only at the end of the decade.[22] One did

---

19. Felsch, *Der lange Sommer der Theorie.*
20. Aronson, "Dear Herbert."
21. Weber, "Individuation as Praxis," 51.
22. Wheatland, *Frankfurt School in Exile*, 268n.

not have to study Marcuse to have an ad hoc connection to the concept of the one-dimensional society. Europe, and Germany in particular, in this context turned into the antithesis of barren everyday American life—a landscape of longing (*Sehnsuchtslandschaft*). In this vein, Jeremy Shapiro remembers "standing on a square in Frankfurt, under some large trees . . . motionless for at least twenty minutes, staring at the trees, the birds, and the sky and feeling the intense excitement of being alive and having such a rich experience."[23]

If those engagements were undertaken with double zeal, how could they have done so with half a heart? To be halfhearted means to have doubts—doubts that, as this article argues, have accompanied the American reception of critical theory, especially regarding Adorno's works, almost from the beginning. It is as if the question that *Telos* used as the name for a conference in 1990, in Elizabethtown, Pennsylvania, persisted throughout the years: Does critical theory have a future? Astonishment would be warranted. Weren't those the same people who had ensured through their own careers—which, with some notable exceptions like Piccone, most *Telos* authors, despite the anti-academic rhetoric, eventually had[24]—that critical theory did enjoy a future long past the life of its first-generation authors? To answer this way would be to substitute ideas for people; the ideas were more fragile than the flood of research literature suggests. The report of the 1990 *Telos* conference, for instance, references in passing, as though it were speaking to insiders, the "official American undertaker" of critical theory and mentions the year 1950.[25] To everyone involved back then, this was an obvious polemical allusion to Martin Jay and his groundbreaking study *The Dialectical Imagination*, published in 1973 and by now translated into eighteen languages; the book had concluded its analysis with 1950, for obvious pragmatic reasons. It received numerous mostly glowing reviews and became something of a gold standard for many studies to come. Lewis Coser, in a private letter, called it "a Kind of *Muster* of how such studies ought to be done, with great respect for the achievement and yet with a great deal of critical distance."[26] But the "critical distance" lauded by Coser was exactly what was criticized in the milieu of *Telos* and *New German Critique*. The book, whose significance for the American discussion and the internation-

23. Shapiro, "My Funeral Music," 273.

24. Despite support by luminaries like Habermas and Daniel Bell, Piccone was denied promotion and tenure by Washington University in St. Louis in 1977. He contested this decision unsuccessfully in court.

25. *Telos*, "Does Critical Theory Have a Future?," 111.

26. Lewis Coser to Martin Jay, March 26, 1973 (German in the original); private collection of Martin Jay.

alization of critical theory cannot be overestimated, was conceived and published at a significant moment. Influenced by the discussions among the New Left (notwithstanding the distance its author maintained from activism), it could rely on testimonies by the first generation like Max Horkheimer, Friedrich Pollock, and, most important, Leo Löwenthal, but it was also infused by discussions inside the Frankfurt tradition. This regards especially its trajectory, that is, whether there is a conceptual break with Horkheimer and Adorno's *Dialectic of Enlightenment*, warranting talk of a "pessimist turn." Similar to accounts of the Institut für Sozialforschung by Jürgen Habermas and Albrecht Wellmer, Jay had posited: "With the shifting of the Institut's emphasis away from class struggle to the conflict between man and nature, the possibility of a historical subject capable of ushering in the revolutionary age disappeared. That imperative for *praxis*, so much a part of what some might call the Institut's heroic period, was no longer an integral part of its thought."[27]

Two of the most prominent critiques in the milieu of *Telos* and *New German Critique* were written by Jacoby and Douglas Kellner. Jacoby, writing in Alvin Gouldner's *Theory and Society*, took issue both with the approach and with the temporal framework of Jay's study:

> Leaving the story as if it ended in 1950, rather than exploding with *One-Dimensional Man*, the rediscovery and republication of the older essays of Adorno and Horkheimer, and the renewal of the Left and a whole series of questions within and on Marxism, is to do an unjustice to critical theory that resists any form of reification. . . . The failure of this successful book is in its distance from the very concepts it is presenting; their living core remains closed to Jay.[28]

Kellner's piece was published in the still very young *New German Critique*, deeming Jay's study "deceptive and disappointing":

> It is deceptive because it fails to explicate the radical Marxist program implicit in the Institute's work in the 1930s and as a result, provides a misleading interpretation of critical theory. It is disappointing because it fails to define adequately what distinguishes critical theory from traditional theory, and it fails to discuss the later transformation of critical theory in which many of its earlier positions were sacrificed.[29]

27. Jay, *Dialectical Imagination*, 279.
28. Jacoby, "Marxism and the Critical School," 237.
29. Kellner, "Frankfurt School Revisited," 131–32.

For those associated with *New German Critique*, the polemical article struck a nerve, setting off an intellectual crisis. "Kellner's accusations," Anson Rabinbach and Andreas Huyssen remarked,

> might have been addressed to us as well: How Marxist was critical theory? Did Jay—or *NGC*—have to address "their program and ideas in terms of our own predicament"? Where did we stand in regard to the "commitment to Socialist revolution"? Did we want to dismiss historians of critical theory for failing to participate in the theoretical reconstruction they were examining? Was this really what our journal should be about?[30]

Without getting into the arguments of Jay or Kellner and Jacoby here—which, among other things, would necessitate a closer look at Jay's reading of critical theory—it bears mentioning that all three were not that far apart from one another, in that they projected huge political expectations onto critical theory. Jay only spelled out the concerns pervading the milieu of *Telos* and *New German Critique*. Both the charge of soulless academicism and the insistence on the Marxist kernel of critical theory indicated first and foremost the persistence of the problem of theory and practice and how much the engagement with the Frankfurt tradition was geared to their unification, to a degree overwhelming theory, putting on it the burden of not just pointing to a revolutionary subject but elaborating its practice as well.

German Words, American History

What is most interesting about these debates—and largely overlooked—is that they can be interpreted as the expression of genuinely American questions that in turn shape the reception and transformation of critical theory in America, which is why it might tell us as much about the Frankfurt tradition as about America (and in that respect, about the differences between the Old and the New Worlds). While one could trace these American peculiarities in many fields, the most explosive and decisive is found in the question of Marxism. Critical theory, as it was formulated at the Frankfurt Institute of Social Research, began and continued as an immanent critique of Marxism—retaining an intimate relationship to the works of Karl Marx, far beyond the frequent charge of political economy being its blind spot.[31] However, many of (Western) Marxism's central categories fell on infertile ground in the United States—an issue most prominently noted by Werner Sombart's *Why Is There No Social-*

---

30. Huyssen and Rabinbach, *"New German Critique,"* 17.
31. See Braunstein, *Adornos Kritik der politischen Ökonomie.*

ism in the United States? (1906), resounding not just in the reception of critical theory but through a whole myriad of works on the political and intellectual history of the United States.[32] The argument was not (and should not be) that Marx's critique of political economy has no analytic value but that Marxism's theory of social change—of revolution—expounded less by Marx than by the Second International, seems at odds with American history and society. It held, broadly speaking, that the growing contradiction between relations of production and the productive forces, resulting in impoverishment and growing collective self-consciousness, would almost inevitably lead to social change. Most of these features, as has frequently been noted, did not echo in the United States. The lack of class consciousness, the openness toward the West, a deeply ingrained promise of upward social mobility, and the two-party system that effectively defused any kind of radicalism had hindered the establishment of a socialist movement or a socialist party that could compare to its European counterparts. Most decisively, notions like "class" and "class consciousness"— the former being dubbed a "cipher for America's exceptionalism"[33]—were volatile at best in the United States. Collective mobilization, albeit militant and sometimes even violent, could rarely rise above the local level. More important, race had been far more powerful in structuring society and collective subjectivity; in fact, it was the major framework for translating social differences. In addition, socialism often had to compete with the idea of Americanism itself, owing to a number of ideological overlaps, as Trent Schroyer noticed in his remarkable essay "Cultural Surplus in America" in *New German Critique*.[34] It is thus not surprising that, insofar as critical theory shared features with Marxism, these were the most intensely debated questions during its American reception. Doubts as to whether concepts like class or class consciousness make sense in the United States could be heard very early on. In 1975 *Telos* arranged a whole symposium on class, during which Jacoby remarked (echoed by Piccone): "If there is no class consciousness for a long period of time, something *is* wrong with your concept of class."[35] Stanley Aronowitz on the same panel was unwilling to let go of the notion of class, because social change could not be thought otherwise; he did, however, frame the problem in Sombartian terms.[36] Piccone later radicalized his critique of the notion of class in the charge that the Frankfurt

32. Sombart, *Why Is There No Socialism in the United States?* See also Laslett and Lipset, *Failure of a Dream?*; Bell, *Marxian Socialism in the United States*; and Buhle, *Marxismus in den USA*.

33. Lenger, *Sozialwissenschaft um 1900*, 83. See also Kamphausen, *Die Erfindung Amerikas*, 261.

34. Schroyer, "Cultural Surplus in America."

35. Aronowitz et al., "Symposium on Class," 154.

36. Ibid., 149n.

School had failed because of the "unwarranted retention of too much traditional Marxist baggage."[37] In fact, when the works of Habermas got more attention—which was more the case in *New German Critique* than in *Telos*—it was certainly due to the attractiveness of his critique of the so-called production paradigm and the suggestions that "communication" and the "public sphere" would provide a better way to conceptualize political conflict. *New German Critique* had proliferated the notion of the public sphere early on, in line with its generally more specific focus on culture, which by definition was a more fluid field, escaping the rigidity of orthodox Marxian terms. While *Telos* stressed ever more the all-pervasiveness of modern administration, *New German Critique* employed an essentially German, Humboldtian idea of culture (and *Bildung*), irreducible to administration. In that way it was possible to evade Adorno's alleged negativism and elitism, by focusing on those authors who were perceived as more open to mass culture and less skeptical, like Benjamin and especially Siegfried Kracauer. This too can be traced back to an American peculiarity. As Lawrence W. Levine argues extensively in *Highbrow/Lowbrow*, the relationship of "high culture" and popular culture worked much differently in the United States than in Europe.[38] Cultural hierarchy or the sacralization of culture, in fact, high culture itself—to which Adorno's critique was always related, resulting in the seemingly immortal yet reductive charge of elitism—in America was a rather young phenomenon, beginning only in the late nineteenth or early twentieth century, not to mention that the bourgeois canon from which Adorno spoke was far away from the American reality. Later phenomena like pop art seemed to thoroughly escape the simple dichotomy of high and low, and called for a more nuanced critique. "Today," Huyssen wrote in 1975, "we must rethink the concept of culture industry and both analyze and activate the contradictions between a passive acceptance of cultural commodities and the possibility of an emancipatory cultural production."[39]

While the profile of *New German Critique* developed during this time, a focus on intellectual history and culture, especially on the Weimar German-Jewish thought, proved rather steady, Piccone and *Telos* reacted more dramatically to the doubts about critical theory and Western Marxism and the frictions, which resulted from the confrontation of German words with American reality. Already in 1977, notwithstanding the enduring presence of both traditions in the journal, Piccone proclaimed: "Looking back over the last

37. Piccone, "Changing Function of Critical Theory," 30.
38. Levine, *Highbrow/Lowbrow*.
39. Huyssen, "Introduction to Adorno," 5.

eight years, it can be said that our historical function has been primarily to provide Marxism with a decent burial."[40] Consequentially, the call to "American-
ize" the journal, that is, to pull back on contributions originating from or concentrating on Europe, had been voiced since the 1970s. Vocally and publicly,
Telos continued its search for a viable theory fitting the American political conditions, against all odds clinging to the promise and ideal of a theory that could
eventually guide practice. Notoriously, this search led Piccone and others in the
mid- and late 1980s to Carl Schmitt, which, in connection to long-brewing
political and personal arguments, resulted in a split inside the journal. Later,
at the beginning of the 1990s, Piccone was convinced that populism would
provide a way to meaningfully analyze society. Only one year after *Telos* had
organized the Elizabethtown conference and had asked the question whether
critical theory had a future, the journal held a second meeting in the same
city that seemed to give an answer: it was called *Populism vs. the New Class*,
featuring as one of the speakers the conservative author Paul Gottfried. Piccone
explained:

> *Telos'* recent populist turn does not constitute a break with the past, but the
> culmination of a quarter century of efforts to relate continental thought to
> American realities, Critical Theory to concrete politics, and to reunite that
> subjective moment vindicated by phenomenological Marxism with its other-
> ness presently alienated in Washington and other administrative centers of
> bureaucratic domination.[41]

The Temporal Core of Critical Theory

While a thorough analysis of this turn would make for another essay, it is clear
that in *Telos*'s case, the historical watershed of 1989 strengthened the doubts
about critical theory, which had been brewing since the 1970s. It is as if history
and truth, which according to Adorno meet in the word, eventually parted ways,
leaving an empty shell that could not speak anymore to a changed present.
"The words were the same, but the spirit was gone," Piccone said accordingly
in an editor's newsletter in 1990.[42] On a similar note, Robert Hullot-Kentor
wrote around the same time that in America Adorno's lifework "was born into
a bottle," and called for a return to Adorno, but a return "to what was never
reached in the first placed."[43] So one is tempted to ask whether Horkheimer

---

40. Piccone, "Internal Polemics," 181.
41. Piccone, "From the New Left to the New Populism," 306.
42. Piccone, Telos Public Sphere, October 1990, 4.
43. Hullot-Kentor, "Back to Adorno," 23.

was correct when he wrote in 1936, in one of critical theory's most programmatic texts, that one condition for its historical success is its transmission "in the strictest possible form." After all, the thought continues with the assertion that "the transmission will not take place via solidly established practice and fixed ways of acting but via concern for social transformation."[44] In nuce, this is the elaboration of a much-referenced yet complex notion in critical theory, the "temporal core" (*Zeitkern*) that every concept and every theory necessarily has. This is not, to be sure to be understood as if a theory loses its validity once the historical moment of its formulation has passed. It retains, for better or worse, a certain autonomy, which did not escape Horkheimer and in fact can be turned back onto critical theory itself: "Documents have a history but a theory does not have its vicissitudes."[45]

References

Adorno, Theodor W. 1998. *Dissonanzen*. Vol. 14 of *Gesammelte Schriften*, edited by Rolf Tiedemann. Darmstadt: Wissenschaftliche Buchgesellschaft.

——. 2007. "Theses on the Language of the Philosopher," translated by Samir Gandesha and Michael K. Palamarek. In *Adorno and the Need in Thinking: New Critical Essays*, edited by Donald A. Burke, Colin J. Campbell, and Kathy Kiloh, 35–40. Toronto: University of Toronto Press.

Anderson, Mark M. 2001. "German Intellectuals, Jewish Victims: A Politically Correct Solidarity." *Chronicle of Higher Education*, October 19. chronicle.com/article/German-Intellectuals-Jewish/2532.

Anonymous. 1970. "The First *Telos* International Conference: 'The New Marxism'; Waterloo, Ontario, October 8–1, 1970." *Telos*, no. 6: 294–317.

Aronowitz, Stanley, Russell Jacoby, Paul Piccone, and Trent Schroyer. 1976. "Symposium on Class." *Telos*, no. 28: 145–66.

Aronson, Ronald. 1971. "Dear Herbert." In *The Revival of American Socialism: Selected Papers of the Socialist Scholars Conference*, edited by George Fischer et al., 3–18. New York: Oxford University Press.

Bell, Daniel. 1967. *Marxian Socialism in the United States*. Princeton, NJ: Princeton University Press.

Braunstein, Dirk. 2011. *Adornos Kritik der politischen Ökonomie*. Bielefeld: Transcript.

Breines, Paul. 1970. "From Guru to Spectre: Marcuse and the Implosion of the Movement." In *Critical Interruptions: New Left Perspectives on Herbert Marcuse*, edited by Paul Breines, 1–21. New York: Herder and Herder.

Buhle, Paul. *Marxismus in den USA*. Berlin: Merve.

Felsch, Philipp. 2015. *Der lange Sommer der Theorie: Geschichte einer Revolte, 1960–1990*. Munich: Beck.

44. Horkheimer, "Traditional and Critical Theory," 241.
45. Ibid., 240.

Genosko, Gary, Samir Gandesha, and Kristina Marcellus. 2007. "Waterloo: The Cradle of Canadian *Telos*." *Review of Education, Pedagogy, and Cultural Studies* 29, nos. 2–3: 175–86.

Grahl, Bart, and Paul Piccone, eds. 1973. *Towards a New Marxism*. St. Louis, MO: Telos.

Hegel, G. W. F. 1991. *Elements of the Philosophy of Right*, edited by Allen Wood, translated by H. B. Nisbet. Cambridge: Cambridge University Press.

———. 2011. *Lectures on the Philosophy of World History*. Vol. 1, *Manuscripts and the Introduction and Lectures of 1822–23*, edited and translated by Robert F. Brown and Peter C. Hodgson. Oxford: Clarendon.

Horkheimer, Max. 2002: "Traditional and Critical Theory." In *Critical Theory: Selected Essays*, translated by Matthew J. O'Connell et al., 188–243. New York: Continuum.

Howard, Dick, and Karl E. Klare, eds. 1972. *The Unknown Dimension: European Marxism since Lenin*. New York: Basic.

Hullot-Kentor, Robert. 2006. "Back to Adorno." In *Things beyond Resemblance: Collected Essays on Theodor W. Adorno*, 23–44. New York: Columbia University Press.

Huyssen, Andreas. 1975. "Introduction to Adorno." *New German Critique*, no. 6: 3–11.

Huyssen, Andreas, and Anson Rabinbach. 2005. "*New German Critique*: The First Decade." *New German Critique*, no. 95: 5–26.

Jacoby, Russell. 1974. "Marxism and the Critical School." *Theorie and Society* 1, no. 2: 231–38.

———. 1981. *Dialectic of Defeat: Contours of Western Marxism*. Cambridge: Cambridge University Press.

———. 2011. "Outside Academe." In *A Journal of No Illusions: "Telos," Paul Piccone, and the Americanization of Critical Theory*, edited by Ben Agger and Timothy W. Luke, 57–61. New York: Telos.

Jay, Martin. 1974. *The Dialectical Imagination: A History of the Frankfurt School and the Institute of Social Research, 1923–1950*. London: Heinemann Educational Books.

Kamphausen, Georg. 2002. *Die Erfindung Amerikas in der Kulturkritik der Generation von 1890*. Weilerswist: Velbrück Wissenschaft.

Kellner, Douglas. 1973. "The Frankfurt School Revisited: A Critique of Martin Jay's *The Dialectical Imagination*." *New German Critique*, no. 4: 131–52.

Laslett, John H. M., and Seymour Martin Lipset, eds. 1984. *Failure of a Dream? Essays in the History of American Socialism*. Rev. ed. Berkeley: University of California Press.

Lenger, Friedrich. 2009. *Sozialwissenschaft um 1900: Studien zu Werner Sombart und einigen seiner Zeitgenossen*. Frankfurt am Main: Lang.

Levine, Lawrence W. 1988. *Highbrow/Lowbrow: The Emergence of Cultural Hierarchy in America*. Cambridge, MA: Harvard University Press.

Piccone, Paul. 1977. "The Changing Function of Critical Theory." *New German Critique*, no. 12: 29–37.

———. 1977. "Internal Polemics." *Telos*, no. 31: 178–97.

———. 2008. "From the New Left to the New Populism." In *Confronting the Crisis: Writings of Paul Piccone*, edited by Gary Ulmen, 287–329. New York: Telos Press.

Schroyer, Trent. 1982. "Cultural Surplus in America." *New German Critique*, no. 26: 81–117.

Shapiro, Jeremy. 2010. "My Funeral Music." In *Listening, Playing, Creating: Essays on the Power of Sound*, edited by Carolyn Bereznak Kenny, 260–79. Albany: State University of New York Press.

Sombart, Werner. 1976. *Why Is There No Socialism in the United States?*, edited by C. T. Husbands, translated by Patricia M. Hocking and C. T. Husbands. White Plains, NY: Sharpe.

Telos. 1989. "Does Critical Theory Have a Future? The Elizabethtown Telos Conference (February 23–25, 1990)." *Telos*, no. 82: 111–30.

Tocqueville, Alexis de. 2010. *Democracy in America: Historical-Critical Edition of "De la démocratie en Amérique,"* edited by Eduardo Nolla. Indianapolis, IN: Liberty Fund.

Weber, Shierry M. 1970. "Individuation as Praxis." In *Critical Interruptions: New Left Perspectives on Herbert Marcuse*, edited by Paul Breines, 22–59. New York: Herder and Herder.

Wheatland, Thomas. 2009. *The Frankfurt School in Exile*. Minneapolis: University of Minnesota Press.